D0459161

Dialectical Criticism and Renaissance Literature

Dialectical Criticism and Renaissance Literature

Michael McCanles

University of California Press, Berkeley, Los Angeles, London

University of California Press
Berkeley and Los Angeles, California

University of California Press, Ltd.
London, England

ISBN 0-520-02694-2
Library of Congress Catalog Card Number: 73-93056
Printed in the United States of America

To My Wife

My praise is plaine, and where so ere profest,
Becomes none more then you, who need it least.

Ben Jonson, *"To Mary Lady Wroth"*

Creation Myth

In the beginning, there was universal Nothing.
Then Nothing said No to itself and thereby begat
                Something,
Which called itself Yes.

Then No and Yes, cohabiting, begat Maybe.
Next all three, in a ménage à trois, begat Guilt.

And Guilt was of many names:
Mine, Thine, Yours, Ours, His, Hers, Its, Theirs—
                and Order.

In time things so came to pass
That two of its names, Guilt and Order,
Honoring their great progenitors, Yes, No, and Maybe,
Begat History.

Finally, History fell a-dreaming
And dreamed about Language—

(And that brings us to critics-who-write-critiques-of-
                critical-criticism.)

Kenneth Burke

Contents

Abbreviations of
Full Titles of Periodicals

ELH	English Literary History
JEGP	Journal of English and Germanic Philology
JHI	Journal of the History of Ideas
MLQ	Modern Language Quarterly
MP	Modern Philology
NLH	New Literary History
PMLA	Publications of the Modern Language Association
SEL	Studies in English Literature
SQ	Shakespeare Quarterly

Preface

This study concerns some major literary productions of the late English Renaissance, but not exclusively. Its purpose is threefold: (1) to develop a dialectical method of analyzing literary works; (2) to exhibit this method in discussion of some specific works by Bacon, Donne, Herbert, Marvell, Milton, and Shakespeare; and (3) to outline a dialectical theory of Renaissance literary history. These topics are distributed somewhat asymetrically throughout the study's introduction and five essays. The introduction takes up the last topic by discussing a central issue still current in modern criticism of past literatures, the dialectic between historicism and formalism. The second topic is the main subject of the first four essays. In Essay One I discuss the major and some of the minor treatises on the "new science" by Francis Bacon, with emphasis on *The Advancement of Learning*, the *Instauratio Magna*, and the *De Augmentis Scientiarum*. Essay Two deals with several poems by Donne, Herbert, and Marvell, with emphasis, in the latter case, on "Upon Appleton House." Essay Three concerns Milton's *Paradise Lost*. And Essay Four takes up eight plays of Shakespeare: *Richard II, 1* and *2 Henry IV, Henry V, Julius Caesar, Troilus and Cressida, Measure for Measure,* and *Hamlet.* Essay Five discusses and synthesizes such conclusions about dialectical analysis as are justified by the first four essays, further develops the historicism-formalism dialectic, and speculates on ways of relating these literary works to their cultural context.

Renaissance literary scholars have been exploring dialectical structures in many works of this period for some time. Recently, the World Shakespeare Congress in Vancouver (*Shakespeare, 1971,* ed. Clifford Leech and J. M. R. Margeson [Toronto: Univ. of Toronto Press, 1972]), published a report detailing the various current critical approaches to Shakespeare, of which "Oscillation Analysis" was singled out as one among six. Of this approach, Elemér Hankiss, chairman of the Investigative Committee on New Research Methods, said:

> Some recent investigations have proved that a peculiar kind of "oscillation" between positive and negative poles of value is one of the basic mechanisms not only of human mind but also of literary expression. The presence and importance of this continuous value-oscillation could be established in lyrical poems, from the simplest folksongs to highly sophisticated twentieth-century poems; in novels, in the description of the heroes, for instance, or in the closures, the concluding passages of the novels; in plays, in Shakespeare's *Hamlet* as well as in O'Neill's or Beckett's plays—and so on. The study of these oscillations may help us to describe, better than we have been able to do so far, the style of different authors and periods, to define literary genres, to distinguish literary works of real aesthetic value from cheap literature, etc. [p. 274]

What in these essays is called "the logic of dialectic" is roughly another name for "oscillation analysis." Lacking heretofore, however, has been a thoroughgoing analysis of the specific features of dialectic in Renaissance literature. Some of this lack I intend to fill here. My indebtedness to the work of many of my colleagues is fully apparent, both in my specific analyses and in the footnotes. For some of my readings I can pretend little originality. For some others, I believe that dialectical criticism supplies some new insights.

Originality in this direction, in any case, is not my prime object. I have attempted here not only to formalize what appears to be a dominant dialectical structure in these works, but to elucidate through dialectic some problems of literary history and criticism of Renaissance literature. The gulf between historicist and formalist criticism plagues Renaissance studies as it does the study of all periods of literature, including the twentieth century. The method and conclusions of my first four analytic essays have implications for this larger problem of relating historicist, "external" approaches to Renaissance literature to formalist, "new critical" approaches. My critique in the introduction and in Essay Five takes in both methods; but if I appear to concentrate on traditional historicist methods, it is only because my own approach shares so much with them in the process of differing radically from them. The first four essays are quite frankly formalist, and adduce relatively little "background" material. My procedure in this will, I hope, be justified in Essay Five.

Some of the topics included in this study correspond to those whimsically and earnestly lined up in a poem printed here before the preface, "Creation Myth" by Kenneth Burke—something I discovered after the fact. Since this study owes much to his work on dialectic, I was not wholly surprised to discover this parallel, although I was delighted. "Creation Myth" repeats in a summary "representative anecdote" and synthesizes many fragments of this myth that Burke has scattered through all of his books. Creation of the world began as a dialectical generation of opposite from opposite (a notion that I find useful in discussing *Paradise Lost*), and this dialectical generation begat many other fragmentations and divisions. "Order" here means, if I interpret Burke's code correctly, man's accommodations to the dialectical nature of things, summed up by "Guilt." Here, the genealogical descent is rapid: from the dialectic between Guilt and Order springs History—the temporal sequence in which these two alternate in mutual, dialectical generation. And from History is born the verbal discursion that parallels the temporal flow of History and articulates it in discrete but syntactically aligned particles. And from Language springs Criticism, and from Criticism springs Criticism-of-Criticism (and so on and on, in a never-ending sequence of ever-increasing self-consciousness). If the movement from Creation to Order to History to Language to Criticism is the way of the world, then the reader will find this study a modest, microcosmic reenactment of this way. Creation, order, and history are the subjects these authors wrote about; language was their constant concern; and criticism is the latter-day family chronicler of his own genealogy.

My indebtedness for the streams of thought that have flowed into these essays during the years of their gestation is broad and, of course, not wholly citable. Various colleagues have aided much in giving me perspective on my ideas in ways that I am not now able to distinguish. My primary indebtedness has been to certain works, ranging from Aristotle to the present, which I cite here to establish in a preliminary fashion both where I have been and where I—and the reader—are going. To Aristotle, through Thomas Aquinas, I owe some of the prime insights that have generated my notion of dialectic, particularly his theory of change, the act-potency schema, and the notion that change is always from opposites to opposites. To Aquinas I am indebted for a doctrine of existential analogy that provided the essential rationalization of the Aristotelian act-potency schema, and first allowed me to understand dialectical logic. As regards Thomistic analogy, I have drawn in the past particularly on two studies: Hampus Lyttkens, *The Analogy Between God and the World: An Investigation of its Background and Interpretation of its Use by Thomas of Aquino* (Uppsala: Almqvist and Wiksells, 1952), and George P. Klubertanz, S. J., *St. Thomas Aquinas on Analogy* (Chicago: Loyola Univ. Press, 1960). Aiding immensely in crystallizing dialectic for me were several works of Kenneth Burke: *A Grammar of Motives* (New York: Prentice-Hall, 1954), *The Philosophy of Literary Form* (New York: Vintage Books, 1957), and *Attitudes Toward History* (Boston: Beacon Press, 1961). In the area of the philosophy of history and the sociology of knowledge, I should mention here Karl Mannheim's *Ideology and Utopia,* R. G. Collingwood's *The Idea of History,* and Ernst Cassirer's *Philosophy of Symbolic Forms,* all cited in the footnotes. My debt to my own colleagues in English Renaissance studies has been enormous. Studies that parallel my own in dealing with antinomical aspects of Renaissance literature include those of Rosalie L. Colie, *Paradoxia Epidemica* (Princeton, N. J.: Princeton Univ. Press, 1966), Norman Rabkin, *Shakespeare and the Common*

Understanding (New York: The Free Press, 1967), and most recently, Stanley Fish, *Self-Consuming Artifacts* (Berkeley: Univ. of California Press, 1972), the manuscript of which the author was kind enough to send me through the University of California Press while it was being completed.

I am indebted to the Department of English of Marquette University for reduced teaching loads, and to the Graduate School for research grants and two half-time Summer Faculty Fellowships. Finally, to my wife, Penelope A. McCanles, my debt is beyond saying, for she has had to live from day to day with the dialectical alternations between passion and drudgery that writing this study has elicited. My thanks for that, and for her careful scrutiny and correction of the final draft, can only be rendered in the dedication of this study to her.

Introduction:

The Dialectic of Historicist and Formalist Criticism

One goal of these essays is to explore how dialectical criticism illuminates several major literary productions of the late English Renaissance so as to answer the question, How can the term "Renaissance" be applied to all of them? Since the first four essays also explore the possibilities of dialectic as an explicative tool, this study as a whole cuts across the usual boundaries separating historicist and formalist criticism. In this respect, I offer here a methodology, also dialectical, whereby these two quarreling factions of literary students may be reconciled. A full exposition of this matter I have left to Essay Five, after the possibilities of dialectical criticism have been illustrated in a practical manner. However, since the organization and procedure of this study may deceptively appear to follow usual models of formalist criticism, my intentions must be stated at the beginning to give the reader an idea of both what and what not to expect. Here, I shall sketch briefly the dialectic between historicist and formalist methods of literary study, to preview how both approaches are joined in the following essays in a way that moves beyond this dialectic. If I seem on occasion to push the trajectories of both factions to rather abstract extremes, this is because the quarrel itself has been carried primarily on the level of theoretical implications, probabilities, and possibilities. Certainly in practice, as much recent literary discussion indicates, historicism and formalism operate as one. This is so much the case that one may wonder if the problem lies not so much in how to join external and internal analysis, as in why the problem itself seems to be so perennially with us. Part of the answer lies, I think, in the fact that, however much both approaches are presently joined in fact, the methodological justifications for such conjunctions are not so easily defined.

The main features of historicism and formalism, as well as the causes of their opposition, can be briefly outlined. One may well note, however, in surveying this quarrel from the 1930s down to the present, that the disagreements of the two factions are very much a function of what they agree upon. First, all seem to agree upon the demarcations between their respective approaches. A general statement of apportionment, with which we may not wholly agree today, occurs in F. W. Bateson's reply to F. R. Leavis, an exchange early in the debate's history. For him, the historical critic deals with such allegedly verifiable "factual" statements as "A derives from B," while the critic's true province should be such statements as "A is better than B." [1] In general, the "new criticism," as it was beginning to be called at that time, concerned not only evaluations, but explanations of fictive works by analyzing the interrelations of their parts, irrespective of external pressures of cultural context. Against this approach, historical critics raised the self-limitations under which the formalists were operating, and called attention to the necessity of taking such pressures into account. The discussion between Cleanth Brooks and Douglas Bush from 1947 to 1953 on Brooks's analysis of Marvell's "Horatian Ode" focuses on where their approaches met and parted. [2]

[1] F. W. Bateson, "A Comment," in *The Importance of Scrutiny,* ed. Eric Bentley (New York: Grove Press, 1948), p. 16, an answer to F. R. Leavis's review of Bateson's *English Poetry and the English Language* in 1935, repr. *ibid.,* pp. 12–16.

[2] Cleanth Brooks, "Marvell's 'Horatian Ode,'" *English Institute Essays,* 1946 (New York: Columbia Univ. Press, 1947), pp. 127–158; Douglas Bush, "Marvell's 'Horatian Ode,'" *Sewanee Review* 60 (1952): 363–376; Cleanth Brooks, "A Note on the Limits of 'History' and the Limits of 'Criticism,'" *Sewanee Review* 61 (1953): 129–135. All three articles are reprinted in *Seventeenth-Century English Poetry: Modern Essays in Criticism,* ed. William R. Keast (New York: Oxford Univ. Press, 1962), pp. 321–358.

The ground of this agreement was still another agreement, the fact that both approaches took as their ultimate goal the elucidation of literary works. In this respect, they tended to agree to split up, along roughly Aristotelian lines, the "causes" of meaning into external efficient and final causes, and internal formal and material causes. Thus the historicist held the superior relevance of biographical studies and cultural context as the (efficient) cause of the work's structure and themes. Insofar as the historicist saw the work as a "product" rather than a "producer" of its culture,[3] he likewise conceived the work's final cause to be its social, political, economic, or religious purposes. Symmetry breaks down here somewhat, because the formalist was likewise concerned with final causes, although he located them wholly within the aesthetic relationship between work and reader. As regards internal causes of meaning, the formalist had the field to himself. For him, the sufficient cause of a work's meaning lay in the achieved organization of its materials into a formal structure. This agreement on divisions of labor, however, was powered by a still more basic agreement-to-disagree about the intelligible relationship between a work's status as "past" and its status as "present" to a modern reader.[4]

The historicists as well as the formalists committed themselves and each other to stances on the literary work's historical status which in turn dictated differing stances on the links between modern reader and past literature. Their agreements-to-disagree were thus matters both of the philosophy of history and culture, and of literary methodology. In line with his commitment to external causes as the sufficient explanation of a work's meaning, the historicist argued, in the words of D. W. Robertson, that

[3] I am indebted for this distinction to Robert Weimann, "Past Significance and Present Meaning in Literary History," *NLH* 1 (1969): 103–104.

[4] For these categories and for much insight into the problems they raise, I am indebted to several recent studies which, taken together, offer much hope that the historicist-formalist dialectic may in fact be resolvable. These include Weimann's essay cited above, Roy Harvey Pearce, *Historicism Once More: Problems and Occasions for the American Scholar* (Princeton: Princeton Univ. Press, 1969), and Wesley Morris, *Toward a New Historicism* (Princeton: Princeton Univ. Press, 1972). Morris's survey of the problem and its history is the best consideration to date of the problematics of the issue and of the trajectories that point to its solution.

"valid criticism of works produced in earlier stylistic periods" can only be achieved "in terms of conventions established at a time contemporary with the works themselves." This is so because "what we call the past is, in effect, a series of foreign countries inhabited by strangers," and we must do our best to discount the partialities arising from our own historical situation in a culture removed from that of the work itself.[5] Here, the work's "past" status justifies attempts at total recreation of past viewpoints, and generates such heuristic entities as "the typical Elizabethan playgoer." The formalist, on the other hand, aware that literatures of all times share several modes of structuring their materials, attempted analyses and judgments which were rendered, as Cleanth Brooks said, "not in terms of some former historical period and not merely in terms of our own: the judgments are very frankly treated as if they were universal judgments."[6] The "timelessness" of formalist criteria and methods was frankly reduced by F. R. Leavis to establishing "a perspective, to determine what of English poetry of the past is, or ought to be, alive for us now."[7]

And yet few denied that the methods of external and internal analysis were both required.[8] The question was not whether the two approaches were necessary, but rather how to justify theoretically their working together. In general, the history of the controversy seems grounded not on mere disagreements regarding emphases, safeguards against "subjectivity," recognitions of the "originality" and "uniqueness" of great literary works, and

[5] D. W. Robertson, Jr., "Some Observations on Method in Literary Studies," *NLH* 1 (1969): 30, 31. A recent scholar puts this division between past and present even more extremely, when he wonders "whether one century's axioms are really possible for the next wholly to recover, whether the axioms of different generations within a single century may not vary markedly, and whether even one decade is not bound to include people with widely divergent views on some major points," Howard C. Cole, *A Quest of Inquirie: Some Contexts of Tudor Literature* (Indianapolis and New York: Bobbs-Merrill, 1973), p. 15.

[6] Cleanth Brooks, *The Well Wrought Urn: Studies in the Structure of Poetry* (New York: Harcourt, Brace, Harvest Book, n.d. [orig. pub. 1947]), p. 217.

[7] *The Importance of Scrutiny*, p. 14.

[8] Cf. Cleanth Brooks, "The Limits of 'History' and of 'Criticism,'" in Keast, *Seventeenth-Century Poetry*, p. 355; F. W. Bateson, in *The Importance of Scrutiny*, p. 18; and Helen Gardner's judicious treatment of the whole problem in *The Business of Criticism* (Oxford: Oxford Univ. Press, 1963), p. 20 and *passim*.

so on, matters with which both sides belabored each other despite the fact that no one seriously questioned them. On the contrary, the continuance of the controversy seems to illustrate, as Roy Harvey Pearce suggests, "that there is a constant and necessary dialectical opposition between the very categories we would synthesize." [9] Robert Weimann develops this notion along lines that I shall pursue: "The past significance of the work of art, its background and origins, is in the last resort indivisible from its present meaning and its survival into the future. The literary historian is confronted with more than the coexistence of these aspects: he has to face both their contradiction and unity." [10] Because neither historicists nor formalists have been able to encompass the "pastness" and "presentness" of the literary work in "both their contradiction and unity," they have found themselves in an irresolvable dialectic. They have, theoretically at least, covertly changed places with each other and back again, because both have equivocated on the relationship between the two dimensions of the literary work's existence. The historicist, despite his insistence on consciousness of one's own historical perspective and the consequent need to recreate the consciousness of past cultures, ultimately aims at an ahistorical view of literature. And the formalist, in systematically denying the relevance of historical perspective, nevertheless implicitly views literary works as functions of historically conditioned perspectives, namely his own.

The historical critic's methodological heritage derives from the body of principles and methods developed through the eighteenth century to the present among historians concerned with matters other than literary history.[11] Historicism is a complex, and sometimes contradictory, set of consequences all derived from a heightened sense of the distance separating one period or culture from another. The historical critic's insistence on discounting present standpoints in order to recreate those of a past culture derives from nineteenth-century and early twentieth-century historians and philosophers of history, who themselves

[9] Pearce, *Historicism Once More*, p. 4.   [10] Weimann, in *NLH* I (1969): 104.
[11] Cf. Chapter 24, "The Historical Method: A Retrospect," in William K. Wimsatt, Jr. and Cleanth Brooks, *Literary Criticism: A Short History* (New York: Knopf, 1965), pp. 522–551.

became increasingly aware that, in Croce's extreme statement, all history is present history. From this realization, and the demands on which it was based, sprang two apparently incompatible historical methodologies, both confusingly called historicism. As Karl Mannheim recognized, citing Troeltsch as his own source, "historicism gave rise to relativism only as a result of demands for an absolutely supra-temporal standard in terms of which historical reality was to be judged." Others more recently, such as Morton White and Ernest Nagel, have penetrated to this essential criterion of "fact" lying behind historicism's cult of historical relativity, and suggest that historicism's revolt against Enlightenment obsession with the "universality of human nature" and an "absolute" rationality accompanying such actually took over this obsession, but turned it upside down.[12] Consequently, two different and apparently opposed conclusions could be drawn. On the one hand, one could insist with Meinecke and Ranke on totally discounting present perspectives and values in the interest of recreating the viewpoint of a past culture, thereby guaranteeing, as far as possible, objectivity. On the other, one could emphasize the impossibility of doing so, and along with Croce, Collingwood, Gentile and others, insist on the presentness of all historical documents to the modern historian. As Giovanni Gentile put the dilemma in its most extreme and anguished form, "Everything is past; nothing is past." [13]

This ambiguous consequence flowing from historicism's demand for some sort of absolute, timeless, ahistorical viewpoint dogs the historical critic as well as his colleagues in departments of history. He seeks, simultaneously, to reap the benefits and avoid the liabilities of two different historical perspectives. In attempting total recreation of past perspectives he ignores the fact, while covertly exploiting it, that all such recreations are necessarily projections

---

[12] Karl Mannheim, "Historicism" (1924), in *Essays on the Sociology of Knowledge,* ed. Paul Kecskemeti (London: Routledge & Kegan Paul, 1952), p. 128; Morton White, "Can History be Objective" in *The Philosophy of History in Our Time,* ed. Hans Meyerhoff (Garden City, N.Y.: Doubleday Anchor Books, 1959), p. 195; Ernest Nagel, "The Logic of Historical Analysis," in *ibid.,* p. 209.

[13] Giovanni Gentile, "The Transcending of Time in History," in *Philosophy and History: Essays presented to Ernst Cassirer,* ed. Raymond Klibansky and H. J. Paton (New York, Evanston, and London: Harper & Row, 1963), pp. 95–96.

from present perspectives. The very notion of doing so is of course historically conditioned, being the consequence of several recent centuries' evolution of historiography. But more to the point, were he actually to achieve the impossible and completely negate his present perspective to recreate himself totally as, for example, "the typical Elizabethan playgoer," he would at once cancel whatever advantages his perspective in the present, outside of the sixteenth century, grants him. Raymond Aron's comments on "the privileges of retrospection" that "compensate for the bondage to which [the historian] is subject" are, or should be, truisms today in literary history as they are in historiography in general. As he goes on to say, "What the creator could not guess at, the historian, thanks to perspective, sees immediately." The historian excels "not merely the spectator, but also the actor, since he has available documents which are by definition inaccessible to those who spontaneously, unconsciously, lived history." [14] To make oneself wholly over into a participant in a past culture is merely to replace one set of partialities with another. Allegedly, such would be a prime achievement for the historical critic; for after all, is it not precisely the partialities of the past culture that putatively give the literary critic the "correct" way of seeing the products of that culture? In attempting such, the historical critic ignores the truth of Bernard Groethuysen's dictum that "What I know, I am no longer; what I am, I know no longer. Life and knowledge cannot be made one." [15] In assuming that "knowing" as an Elizabethan depends on his "being" an Elizabethan, he likewise presupposes that an Elizabethan is in full contact with the fundamental categories of truth and value that underlie his culture. But in fact just the opposite is true. Clearly, the capacity to write studies of "the Elizabethan world picture," "the political orthodoxies of the Tudors," and "the metaphysical 'mode' " do not derive from living in Renaissance England. Such documents as historical critics adduce on these matters, which state general summaries of conventional material, do by that very fact destroy

[14] Raymond Aron, *Introduction to the Philosophy of History,* trans. George J. Irwin (Boston: Beacon Press, 1962), p. 80.
[15] Bernard Groethuysen, "Towards an Anthropological Philosophy," in *Philosophy and History,* p. 86.

whatever illusion of a transhistorical perspective they suggest. As shall become clear later in this study, statements of the world view of a particular culture made by members of that culture are always partial and incomplete by that very fact.

What in fact the historical critic does, is seek covertly to reap the advantages of both cultural recreation and present perspective; nor does his equivocation stop here. In seeking to discount present perspectives, he must perforce project a standpoint that is really outside of history altogether, because only such a perspective allows both past and present to be available to him. As Martin Heidegger points out, artifacts that were made in the past may still exist in the present, and therefore their "pastness" is not automatically given. On the contrary, "our going back to 'the past' does not first get its start from the acquisition, sifting, and securing of such material; these activities presuppose *historical Being towards* the Dasein that has-been-there [the original creator of these in the past]—that is to say, they presuppose the historicalness of the historian's existence." [16] Consequently, the literary critic's attempt to negate his own historicalness would lead, if followed out thoroughly, to a complete incapacity to understand any historical existence, either of the past or of his own. But, as has been pointed out, in fact he does no such thing, but seeks rather to be at once immersed in history (the past) and outside of history.

The formalist's theory is likewise at odds with his practice, in that he equivocates with the same terms but in reverse. Like the historicist, the formalist grants the irrevocable pastness of the past, but emphasizes as a consequence that literary artifacts surviving the demise of their own culture become totally recreated only when they lie before him in the present. This present is also treated as if it were an "eternal present," as Brooks suggests in the quotation cited above. If the work results primarily from its intrinsic causes, then matters of external, cultural pressures can be, at best, of subordinate consequence. All writers, especially major ones, took over traditional materials and made them new. And though the conventions, values, and structures available to

[16] Martin Heidegger, *Being and Time,* trans. John Macquarrie and Edward Robinson (New York and Evanston: Harper & Row, 1962), pp. 431–432, 446.

the writer in his own time may have passed away, his own creations of conventions, values, and structures remain intact and
"eternally present." Further, the formalist desires to discover
perennial principles of fictive structure that hold sway *mutatis
mutandis* through all periods of literary activity, thereby risking,
as the historicists never tire of pointing out, sources of creativity
wholly indigenous to one time and place.

The formalist's projection of an ideal continuum in which all
literary works are eternally present only succeeds in substituting
one cultural context for another: his own. Like the historicist, he
also attempts to project a timeless, ahistorical standpoint from
which to view the work "as it is"; and like the historicist, he too
equivocates in the uses to which he puts this standpoint. For one
thing, the formalist performs an act of historical recreation in the
very act of reading and understanding a work, as F. O. Matthies-
sen pointed out in noting that "aesthetic criticism" "inevitably
becomes social criticism, since the act of perception extends
through the work of art to its milieu." [17] But more important, the
formalist's ahistorical standpoint violates itself to the exact degree that he uses methods of analyzing literary structure that are
the products of literary developments in the late nineteenth and
twentieth centuries. The very notions of "organic form," "structure of meaning," "ambiguity," and the rest derive from conceptions of literary structure for which such writers as Flaubert,
James, Conrad, Joyce, and Eliot were primarily responsible. Now
it may well be that such notions work with past writers; but if
they do, it is not because they have some sort of transhistorical
validity, but for precisely the opposite reason: that they are part
of a continuous evolution of creation and criticism through the
history of Western literature. But having projected his standpoint
out of history, the formalist deprives himself, as does the historicist, of precisely the advantages granted by his perspective in
the present: he deprives himself of means for discriminating the
usefulness of his critical tools in general from their relevance
vis-à-vis past works. In refusing to take account of historical perspective, in treating all literary works as present, he loses the

---

[17] Paraphrased from *Henry James: The Major Phase,* by Wesley Morris in
Toward a New Historicism, p. 131.

capacity to weigh his own perspective against those of past cultures, so as to judge both their similarities and their differences.

The dialectic between historicists and formalists thus derives from an inability to synthesize the dual historical status of literary works themselves. In each seizing one dimension to the exclusion of the other, critics on both sides end up having to take account of the pressure that this dual dimension exerts, and to oscillate covertly back and forth between several perspectives, trying to derive the respective advantages of each, as if such were not impossible. The present state of this question has for the most part emphasized its paradoxes and the difficulties of resolving them. Beside Roy Harvey Pearce and Robert Weimann who were cited before, others have recently framed in similar terms the problems raised by the literary work's dual status. Murray Krieger tries to accommodate the literary work as at once the "bearer" and "creator" of its culture. He views the work's dual status as essentially "miraculous," in that it faces toward its existential, cultural situation primarily by being itself an autonomously organized internal structure.[18] E. D. Hirsch, Jr., would make the choice between "past meaning" and "anachronistic" meaning a purely ethical matter, without grounds in either literary theory or metaphysics, and thereby takes for granted the gulf between the two.[19] And Wesley Morris has declared that "the new historicist, who would make the tautological necessities of his theory meaningful, must combine the two, must see literature both as a part integrally absorbed into the whole and as a part individually rising out of the whole."[20]

The organization of the following five essays attempts to do justice to both dimensions of the works I discuss. The first four essays are discrete internal analyses to be read as such in their own right, and they point toward a synthesis to be defined in Essay Five. As I shall argue in Essay Five, the resolution of the historicist-formalist dialectic can be achieved only by taking account

[18] Murray Krieger, *A Window to Criticism: Shakespeare's Sonnets and Modern Poetics* (Princeton: Princeton Univ. Press, 1964), pp. 206–207, and *passim*.

[19] E. D. Hirsch, Jr., "Three Dimensions of Hermeneutics," *NLH* 3 (1972): 245–261.

[20] Morris, *Toward a New Historicism*, p. 15.

of the "paradox," as Helen Gardner calls it, by which "the more we put a poem into the past, establish it in its historical context, and interpret it by its own age's aesthetic canons, the more its uniqueness and individuality appear." A great literary work of the past is "extra-historical," she says, precisely because it is the "expression and creation of a human mind and personality and so (is) ultimately irreducible into anything but itself." [21] The logic of dialectic will provide a basis, in other words, for grasping under a single principle a literary work's place in its culture as well as its uniqueness.

Though the first four essays analyze individual works in a formalist manner, taken together they are intended collectively as reciprocal contexts of one another. To elucidate the structures of several works roughly contemporary with each other is necessarily to play the roles of both critic and literary historian. However, such historical generalizations, demarcations, labels, and areas of study, which are the usual categories of historical criticism and literary history, are really, nominalistically speaking, convenient fictions. Their significance is only as valid as the conclusions that a study of individual texts will justify. Consequently I begin, in the first four essays, with internal analyses that are frankly formalistic. These essays progressively develop and accrete general conclusions that are more fully elaborated in the fifth essay, where I take up the theoretical dimensions of historical interrelationships.

Essays One through Four discuss four different ways of accommodating the logic of dialectic. They progress from philosophical prose that overtly denies the dialectical logic inherent in its key terms—Bacon's new science—to dramatic fictions—eight plays of Shakespeare—wherein dialectic is most overtly accommodated. The intervening discussions of three metaphysical poets and *Paradise Lost* move between these two extremes, showing how a denial of dialectic can become likewise a tool for incorporating acceptance of it in fictive discourses.

Dialectic occurs when men attempt to force on a "both-and" reality an "either-or" reading of it. Whether in literary fictions or, for that matter, in the actual world agents attempt to resolve

[21] Gardner, *The Business of Criticism*, p. 20.

conflicts and contradictions between antinomical concepts, ideological positions, and doctrines by reducing these antinomies to one conflicting side, and ignoring or denying the other. In so doing, they only invite back on themselves the attacks of other men (or other concepts, other ideologies) which embody the oppositions and contradictions they have denied. A discourse that commits itself to antinomical categories as its key terms is, whatever it may be about, a verbal action the end of which is to extricate itself from the dialectical logic implicit in those categories. This dialectical logic asserts itself in proportion to the argumentative force directed at escape from it. A main point this study makes about dialectical logic and its uses in constructing and interpreting verbal discourses is that dialectic becomes inevitable to the exact degree dialectic is denied. And conversely: to the degree dialectic is overtly accommodated, built into a writer's discourse, the ironies and disruptions dialectic causes are, if not wholly avoided, at least controlled.

Consequently, these four essays progress on the basis of a kind of shifting proportion. In Bacon's prose the greatest resistance to dialectic is balanced by the greatest incidence of unintentional dialectic. As dialectic is progressively accommodated (by the metaphysical poets, Milton, and Shakespeare), the proportion of unplanned eruptions of dialectic into the surface of the discourse progressively abates. This is, of course, a nonchronological progression. Nor does it intend some sort of causal connection between Bacon and the metaphysicals, the metaphysicals and Milton, and so on. Rather, this arrangement is intended to clarify how several works sharing a common dialectical structure become by that reason individual and unique in their use of it. This is, in fact, also a main point this study attempts to make: that these works differ according to the same dialectical structure that links them together. Dialectical logic explains not only the uniqueness of these works (the formalist's enterprise), and not only what they share (the domain of the historicist); rather, dialectic moves beyond this split to explain how likeness and difference, harmony and conflict create each other.

Each analysis introduces dialectical terms only in an ad hoc manner, and I do not attempt to develop the dialectical paradigms governing these terms until the fifth essay. There are two reasons for this. For one, I believe and hope that dialectic is not forced on these works, and I would like its relevance to them to arise out of readings that take into consideration only the verbal actions they overtly display. More important, however, is the second reason. My discussion of the historicist-formalist dialectic entails the notion that formal analysis is already implicitly historical scholarship. Nevertheless, the two are not the same. By excluding from my analysis in the first four essays any extended reference to background material, I am attempting here to act out one of my main contentions: that considerations of historical context must wait, perhaps even be deliberately ignored, in order to develop materials for such considerations out of analysis temporarily limited to individual texts. And since the contextual relations among these texts will be established in the fifth essay according to the same dialectical logic that governs their internal structure, a full illumination of the first depends on an examination of the second. However, lest the reader lose sight of the main argument of these essays, they are linked by short transition sections that generalize their specific conclusions and prefigure the more theoretical discussion of Essay Five.

ESSAY one

Myth and Method in the Scientific Philosophy of Francis Bacon

Like Descartes, Spinoza, and Leibniz after him, Bacon overtly refused to accommodate the ambiguities of dialectical relations. On the contrary, his "new science" attempts an all-inclusive system of the natural world, characterized by clear, univocal distinctions and identities. I shall examine in this first essay the strategies and strengths available to philosophical prose for accomplishing such a system, as well as this system's inability to resolve the dialectical tensions built into its key terms. Bacon's overt attempt to force an either-or reading on the structures of the natural world and human thought will illuminate the both-and readings of these realms achieved variously by the metaphysical poets, Milton, and Shakespeare. The kind of system Bacon envisioned, wherein all natural phenomena are reduced to a few essential "forms" in a pyramid of abstract laws, could not accommodate the ambiguities of definition, terminology, and reference that dialectic enforces. For this reason dialectic emerges covertly in Bacon's prose because the seeds are already implanted in it. If dialectic becomes inevitable to the degree that it is denied, then the new science clearly manifests such inevitability.

VISION METHODIZED

Justifying his allegorization of various Greek myths in the *De sapientia veterum* (1609), Bacon asserts that in "the old times, when the inventions and conclusions of human reason . . . were as yet new and strange," fables were used not "as a device for shadowing and concealing the meaning, but as a method of making it understood." "For," Bacon says, "as hieroglyphics came before letters, so parables came before arguments." [1] The *De sapientia veterum* will "uncover" the meanings of these myths, and bring them from the darkness of shadowy parables into the light of conceptual arguments.

Though he elsewhere moves through visionary and mythic insights into methodical, systematic statement, as in the *Principles and Origins According to the Fables of Cupid and Coelum* and the myth of Pan in the *De augmentis* (Book 2), Bacon's usual method is literal and systematic exposition. Commentators such as Anderson, Farrington, and Rossi appropriate the model set forth in the "Plan of the Work" prefacing the *Instauratio Magna* of 1620.[2] And certainly Bacon thought that his new science depended radically on the inner coherence of its method.[3] The definitive Spedding-Ellis edition of Bacon's works ratifies this approach, arranging Bacon's various *opuscula* according to their possible place in Bacon's six-part schema.[4] I would suggest, however, that the origins and goals of Bacon's new science are visionary and mythical; that for this reason he only imperfectly clothed it in systematic, methodical language; and that the visionary imperatives governing the new science emerge from recurrent patterns of poetic statement, image, and metaphor.

[1] *The Works of Francis Bacon,* ed. James Spedding, Robert Leslie Ellis, and Douglas Denon Heath (London: Longman, 1857–1874), 6:698. Hereafter referred to in the text as SE, followed by the appropriate volume and page numbers.

[2] Fulton H. Anderson, *The Philosophy of Francis Bacon* (Chicago: Univ. of Chicago Press, 1948); Benjamin Farrington, *Francis Bacon: Philosopher of Industrial Science* (New York: Henry Schuman, 1949); Paolo Rossi, *Francis Bacon: From Magic to Science,* trans. Sacha Rabinovitch (London: Routledge & Kegan Paul, 1968).

[3] *Of the Advancement of Learning,* SE 3:357; *De dignitate et augmentis scientiarum,* SE 4:362–363; *Novum organum,* SE 4:29, 62–63.

[4] Spedding takes responsibility for "the general distribution of the Philosophical works into three parts,—whereby all those writings which were either published or intended for publication by Bacon himself as parts of the Great Instauration are (for the first time, I believe) exhibited separately, and distinguished as well from the independent and collateral pieces which did not form part of the main scheme, as from those which, though originally designed for it, were afterwards superseded or abandoned" (SE 1:viii).

The preface to the *De sapientia veterum* states one of these patterns: the "darkness" of poetic fable versus the "light" of conceptual argument. The "translations" from myth to concept here enact a part of his program which he had earlier—1603— called for in more direct terms:

> But do you suppose, when all the approaches and en- trances to men's minds are beset and blocked by the most obscure idols (*obscurissimis idolis*)—idols deeply implanted (*haerentibus*), and, as it were, burned in—that any clean (*sinceras*) and polished surface remains in the mirror of the mind on which the genuine natural light (*nativis radiis*) of things can fall? [5]

When discussing epic poetry in the *De augmentis,* Bacon sets in opposition men's desire to behold "a more ample greatness, a more perfect order and a more beautiful variety than [he] can anywhere (since the Fall) find in nature"; and reason and his- tory, that buckle and bow down "the mind to the nature of things" (SE 4:315–316). The light-dark opposition in Bacon's vision of the new science is analogous to that between reason and poetry. As regards both, Bacon chooses a conceptual and methodical mode of exposition at the expense of a metaphorical and rhetorical one. His strictures on Ciceronian rhetoric and praise of aphorism as well as his attack on the Idols of the mind no doubt come to mind here as well. Clearly, Bacon was con- sciously committed to "buckling" and "bowing down" the vi- sionary and mythical insights which generated his new science to a rigorous test by methodic translation into conceptual system. However, Bacon only incompletely succeeded in this translation. What was accomplished with Greek myth was not so easily achieved with the Baconian myth.

Certain anomalies remain unresolved where his experimental method attempts to correct the weaknesses of man's knowing powers, and also where he defines the ultimate goals of this method. First, there is Bacon's ambivalent ideal of a "true and lawful marriage between the empirical and the rational faculty,

---

[5] Benjamin Farrington, *The Philosophy of Francis Bacon* (Chicago: Univ. of Chicago Press, 1966), p. 62; Latin text, SE 3:529.

the unkind and ill-starred divorce and separation of which has thrown into confusion all the affairs of the human family" (SE 4:19). All of Bacon's statements on this matter leave unresolved whether in this marriage the senses are the male faculty fecundating the passive "mirror-like" reason, or whether reason begets actively on the fallible body of the senses the issue of general axioms. Another apparent contradiction occurs in Bacon's various statements on man's knowing faculties *vis-à-vis* the complex forms of nature. At one extreme Bacon insists on the "so differing . . . harmony . . . between the spirit of man and the spirit of nature" (*De aug.*, SE 4:433), and at the other he says that "whatsoever is not God but parcel of the world, he [God] hath fitted it to the comprehension of man's mind, if man will open and dilate the powers of his understanding as he may" (*Valerius Terminus,* 1603, SE 3:221). Finally, despite criticizing Aristotelian philosophy for projecting final causes, Bacon was not adverse to stating at least in general terms the ultimate purpose of the new science. For instance, he speaks of "the glory of the Creator and the relief of man's estate" in *The Advancement of Learning* (SE 3:294), and in expanding on this *locus classicus* in *De augmentis* he predicts that metaphysics (as he redefines it) will enfranchise "the power of men to the greatest liberty, and lead it to the widest and most extensive field of operation" (SE 4:362). In the *Description of the Intellectual Globe* (1612) he says that "he who knows the universal passions of matter and thereby knows what is possible to be, cannot help knowing likewise what has been, what is, and what will be, according to the sum of things" (SE 5:512). But these statements concern means toward still further ends, and sum up what Bacon said (following Democritus [6]) in *The New Organon,* namely that "Nature to be commanded must be obeyed" (SE 4:47). Even *The New Atlantis* envisions science conferring on future ages only a vaguely conceived and undifferentiated blessing. In contrast I find buried in discussions of otherwise unrelated matters numerous hints at a much more broadly projected *telos* for the new science, hints that Bacon uniformly does not develop and of which he does not even show an awareness.

[6] R. A. Tsanoff, "Francis Bacon and Philosophic Thought," *Rice University Pamphlets* 13 (1926):7.

In the arguments of a man otherwise devoted to extrapolating with careful self-criticism the implications of his informing idea, these odd gaps and blurs suggest a broader difficulty. Statements, motifs or fragments of ideas, images, and metaphors occurring and recurring through Bacon's scientific treatises disclose a mythic model that both parallels his conceptual system, and to a large extent runs counter to the logical requirements of that system.[7] This myth points beyond the system which imperfectly embodies it to a vision of human power that human reason can only reach for but never grasp. These repeated patterns can be divided into three somewhat overlapping groups. The first concerns a norm of intuition that measures human knowledge by immediate contact between mind and the phenomena of nature. The second envisions the human mind purified of all normal abstractive functions and thereby prepared for intuitive identification with the natural world. The third includes the secularized "conversion" and "resurrection" in full command of nature which the new scientist "merits" by humbling himself before nature and becoming again as a little child. These patterns coalesce into a vision of man who, having achieved complete knowledge of and absolute power over the natural world, is released finally from his own body into an angelic existence of total, timeless freedom.[8]

Bacon himself distinguished between myth and method when he opposed "Heroical Poetry" to the products of reason (part of this passage I have already alluded to above):

[7] My assertion that Bacon was attempting to construct a coherent system is not touched by Bacon's well-known strictures on the methods of earlier philosophers, who, as Bacon said, settled too quickly and easily for conceptual systems. Bacon's preference for discrete aphorisms actually refers to the discourse for recording the beginnings of experimentation; aphorisms were seen by him as guards against too rapid extrapolation of universal laws, not as substitutes for them. Cf. Brian Vickers, *Francis Bacon and Renaissance Prose* (Cambridge: University Press, 1968), Ch. 3, "The Aphorism," esp. pp. 82–83.

[8] The important place of image and metaphor in Bacon's articulation of his new science has become increasingly recognized in the last decade, reversing the earlier denigration following L. C. Knight's attack on Bacon's figurative language in *Explorations* (New York: New York Univ. Press, 1964; orig. publ. 1947). Cf. Elizabeth Sewell, *The Orphic Voice* (New Haven: Yale Univ. Press, 1960); A. Righter, "Francis Bacon," in *The English Mind*, ed. H. S. Davies and G. Watson (Cambridge: University Press, 1964); W. R. Davis, "The Imagery of Bacon's Late Work," *MLQ* 27 (1966): 162–173; and Vickers, *Francis Bacon and Renaissance Prose*.

> For if the matter be attentively considered, a sound argu-
> ment may be drawn from Poesy, to show that there is
> agreeable to the spirit of man a more ample greatness,
> a more perfect order, and a more beautiful variety than it
> can anywhere (since the Fall) find in nature. And there-
> fore, since the acts and events which are the subjects of
> real history are not of sufficient grandeur to satisfy the hu-
> man mind, Poesy is at hand to feign acts more heroical;
> . . . [SE 4:315–316]

Poetry stands to science as fruitless but pleasing fantasy stands
to natural laws that assure an authentic "more ample greatness."
Bacon did not reject "sufficient grandeur to satisfy the human
mind," nor did he envision anything other than "acts more
heroical" than had ever been achieved before. Rejected, rather,
were mentally constructed systems (whether philosophic or
poetic) that reflected not the natural world, but mental fantasies. Nevertheless, Bacon's method of investigation is a means
to an end in itself not methodic but mythical, or in Bacon's
sense of the term, "poetic." And I suggest that these mythical
final causes will appear in Bacon's otherwise strictly methodical
discourse only through scattered and oblique allusions, mainly
because they are the very thing Bacon felt must be suppressed
if his method was to succeed.

The mythic model energizing Bacon's method is made up of
patterns that reach to one another across the boundaries of the
various treatises, through parallelism, association, and repetition.
Whereas image and metaphor are overtly subordinated to systematic argument, for my purposes I reverse this relationship,
and see these metaphors as embodying the mythic ends of the new
science. Bacon continually illustrates his conceptual arguments
with concrete images, suggesting elements in his myth recalcitrant
to entering a logical scientific grammar. In other words, since the
mythic element in Bacon's writing is that part of his radical
vision of ends and goals for which he had not achieved a completely methodical correlate, it will show up in statements that
are really hortatory under the guise of being pragmatically
directional. One might even wonder whether Bacon's continual
emphasis on workability does not compensate for the envisioned

ideals that his method had not in fact practical instruments for realizing. In any case, the occurrence of image and metaphor in the midst of Bacon's systematic exposition, suggesting the system's failure to effect wholly the translation from myth to method, allows them to become for us chinks releasing light onto the mythic model which fascinated Bacon and led him to systematic exposition in the first place.

THE IDEAL OF INTUITION

The ideal of intuition identifies "true" human knowledge with an immediate cognition of the natural world which discounts the constructs of conceptual reasoning. Images and statements joining the light of nature with the human mind, conceived as an unwarped, polished mirror, mediate this ideal; they occur often in Bacon. Related to this cluster is the doctrine of the Idols, fictions of the mind which Bacon describes as clouding and distorting this mirror. An early appearance of the cluster brings together all three elements, *The Masculine Birth of Time* (1603): "But do you suppose, when all the approaches and entrances to men's minds are beset and blocked by the most obscure idols— idols deeply implanted and, as it were, burned in—that any clean and polished surface remains in the mirror of the mind on which the genuine natural light of things can fall?" [9]

In the same work Bacon attacks the followers of Aristotle "who turned themselves away from the perambulation of our globe and from the light of nature and of history." Against these and others he affirms that "generally speaking science is to be sought from the light of nature (*naturae lumine*), not from the darkness (*obscuritate*) of antiquity." And indeed, the new science is envisioned as "set up in the midst" of nature as "one bright and radiant light of truth (*veritatis lumen clarum et radiosum*), shedding its beams in all directions and dispelling all errors in a moment." [10] In the *Cogitata et Visa* (*Thoughts and Conclusions*) of four years later (1607) Bacon extends the image of the mirror, when he says that the unaided mind is "a mirror (*speculi*) so

[9] Farrington, *The Philosophy of Francis Bacon*, p. 62.
[10] *Ibid.*, pp. 63, 69, 70; Latin text SE 3:535, 537.

uneven as to distort the rays which fall upon it by its angularities. It is not a smooth flat surface." And a year later, in the *Redargutio Philosophiarum (The Refutation of Philosophies)*, Bacon further specifies the purified mind as a flat mirror, when he calls for "leveling a special path on account of the inveterate prejudices and obsessions of our minds." [11] The image of "leveling" illuminates Bacon's goal of conforming all minds to a process of experimentation ideally impersonal and quasi automatic. This in turn is linked with the doctrine of the Idols, whereby Bacon would eradicate subjectivity and create scientific minds all capable of seeing the same things in the same way. The opposition between light and dark occurs again in *The Refutation of Philosophies*, where Bacon sets "the light of nature, that is to say, the enquiry into particulars," against "the obscure and tortuous recesses and caverns of the imagination." For him the norm, reminding us somewhat of Descartes later on, is "some crystal clear thought *(liquido cogitarent)*" which man may "set up in the midst" as "some one clear source of light and truth." [12]

Extending this pattern are occasional words and images that describe the perfect intellectual mirror achieved through a kind of washing and purging. For instance, in *The New Organon* he speaks of removing the Idols of the mind so that "the understanding" be "thoroughly freed and cleansed *(expurgandus)*," and he sees "these expiations and purgings of the mind *(expiationibus et expurgationibus mentis)*" as necessary for the proper working of his new logic (SE 4:69, 70; 1:179). Likewise, in the earlier *Thoughts and Conclusions*, Bacon had found the unaided mind not "so scoured and clean *(vacuum et purum)* as to admit the genuine native images of things without some colouring from the imagination." [13]

This pattern of light-mirror-purgation, through which Bacon so often envisions a perfect cognition of the natural world, obviously governs and parallels his systematic development of empirical experimentation. Bacon's attempt to establish "forever a

[11] *Ibid.*, pp. 88, 103; Latin text SE 3:607.

[12] *Ibid.*, pp. 118, 124; Latin text SE 3:577. Further examples of the light-mirror pattern occur in *Valerius Terminus*, SE 3:217, 224, 241; *The New Organon*, SE 4:27, 54, 57, 109; *De augmentis*, SE 4:431.

[13] Farrington, *The Philosophy of Francis Bacon*, p. 88; Latin text, SE 3:606.

true and lawful marriage between the empirical and the rational faculty" in *The New Organon* had already been foreseen in *The Masculine Birth of Time,* but with an interesting addition. The philosopher speaking in the first person says: "My dear, dear boy, what I purpose is to unite you with *things themselves* in a chaste, holy, and legal wedlock." [14] What "things themselves" are varies significantly for Bacon from place to place, but this at least is certain: "things themselves" are the residue left when all obscurities and impurities are purged from the mirror of the mind. The need to make the mind an exact reflection of "things themselves" is a constant in Bacon's writings. That this ideal also entails certain conditions that block its fulfillment is only one paradox that the mythic element in Bacon's method brings to light.

Bacon defined "objective knowledge" through a sharp distinction between the (biased) contributions of the mind on the one hand, and the natural world "in itself" on the other. In this respect Bacon assumed with many Renaissance thinkers the split between intuitive and abstractive cognition which William of Ockham had laid in the fourteenth century as the foundation of nominalist epistemology. In the early *Rules for the Direction of the Mind* (1628), written two years after Bacon's death, Descartes defined "science in its entirety" positively as "true and evident cognition," and negatively as that about which the mind is in no doubt whatsoever. Then he describes the kind of intuition which grasps the first principles of science:

> By *intuition* I understand, not the fluctuating testimony of the senses, nor the misleading judgment that proceeds from the blundering constructions of imagination, but the conception which an unclouded and attentive mind gives us so readily and distinctly that we are wholly freed from doubt about that which we understand. Or, what comes to the same thing, *intuition* is the undoubting conception of an unclouded and attentive mind, and springs from the light of reason alone; . . . Thus each individual can mentally have intuition of the fact that he exists, and that he

14 *Ibid.,* p. 72; italics in Farrington's text, but not in the original (SE 3:538).

thinks; that the triangle is bounded by three lines only, the sphere by a single superficies, and so on.[15]

For Descartes intuition is intellectual vision as opposed to the senses and the imagination. For Bacon, the intuitive ideal is usually located in immediate contact between the senses and the natural world. Despite this important difference, both thinkers agree in defining contact between human cognition and first principles (conceptual for Descartes, "things themselves" for Bacon) against the obscuring and "impure" parts of human knowing faculties, and both are literally agreed in finding the imagination one of these.

A position earlier than Bacon's but closer to it in substance is Nicholas of Cusa's. He attempts in the *De docta ignorantia* (1440) to describe an adequate human knowledge of the Infinite Divine (if such were in fact possible). To achieve this, however, is to achieve "abolition of all structures on the part of the human mind." [16] Arguing Cusa's influence on Leonardo da Vinci, Ernst Cassirer finds the latter distinguishing between two opposed groups. The first are the "primitives" who follow "only one pattern and one model for their work: experience." The others, strikingly like those criticized by Bacon, "abandoned nature and reality and lost themselves in a world of merely conceptual distinctions (*discorsi*)." [17] Linked with Bacon at least through the empiricism that both owed in part to Bernardino Telesio (1509–1588),[18] Tommaso Campanella distinguished sharply between intuition and mental abstraction: "[He holds as a norm] the direct authentication of something which is given; it is the immediate apprehension of being, which is achieved without reasoning, through a kind of total fusion of knowledge with its object.—Understood in this way, sense is opposed to reason as

[15] *The Philosophical Works of Descartes*, trans. Elizabeth S. Haldane and G. R. T. Ross (New York: Dover Publications, 1955), I: p. 7.

[16] Giuseppe Bufo, *Nicolas de Cues, ou la métaphysique de la finitude* (Paris: Éditions Seghers, 1964), p. 41: "la suppression de toute construction de la part de l'esprit humain."

[17] Ernst Cassirer, *The Individual and the Cosmos in Renaissance Philosophy*, trans. Mario Domandi (New York: Harper Torchbooks, 1964), p. 48.

[18] Cf. *On the Principles and Origins According to the Fables of Cupid and Coelum*, SE 5:492.

intuition is opposed to discourse. . . ." [19] And in the sceptical
stream of Renaissance thought a similar ideal grounds a philosophical faith quite the opposite of Bacon's. For instance, Francis Sanchez (1552–1632) in his short treatise *Quod nihil scitur*
(*That Nothing is Known* [1581]) insists that "knowledge is
perfect cognition of a thing." What characterizes this "perfect
cognition" is, in Richard Popkin's paraphrase, the "immediate,
intuitive apprehension of all the real qualities of an object." Opposed to intuition are generalizations which "go beyond this
level of scientific certainty and introduce abstractions, chimeras,
etc." [20]

Though the distinction between intuition and discursive thought
goes as far back as Plato and Aristotle, the distinction in the
Renaissance derived from a source closer to home. This source
was William of Ockham (c. 1290–1349), whose distinction between intuitive and abstractive cognition explains the curious
difficulties Bacon faced in trying to formulate his own norm of
intuition.[21] As far as one can tell, this split originates for Ockham in an *a priori* demand for direct correspondence between the
forms of mental conception and the structures of the material
world. In any case, Ockham's insistence on the total distinction
between these two realms can be explained by the failure of this
demand to be realized. For, finding this demand to fail, Ockham
held that only the mind's direct intuition through the senses of
discrete material objects, an intuition defined explicitly against
abstraction, can bring the intellect into contact with the actual
existence of these objects. The difficulty with this distinction is

[19] Leon Blanchet, *Campanella* (Paris: Librairie Félix Alcan, 1920), p. 282: "la
constatation directe de quelque chose qui est donné; c'est l'appréhension immédiate
de l'être, qui se fait sans raisonnement, par une sorte de fusion complète de la
connaissance avec son objet.—Ainsi compris, le sens s'oppose à la raison comme
l'intuition s'oppose au discours. . . ."

[20] Richard H. Popkin, *The History of Scepticism from Erasmus to Descartes*
(Assen: Van Gorcum, 1960), p. 40: "scientia est rei perfecta cognitio." For a
discussion of the significance of the "mirror" topos in still other Renaissance figures
such as Ficino, the Cambridge Platonists, and Milton, and of its connection with
the ideal of intuition, cf. Gordon W. O'Brien, *Renaissance Poetics and the Problem
of Power* (Chicago: Inst. of Elizabethan Studies, 1956).

[21] For the all-pervasive influence of nominalism in the late medieval and Renaissance universities, cf. Walter J. Ong, S. J., *Ramus, Method and the Decay of
Dialogue* (Cambridge: Harvard Univ. Press, 1958), esp. ch. VI.

that it remains a solution "by default," and results in an ambiguous attitude toward abstractive concepts, as well as the systems that the mind constructs from them. One can emphasize either their incapacity to mirror "things as they are," or the fact that they are the only instrument available to men for understanding and articulating the data given in intuition.

For Ockham, the mind fragments the individual, integral, and discrete bodies of the natural world into distinct concepts in order to articulate its understanding of them, thus placing the structures of both at odds with each other. Consistent with this split is the distinction between intuitive and abstractive cognition:

> Intuitive cognition of a thing is cognition that enables us to know whether the thing exists or does not exist, in such a way that, if the thing exists, then the intellect immediately judges that it exists and evidently knows that it exists, unless the judgment happens to be impeded through the imperfection of this cognition.[22]

In turn he defines abstractive cognition in this fashion:

> We must realise . . . that the term "abstractive cognition" can be taken in two senses. In one sense it means cognition that relates to something abstracted from many singulars; and in this sense abstractive cognition is nothing else but cognition of a universal which can be abstracted from many things. . . .
>
> Abstractive cognition in the second sense abstracts from existence and non-existence and from all the other conditions which contingently belong to or are predicated of a thing.[23]

Ockham further divides abstractive cognition into the abstractive concepts of singular things accompanying intuition, and abstractive concepts of universals.[24] About this he says:

[22] Prologue to the *Ordinatio Ockham,* Q. 1, in *Ockham: Philosophical Writings,* ed., Philotheus Boehner (Edinburgh: Nelson, 1957), p. 23.

[23] *Ibid.,* pp. 22–23.

[24] Sebastian Day, *Intuitive Cognition: A Key to the Significance of the Later Scholastics* (St. Bonaventure, N.Y.: Franciscan Inst., 1947), p. 185.

> It must, however, be understood that there are two sorts
> of universal. There is one sort which is naturally univer-
> sal; in other words, is a sign naturally predicable of many
> things, in much the same way as smoke naturally signifies
> fire, or a groan the pain of a sick man, or laughter an
> inner joy. Such a universal is nothing other than a content
> of the mind; and therefore no substance outside the
> mind and no accident outside the mind is [sic] such a
> universal.[25]

The universal is abstracted from as many concepts as there are
discrete intuitions,[26] and thus reflects nothing in the material
world. Articulate and conscious thought is by its very nature
abstractive: to think is to abstract.

> To sum up: The mind's own intellectual acts are called
> states of mind. By their nature they stand for the actual
> things outside the mind or for other things in the mind,
> just as the spoken words stand for them by convention.[27]

Ernest Moody sums up nicely Ockham's statements on universals and their place in human knowing:

> It remains, therefore, that the universal which is a prin-
> ciple of finite human knowledge, and which alone concerns
> the philosopher as such . . . is the *universale post rem.*
> This is the concept or act of understanding which is
> proper to individual human minds, and which is a natural
> or immediate sign of the finite causes of change with
> which the science of nature is concerned. Porphyry's ques-
> tions [about the ontological status of universals], conse-
> quently, receive the following answers: (1) Universals
> exist only in the mind. (2) Being acts of the understand-
> ing, which is incorporeal, they are incorporeal. (3) Being
> acts of the understanding, which is not a sensible or ma-

[25] *Summa totius logicae,* I, c. xvi, Boehner, *Ockham,* p. 34.
[26] *Ordinatio Ockham,* 2.8, Q, quoted and paraphrased in Frederick Copleston,
S. J., *A History of Philosophy, Vol. III: Ockham to Suraez* (Westminster, Md.:
Newman Press, 1959), pp. 56–57.
[27] *Expositio super librum Perihermenias,* Boehner, *Ockham,* p. 44.

terial thing, they cannot be said to be *in* sensible things nor of the being of sensible things.[28]

This gulf creates both the demand for concept-object correspondence, and the realization of concept-object split. Once the problem of "true" knowledge was set on these grounds, the split between concept and object became both a distinction to be insisted upon, and a rift to be healed, with both options generating the necessity of its opposite. The "ideal" cognition would preserve the differences between concepts and things, while identifying the two nevertheless in a mirrorlike fashion; in short, the "ideal" was self-contradictory.

Bacon manifests his indebtedness to the Ockhamist split in various ways. For instance, in the section on Pan in the *De sapientia veterum,* Echo is allegorized into contributing to Baconian science:

> And it is excellently provided that of all discourses or voices Echo alone should be chosen for the world's [Pan's] wife. For that is in fact the true philosophy which echoes most faithfully the voice of the world itself, and is written as it were from the world's own dictation; being indeed nothing else than the image and reflexion of it, which it only repeats and echoes, but adds nothing of its own. [SE 6:714]

The comparison of the purged intellect to an unwarped mirror likewise adumbrates this notion. About the senses he says, for instance, that "the testimony and information of the sense has [sic] reference always to man, not to the universe; and it is a great error to assert that the sense is the measure of things" (SE 4:26). About the intellect itself, Bacon, after expressing the wish that "human intellect were even, and like a fair sheet of paper with no writing on it," insists that the unaided mind cannot be trusted because "in forming its notions" it "mixes up its own nature with the nature of things" (SE 4:26–27). If we remember the Aquinian dictum that whatever is received into the

[28] Ernest A. Moody, *The Logic of William of Ockham* (New York: Sheed and Ward, 1935), p. 94.

mind is received according to the mode of the receiver, we see
how radically Bacon has discounted constructs indigenous to human thought. For Bacon, as for Ockham, whatever is received
into the mind according to the modes of the mind ceases to reflect
physical objects themselves.

How the mind can operate having been stripped of its distinguishing functions is a problem to which Bacon does not so
much provide a solution, as "exhort" one. The hortatory elements in Bacon's writings become visible at those points where
his vision of the new science calls for solutions at once necessary and impossible. Futility is oddly rendered by statements that
treat self–contradictions as readily resolvable. The imperative that
the mind not "mix up its own nature with the nature of the
things" is just such a hortatory statement, and signals a major
eruption from the stratum of mythic wish into the methodic
implementation of the new science. Such statements present
"what ought to or should be achieved" in terms of "what can
be achieved." And what "ought to be achieved" expresses most
obviously an inherently self-contradictory imperative, when stated
in a methodical grammar ruled by noncontradiction, the grammar of the new science.

Whereas Bacon criticizes both sense knowledge and abstract
knowledge because they "mix" something of themselves with the
data derived from material objects, he may also downgrade one
at the expense of the other. He attacks past philosophies for
elaborating mental constructs at the expense of empirical evidence
in *The Masculine Birth of Time* and *The Advancement of
Learning*. For instance, in the latter we find one of his better-
known statements on the subject:

> For the wit and mind of man, if it works upon matter,
> which is the contemplation of the creatures of God, work-
> eth according to the stuff, and is limited thereby; but if it
> work upon itself, as the spider worketh his web, then it is
> endless, and brings forth indeed cobwebs of learning, ad-
> mirable for the fineness of thread and work, but of no sub-
> stance or profit. [SE 3:285–286]

While insisting on a return to nature itself, Bacon fully recognized that the mind is the only instrument capable of correcting

the errors of the senses, and on this corrective function Bacon's ideal of the true marriage between the rational and empirical faculties rested. "To the immediate and proper perception of the sense," he said, "I do not give much weight; but I contrive that the office of the sense shall be only to judge of the experiment, and that the experiment itself shall judge of the thing" (SE 4:26). Thus Bacon escaped one consequence of the Ockhamist split between intuition and abstraction, in that a liaison would be possible once the differences were recognized and understood. However, this marriage had more subtle obstacles to overcome. The norm of direct correspondence between the forms of thought and things introduces still other ambiguities. These appear primarily in the laws of the new science itself, which Bacon envisioned composed simultaneously of atomistic particles of thought and of abstract concepts.

Bacon's theory of induction signals his inability to fit his vision to the requirements of systematic exposition and testing. He attacks syllogistic deduction, giving an analysis of propositions and terms wholly indebted to nominalist logic:

> . . . the syllogism consists of propositions; propositions of words; and words are the tokens and signs of notions. Now if the very notions of the mind (which are as the soul of words and the basis of the whole structure) be improperly and overhastily abstracted from facts, vague, not sufficiently definite, faulty in short in many ways, the whole edifice tumbles. [SE 4:24] [29]

[29] In his *Expositio super viii libros Physicorum*, Ockham is careful to make explicit the relation between propositions and their components on the one hand, and the world of discrete singulars on the other: "Now the fact is that the propositions known by natural science are composed not of sensible things or substances, but of mental contents or concepts that are common to such things. Hence, properly speaking, the science of nature is not about corruptible and generable things nor about natural substances nor about movable things, for none of these is subject or predicate in any conclusion known by natural science. Properly speaking, the science of nature is about mental contents which are common to such things, and which stand precisely for such things in many propositions, though in some propositions these concepts stand for themselves, as our further exposition will show. . . . The subject of such a proposition is a mental content or a word; which is our intended conclusion. . . . A real science is not about things, but about mental contents standing for things: for the terms of scientifically known propositions stand for things. . . . The real sciences are about mental con-

Such a critique dictates a system of abstractions founded as firmly in the non-abstract as possible. Bacon's dilemma is summed up by Paolo Rossi:

> [There] is in fact more and other than an antipathy [toward language]: Bacon's attitude stems from his mistrust of language—as of all the products of the human mind—because, though it is indispensable to humanity as such, it tends to hinder the true understanding of reality by coming between man and the world he inhabits.[30]

Bacon's insistence on a cooperative marriage between the senses and the mind comes across as less the beginning of a viable method, and more an exhortation covertly elicited by its inherent impossibility. As Rossi implies, Bacon had to insist that the intellect was both the indispensable tool of the new science, and the main obstacle to it. Deductive "proceeding has been to fly at once from the sense and particulars up to the most general propositions, as certain fixed poles for the argument to turn upon." In contrast, his "plan is to proceed regularly and gradually from one axiom to another, so that the most general are not reached till the last; but then when you do come to them you find them to be not empty notions, but well-defined, and such as nature would really recognize as her first principles, and such as lie at the heart and marrow of things" (SE 4:25.) [31] Later, he says such principles are "extracted not merely out of the depths of the mind, but out of the very bowels of nature"; for he proposes to "sink the foundations of the sciences deeper and firmer" and he begins "the inquiry nearer the source than men have done heretofore" (SE 4:25). Leaving aside the often-noticed fact that this proceeding ignores the working hypothesis and even implicitly

---

tents, since they are about contents which stand for things; for even though they are mental contents, they still stand for things," Boehner, *Ockham,* pp. 11–12.

[30] *Francis Bacon: From Magic to Science,* p. 170.

[31] Also in Book 1 of *The New Organon* (*Aph.* 38): "For since all Interpretation of Nature commences with the senses, and leads from the perceptions of the senses by a straight, regular, and guarded path to the perceptions of the understanding, which are true notions and axioms, it follows of necessity that the more copious and exact the representations of the senses, the more easily and prosperously will everything proceed" (SE 4:192).

denies its validity, we may ask just what makes Bacon's principles more valid for him than those he defines them against. The key distinction is between "fly up" and "gradual." Now it is quite clear that Bacon's new science would consist of logical interrelations no different, in general, from those in Aristotle's *Metaphysics*. The two differ for Bacon in that the foundations of the new science are grounded in empirical observations, and not mediated by still other principles. As the laborious tables and procedures in Book II of *The New Organon* demonstrate, however, Bacon had great difficulty making the transition from physical data to purely conceptual principles founded on these data.

This transition rather confounds the two sides than builds a bridge between them. This is indicated by the ambiguities of Bacon's "forms," which equivocate between abstract concepts at one place and atomistic pieces of matter at another. The question of just what Bacon meant by his "forms" has been one of the great siren calls luring the Bacon scholar. Ellis, as a preface to an extended discussion of them in his immensely helpful introduction to Bacon's philosophy, says that they are not an important part of the new science (SE 1:28). A quick summary of several discussions of these ambiguous entities will, I think, indicate the possibilities that Bacon's own indecision seems to allow.

Paul Shorey, for instance, finds the "Baconian doctrine of forms" to be "the Platonic idea conceived as the as yet unknown law of a quality or effect to be investigated." Similar to this opinion is Rossi's: the "Form is . . . a relation between simple natures." Through these relations man might "discover every organisation and movement from which a given simple nature can result." In these two cases the forms are the few, essential principles governing the wide variety of complex physical phenomena. At the other extreme is Ellis's notion that the form stands to the visible, phenomenal "Nature" of a physical object as a primary quality stands to a secondary quality, and that "the thing and its Form differ only as 'apparens et existens, aut exterius et interius, aut in ordine ad hominem et in ordine ad universum.' " As Ellis goes on to say, "That [the form] is after all only a physical conception appears sufficiently . . . from the fact of its being made the most important part of the subject-matter of the natural sciences" (SE 1:31). However, Ellis is quite aware of Bacon's tendency to see the form as simultaneously a physical entity and a law governing physical entities. In agreeing, Anderson says Bacon "finally comes . . . to regard forms both as the constituents of things and as the laws of their activity." And in distinguishing most scrupulously the possible meanings of the term, the English philosopher C. D. Broad discovers four different but related ways in which Bacon seems to use it. These run from the most material, the notion that there are in the world certain physical substances irreducible to one another, to the most abstract, "the various generic physical properties, such as colour, temperature, etc., [which] are wholly incomparable with each other and cannot be regarded as species of any one genus." The other two possibilities include the notion that the number of "different kinds of material substance is comparatively small, and that the apparent multiplicity of kinds arises from the various proportions in which these few are mixed and compounded"; and "the various specific modifications of a single generic property, such as colour" may yet be distinguished as all species of this genus (i.e., form) by quantifiable proportions.[32]

These do not exhaust the differing opinions possible on this matter. And if Broad's distinctions are in part difficult to perceive, this is due to the ambiguous texts on which they are founded:

1. For though in nature nothing really exists beside individual bodies, performing pure individual acts according to a fixed law, yet in philosophy this very law and the investigation, discovery, and explanation of it, is the foundation as well of knowledge as of operation. And it is this law, with its clauses, that I mean when I speak of *Forms;* a name which I the rather adopt because it has grown into use and become familiar. [*Aph.* 2]
2. But whosoever is acquainted with Forms, embraces

[32] Paul Shorey, *Platonism Ancient and Modern* (Berkeley: Univ. of California Press, 1938), p. 183; Rossi, *Francis Bacon: From Magic to Science*, p. 202; SE 1:29–30; Anderson, *The Philosophy of Francis Bacon*, p. 79; C. D. Broad, *The Philosophy of Francis Bacon* (Cambridge: University Press, 1926), pp. 37–39.

the unity of nature in substances the most unlike. . . .
[*Aph.* 3]

3. For a true and perfect rule of operation then the direction will be *that it be certain, free, and disposing or leading to action.* And this is the same thing with the discovery of the true Form. For the Form of a nature is such, that given the Form the nature infallibly follows. Therefore it is always present when the nature is present, and universally implies it, and is constantly inherent in it. Again, the Form is such, that if it be taken away the nature infallibly vanishes. Therefore it is always absent when the nature is absent, and implies its absence, and inheres in nothing else. Lastly, the true Form is such that it deduces the given nature from some source of being which is inherent in more natures, and which is better known in the natural order of things than the Form itself. For a true and perfect axiom of knowledge then the direction and precept will be, *that another nature be discovered which is convertible with the given nature, and yet is a limitation of a more general nature, as of a true and real genus.* [*Aph.* 4]

4. The rule or axiom for the transformation of bodies is of two kinds. The first regards a body as a troop or collection of simple natures. In gold, for example, the following properties meet. It is yellow in color; heavy up to a certain weight; malleable or ductile to a certain degree of extension; it is not volatile, and loses none of its substance by the action of fire; it turns into a liquid with a certain degree of fluidity; it is separated, and dissolved by particular means; and so on for the other natures which meet in gold. This kind of axiom, therefore, deduces the thing from the forms of simple natures. For he who knows the forms of yellow, weight, ductility, fixity, fluidity, solution, and so on, and the methods for superinducing them, and their gradations and modes, will make it his care to have them joined together in some body, whence may follow the transformation of that body into gold. [*Aph* 5] [SE 4:12off.]

The second kind of axiom in Aph. 5 refers to the "latent process" which joins simple natures, and does not concern us here.

In text 1, forms are laws controlling discrete physical bodies; in text 2, forms are a kind of unifying principle which "embraces" the various diverse natures in physical bodies. This principle can be either an abstract idea, which Shorey compared to a Platonic form, or a physical substratum underlying secondary qualities, Ellis's interpretation. Text 3 connects forms and natures in such a way that the first could either (following Ellis) constitute physical objects themselves, or become abstract genera of which, presumably, the natures are species. The section on convertibility in italics adds further ambiguity, in that the specific nature in a specific body is convertible with a "nature" which is yet broader in extension than the first. In light of examples later in Book II, Bacon seems to aim at a generic principle or quality, different versions of which may yet be present in different bodies. The attempt to arrive at the common "form" of heat in the later aphorisms bears this inference out. Text 4 illustrates a similar ambiguity. The simple natures that make up gold seem to be both atomistic and irreducible parts ("troop or collection of simple natures"), and abstract, generic categories of physical qualities ("yellow, weight, ductility, fixity, fluidity, solution, and so on").

My answer to the question "Are the forms material constituents of physical bodies, or abstract laws governing the constituents of physical bodies" is quite simply that Bacon covertly required that they be both. Thus, to cite two further apparently irreconcilable passages, he could at one time insist that "the Form of a thing is the very thing itself, and the thing differs from the form no otherwise than as the apparent differs from the real, or the external from the internal, or the thing in reference to man from the thing in reference to the universe" (SE 4:137). And still later, this point is overtly developed in a seemingly incompatible direction:

> And even in the case of simple natures I would not be understood to speak of abstract forms and ideas, either not defined in matter at all, or ill defined. For when I speak of Forms, I mean nothing more than those laws and determinations of absolute actuality which govern and consti-

tute any simple nature, as heat, light, weight, in every
kind of matter and subject that is susceptible of them.
Thus the Form of Heat or the Form of Light is the same
thing as the Law of Heat or the Law of Light [SE 4:146]

The form is first an abstract law or category of qualities, then
an immanent constituent of physical bodies themselves. Bacon, in
both assuming and yet trying to escape the Ockhamist split,
oscillated covertly back to the demand for total correspondence
between the structures of concepts and objects. The impossibility
of this correspondence plus the insistence that nothing less than
correspondence will suffice together cause this equivocation.
Bacon's ideal of a science that moves gradually from intuition
of material things to the most general laws thus appears to be a
coalescence of the incompatible demands that this ideal, as he
formulated it, forced upon him. This science would have to be
(impossibly) both abstract and concrete, built up out of elements which are simultaneously atomic particles of matter and
atomistically conceived abstract qualities. In this way did his
mind envision establishing "forever a true and lawful marriage
between the empirical and the rational faculty."

Perhaps nowhere else do the patent incongruities in Bacon's
method manifest so clearly the hortatory, mythic element in his
vision. But, I might add, nowhere else does Bacon grapple so
closely with the methodical consequences of that vision. The
call for a new experimental method is of course at the heart of
the new philosophy. Whether Ellis is right or not about the importance of forms, Bacon failed because his method required a
total coalescence of mind and matter that the method also made
impossible. Since the norm of concept-object correspondence and
the result by default of concept-object split were both grounded
on the irreducible differences between intuitive and abstractive
cognition, both positions could only lead each other around in
dialectical oscillation.

THE PURIFICATION OF THE MIND

Bacon had acute if limited insight into the psychological as
well as epistemological debilities of the human mind. His criti-

cism links a distrust of any knowledge the mind achieves without labor, with systematic discounting of mental constructions, the doctrine of the Idols. Relevant to the latter point, Bacon now and again insists that the refusal of man's mind to bow down before nature as something made by God, in desiring to remake nature in its own image, constitutes a secular version of the sin of idolatry.

In *The Advancement of Learning* Bacon attacks poetry because "the use of this Feigned History hath been to give some shadow of satisfaction to the mind of man in those points wherein the nature of things doth deny it" (SE 3:343). The same complaint is made against previous philosophers in the *Thoughts and Conclusions* two years later (1607), where he says that "they seek only mental satisfaction, or a lucrative profession, or some support and ornament for their renown." [33] In seeking this satisfaction, the mind tends to desire too much perfection and symmetry in the system it creates: "What the philosophers are concerned with is that their art should be held perfect." Systems of this sort "make a show of presenting a complete whole," and against such Bacon states his early preference for an aphoristic style.[34] In *The New Organon,* wherein he delivers his most definitive criticism of man's capacity for "admiring and almost adoring the human mind" (SE 4:27), Bacon continually disabuses the reader of opinions that are adopted "either as being the received opinion or as being agreeable to [the human understanding]" (SE 4:56). He says at one point, quite unequivocally: "And generally let every student of nature take this as a rule,—that whatever his mind seizes and dwells upon with peculiar satisfaction is to be held in suspicion, and that so much the more care is to be taken in dealing with such questions to keep the understanding even and clear" (SE 4:60).

Of the four Idols themselves, the Idols of the Theater are specifically defined by Bacon as "stories" presented in the "philosophical theater" which like the plays of poets "are more compact and elegant, and more as one would wish them to be, then true stories out of history" (SE 4:63). Bacon also criticizes the mind's desire for mental satisfaction because it substitutes the fictitious symmetry of system for learning that controls nature.

[33] Farrington, *The Philosophy of Francis Bacon,* p. 76.   [34] *Ibid.,* pp. 74, 75.

In *De augmentis* (1623) Bacon, distinguishing the Magistral and the Initiative modes of discourse, notes that the former "is fit to win consent or belief, but of little use to give directions for practice." It "more satisfies the understanding" because it carries its own demonstrations within itself and does not look to the "actions in common life" which "are dispersed, and not arranged in order" (SE 4:451).

A corollary to Bacon's strictures on the desire for specious satisfaction is that the new science can be achieved only "by slow and faithful toil" as it "gathers information from things and brings it to the understanding."[35] In *The Refutation of Philosophies* (1608) he criticizes "those who take up philosophy, not as an anxious and laborious sphere of duty but as a sort of holiday excursion."[36] In *The Advancement of Learning* Bacon connects the avoidance of this labor with the mind's delight in its own fancies: "So whosoever shall entertain high and vaporous imaginations instead of a laborious and sober inquiry of truth, shall beget hopes and beliefs of strange and impossible shapes" (SE 3:362). Furthermore, impressing our own image on nature has ethical overtones for Bacon missing in the Ockhamist reading of abstraction:

> For we copy the sin of our first parents while we suffer for it. They wished to be like God, but their posterity wish to be even greater. For we create worlds, we direct and domineer over nature, we will have it that all things *are* as in our folly we think they should be, not as seems fittest to the Divine Wisdom, or as they are found to be in fact; and I know not whether we more distort the facts of nature or our own wits; but we clearly impress the stamp of our own image on the creatures and works of God, instead of carefully examining and recognising in them the stamp of the Creator himself (*The Natural and Experimental History for the Foundation of Philosophy* [1622]). [SE 5:132]

In place of repeating our first parents' sin, Bacon exhorts us "to approach with humility and veneration to unroll the volume of Creation, to linger and meditate therein, and with minds washed

---

[35] *Thoughts and Conclusions,* in *Ibid.,* p. 89.   [36] *Ibid.,* p. 110.

clean from opinions to study it in purity and integrity." From the religious overtones of this passage it is not unreasonable to assume that Bacon conceived man's attempts to impress his own conceptions on nature as nothing less than idolatry. In the early *Valerius Terminus* he makes a statement tantamount to this: ". . . In the inquisition of nature they have ever left the oracles of God's works, and adored the deceiving and deformed imagery which the unequal mirrors of their own minds have represented unto them" (SE 3:224).

Thus Bacon equates the mind's delight in its own constructions with the imposition of these constructions on nature, which results in the twin evils of useless learning and idolatry. The doctrine of the Idols in *The New Organon* thus contains religious imperatives secularized. Just as the sinner must first realize his sinfulness before he can begin to repent, so likewise conversion to the new science requires first a careful analysis of the weaknesses of the human knowing faculties. As Moody Prior formulates this part of Bacon's program, "If the past was to be swept aside, the mind wiped clear, and a new way charted, the positive program could begin only after all established illusions about man himself had been anatomized and taken into account." [37]

The doctrine of the Idols is well known. In criticizing them Bacon in reality asks man to discount tendencies indigenous to the human mind. Only of the last Idols, those of the Theater, does Bacon say that they are not "innate." [38] These Idols include various philosophies that men over the ages have come to accept, but which violate in one way or another the canons of the new science. The third, the Idols of verbal imprecision enforced by "the apprehension of the vulgar" (SE 4:55), are perhaps not innate, in that a precise scientific language is possible. The first two groups of Idols, those of the Tribe and of the Cave, Bacon treats as strictly innate. Of the first Bacon says

[37] Moody E. Prior, "Bacon's Man of Science," *JHI* 15 (1954):349.

[38] SE 4:62; in the *De augmentis* (SE 4:431), after giving the first three Idols as in *The New Organon,* Bacon says of the fourth: "There is also a fourth kind which I call the Idols of the *Theatre,* superinduced by corrupt theories or systems of philosophy, and false laws of demonstration. But this kind may be rejected and got rid of: so I will leave it for the present. The others absolutely take possesion of the mind and cannot be wholly removed."

they "have their foundation in human nature itself, and in the tribe or race of men" (SE 4:54). By these, men believe that "the sense of man is the measure of things." The Idols of the Cave are similar delusions, peculiar to the subjective dispositions in individual men: "So that the spirit of man (according as it is meted out to different individuals) is in fact a thing variable and full of perturbation, and governed as it were by chance" (SE 4:54). Bacon assimilates to the first two groups his criticism of the mind's delight in symmetry and order.

But all four types of Idols, if not strictly innate, are at least produced by tendencies innate in the human mind. For instance, Bacon says the Idols of the Theater are like invented stories which "are more compact and elegant, and more as one would wish them to be, than true stories out of history." And if human language is a necessary tool of articulation and discourse, then the tendency to invent "names of things which do not exist" or "of things which exist, but yet confused and ill-defined, and hastily and irregularly derived from realities" is a natural tendency, however correctable. Bacon does not simply point out "mistakes," errors in calculation such as a man might make in geometry without bringing into question the axioms of Euclid. On the contrary, Bacon gives us something larger and less precisely defined. He is commenting on *a priori* tendencies that seem built into the very structure of human thinking and define it, rightly or wrongly, as specifically human. My point is that Bacon's calling these Idols blemishes on the mirror of the mind can be understood only as a reflex of his ideal of that mirror: a cognitive faculty from which everything specifically human is subtracted, leaving only the data of nature itself, pure and uncontaminated by conceptual constructs, emotional subjectivity, refined from the human contributions of articulate language, and totally isolated from desires of human fantasy. On the one hand, Bacon wants the human mind to possess "a true model of the world, such as it is in fact," while on the other hand his critique of human mental capacities denies that such is possible. He wants an abstract system which in order to be ontologically valid cannot be an abstract system; he wants a human knowledge in which everything that specifically defines the term "human knowledge" is purged and removed; in short, he wants knowledge without a knower, thought without a thinker, and, finally, the ultimate paradox, knowledge and thought that can be valid only at the expense of being the negation of knowledge and thought.

We have discovered here another embarrassment which dogs Bacon's attempt to methodize his vision of the new science. The limitations of conceptual abstraction lead to an ideal of a completely nonconceptual knowledge (that is, intuition), which, to be articulated at all, must nevertheless be conceptualized. In Bacon's myth of the new science all of these antinomies are envisioned as ideally resolved. But when these resolutions enter the realm of systematic method where the law of noncontradiction holds sway, they necessarily break apart again, showing by the equivocations that characterize them their origins in a mythic vision of a seamless whole. And as long as these equivocations remain unresolved in the realm of method, statements overtly presenting the coalescence of mind and matter, thought and intuition are in reality only exhortations that such be the case.

THE REDEMPTION OF THE MIND

The source of these paradoxes lies at the heart of the Baconian enterprise, the conviction that if man is ruthless and thorough enough in searching out the limitations of his cognitive faculties, this humbling would be ultimately rewarded with an "instauratio magna," a great new return to man's original innocence. This innocence was Bacon's historical analogue for man possessed, without need for struggle, of knowledge of and power over his universe. Metaphors and allusions drawn from the Christian story of fall and redemption appear often enough in Bacon's treatises to allow us to call his enterprise a secular analogue to the Christian myth of redemption itself.

Bacon makes this parallel explicit in the *Valerius Terminus:*

Nay it is a point fit and necessary in the front and beginning of this work without hesitation or reservation to be
professed, that it is no less true in this human kingdom of
knowledge than in God's kingdom of heaven, that no man

shall enter into it *except he become first as a little child.* [SE 3:224; italics in original]

In *The New Organon* Bacon insists that this childlike state can be achieved only after the mind is cleansed of its Idols:

> So much concerning the several classes of Idols, and their equipage; all of which must be renounced and put away with a fixed and solemn determination, and the understanding thoroughly freed and cleansed; the entrance into the kingdom of man, founded on the sciences, being not much other than the entrance into the kingdom of heaven, whereinto none may enter except as a little child. [SE 4:69]

Finally, in the still later *Natural and Experimental History* Bacon relates this motif to the notions of purgation and of humbling the mind before nature:

> [Man should] approach with humility and veneration to unroll the volume of Creation, to linger and mediate therein, and with minds washed clean from opinions to study it in purity and integrity. For this is that sound and language which went forth into all lands, and did not incur the confusion of Babel; this should men study to be perfect in, and becoming again as little children condescend to take the alphabet of it into their hands, and spare no pains to search and unravel the interpretation thereof, but pursue it strenuously and persevere even unto death. [SE 5:132–133]

The parallels Bacon draws between the humbling of spirit counseled by Christ and the humbling of the mind before the truths of nature are explicit, intended, and quite suggestive. Paolo Rossi, in commenting on passages like these, finds that "for Bacon the freeing of minds depends upon a revision of man's attitude to the world, and is part of the reform of knowledge, but also of a more vital reform bearing on ethics and religious faith." [39] But for our purposes Bacon's allusions to the Christian myth

[39] Rossi, *Francis Bacon: From Magic to Science,* p. 163.

of fall and redemption bear a somewhat different relation to the new science. Whatever part the new science was to play in the larger religious reform of mankind, biblical myth provides metaphors for a scientific vision that he could only partly express in a conceptual, methodical fashion. The need to become again as a little child to enter the kingdom of science expands exhortations Bacon gives in more methodical terms elsewhere. The "scientist-as-child," for instance, has purged his mind of all Idols and of "natural" desires to impose his own mental constructs on nature. The great instauration would return man to a state before the Fall, and even points anagogically to a final secular "resurrection," where man is freed from the confinements of the natural world.

Before introducing the six-part "Plan of the Great Instauration," Bacon says: "It being part of my design to set everything forth, as far as may be, plainly and perspicuously (for nakedness of the mind is still, as nakedness of the body once was, the companion of innocence and simplicity), let me first explain the order and plan of the work" (SE 4:22). Bacon uses the Eden myth for two purposes. First, he defends the desire for knowledge from charges that it repeats the Fall and is therefore sinful. For him, Adam fell not from desiring knowledge of nature (which he had already by right), but rather "it was the proud knowledge of good and evil, with an intent in man to give law unto himself and to depend no more upon God's commandments, which was the form of the temptation" (SE 3:265). Second, by thus divorcing the desire for knowledge from the Fall, Bacon sets up the pre-lapsarian state of man as the norm against which to measure the goals of the new science. For instance, he says in *Valerius Terminus* that the goal of the new science

> is a restitution and reinvesting (in great part) of man to the sovereignty and power (for whensoever he shall be able to call the creatures by their true names he shall again command them) which he had in his first state of creation. And to speak plainly and clearly, it is a discovery of all operations and possibilities of operations from immortality (if it were possible) to the meanest mechanical practice. [SE 3:222]

Finally, in the *Natural and Experimental History* Bacon refers to man's tendency to "impress the stamp of our own image on the creatures and works of God," as a kind of second Fall: "Wherefore our dominion over creatures is a second time forfeited, not undeservedly." For though after the Fall "some power over the resistance of creatures was still left to him," nevertheless "because we desire to be like God and follow the dictates of our own reason, we in great part lose" (SE 5:132).

It should now be clear to what extent the myth of Eden and the Fall becomes a central nexus wherein meet some of the essential elements in Bacon's philosophy. Bacon takes the prelapsarian state, conceived by some Protestant reformers as the state to which regenerate man is returned, and makes it a paradigm of the new instauration.[40] (The word "instauratio," meaning "renewal," itself carries this quasi-religious significance.) The cost of this instauration is indeed nothing less than everything: inherited ideas and systems, desires and modes of thought indigenously human, the whole history of human thought up to Bacon's time, everything, in short, that might stand between cognition and immediate contact with and control over nature are deliberately stripped away. The reward of this purgation is the great "regeneration": renewal of Adam's state before the Fall, man repossessed of his rightful inheritance, "when the end of work is but for exercise and experiment, not for necessity; for there being then no reluctation of the creature, nor sweat of the brow, man's employment must of consequence have been matter of delight in the experiment, and not matter of labour for the use" (SE 3:296).

There is, then, an element of historical and religious primitivism in Bacon's thought, which parallels his epistemological primitivism, the ideal of unmediated intuition. One is reminded of a similar parallel in the puritanism of Bacon's upbringing, between returning to the "purity" of the primitive church, and

[40] Cf. Perry Miller, *The New England Mind: The Seventeenth Century* (Boston: Beacon Press, 1961), p. 184: "The great William Perkins, for instance, defined three elements in the original righteousness: the substance of the body and soul, the faculties of reason and will, and the integrity of the faculties; in the fall the third was lost and must be restored in regeneration, so that conversion 'is not the change of the substance of man, or of the faculties of the soule, but a renewing and restoring of that purity and holiness, which was lost by mans fall.'"

transcending symbol and human reason to an unmediated confrontation with the Holy Spirit. To achieve this freedom man must sweat for it, curb his yearning for quick results and mental satisfaction. He must, as it were, crucify the desires for knowledge and power in the old man before he can achieve the knowledge and power reserved for the new man of science, the man who, to enter the kingdom of science, becomes again as a little child.

A further example of this quasi-religious primitivism is Bacon's notion of metaphyiscs. In the treatise *On Principles and Origins According to the Fables of Cupid and Coelum*, after examining four relations available between abstract principles and material objects, he chooses that by which ". . . the principle of things [is made] one in substance, and that fixed and invariable; [by which is deduced] the diversity of beings from different magnitudes, configurations, and positions of that same principle" (SE 5:469). The science of ultimate principles was for Bacon the *Philosophia Prima*, the governing science of all of the other sciences. Robert McRae sums up this particular aspect of Bacon's vision:

> As a result knowledge is organized as a pyramid, and the sciences in this pyramid are related to one another in the order of their generality. At the base of the pyramid is Natural History. On that is built Physics, which has two parts, one less general and one more general. On Physics is built Metaphysics, which subsumes the axioms of Physics under axioms of still greater generality. At the vertical point, if it should ever be reached, there is the Summary Law of Nature, a single law of the maximum generality embracing everything. The distinction between these sciences is simply one between levels of generality in the knowledge of nature.[41]

Though Bacon states most definitively the essential characteristics of *Philosophia Prima* and the "summary law of nature" in the later works, particularly the *De augmentis,* some of them were

41 Robert McRae, "The Unity of the Sciences: Bacon, Descartes, and Leibniz," *JHI* 18 (1957):32.

in his mind from the start. For instance, in *The Advancement of Learning,* when speaking of Metaphysics, he says that "always that knowledge is worthiest, which is charged with least multiplicity; which appeareth to be Metaphysic" (SE 3:357). In the same work, he describes a knowledge supreme in its simplicity, which joins all more complex and less general disciplines as the single trunk of a tree joins all of its branches (SE 3:346). And if all lower sciences meet in one, then the man who possesses knowledge of that science likewise possesses power. Thus of Metaphysics he says in the *De augmentis:*

> But the use of this part of Metaphysic, which I reckon amongst the deficient, is of the rest the most excellent in two respects; the one, because it is the duty and virtue of all knowledge to abridge the circuits and long ways of experience (as much as truth will permit), and to remedy the ancient complaint that "life is short and art is long." And this is best performed by collecting and uniting the axioms of sciences into more general ones, and such as may comprehend all individual cases. . . . The second respect which ennobles this part of Metaphysic, is that it enfranchises the power of men to the greatest liberty, and leads it to the widest and most extensive field of operation. . . . But whosoever knows any Form, knows the utmost possibility of superinducing that nature upon every variety of matter, and so is less restrained and tied in operation, either to the basis of the matter or to the condition of the efficient. . . . [SE 4:361–362]

The highest state of knowledge that man can reach, however, is only Metaphysics, wherein are collected and united "the axioms of sciences into more general ones, and such as may comprehend all individual cases." But "as for the cone and and vertical point ('the work which God worketh from the beginning to the end,' namely, the summary law of nature) it may fairly be doubted whether man's inquiry can attain to it" (SE 4:361–362). In *On Principles and Origins* he elaborates this point:

For the summary law of being and nature, which pene-
trates and runs through the vicissitudes of things (the
same which is described in the phrase, "the work which
God worketh from beginning to the end"), that is, the
force implanted by God in these first particles, from the
multiplication whereof all the variety of things proceeds
and is made up, is a thing which the thoughts of man may
offer at but can hardly take in. [SE 5:463]

To possess this law, or even the few general axioms which
stand just below this law, is to possess at once the whole of nature in intention; that is, to possess the ultimate "form of forms."
Such laws would contain implicitly all the possible specific forms
which are the building blocks of material objects. Therefore,
sense intuition and the summary law of nature constitute the
two outer limits of the complex operations described at length
in Book 2 of *The New Organon*. Furthermore, the cognitive conditions and values of both ends of this process are functionally
identical. Whereas sense data yield intuitive knowledge of discrete, "simple" bodies, the summary law yields the equal but
opposite simplicity of a single law governing all bodies. And
whereas intuition stands as ultimate in its unmediated contact
with bodies, the summary law is likewise ultimate as that law beyond which there are no higher concepts. Bacon defines both intuition and the summary law against the complex, discursive,
and provisional steps which lie between them. Their functional
identity within Bacon's vision of the new science thus does not
abrogate their essential differences. In this respect the summary
law of nature is in its own realm a cognate to the Edenic state
of man before the Fall, wherein he possessed naturally the total
knowledge of nature that he must now, after the Fall, approach
only with labor and care. It incorporates that ideal of purity and
light running through all of Bacon's norms of what knowledge
should be, whether he is speaking of the destruction of the mind's
Idols, or more positively of his projected method of experimentation.

MAN AS ANGEL

Nowhere does the discrepancy in Bacon's vision of the new science appear more palpable than in his formulations of its ultimate purposes. Why Bacon never brought himself to state these more fully is difficult to answer. I suggested in the first section of this essay that Bacon could not deal with this mythical, teleological dimension of his new science because he rejected a too quick grasping for ideal fantasies and wishes. One can only wonder to what extent Bacon's sensitivity to such desires derives from their existing in his own ideal. Harold Fisch speculates suggestively along the same lines, when he says:

> Bacon's overt intention, then, is to design a neutralized Nature capable of being handled efficiently by the scientist and stripped of the obscurities of medieval realism and imaginative fantasies of all kinds. He protests against the introduction of Biblical motifs and images into Natural Philosophy by Fludd and Paracelsus. But the strange thing is that Bacon was himself a man of imagination, a poet, as Shelley insisted, and though he fought back against this impulse in himself, the fact is that the Idols of the Cave, the Theatre, and the Market-Place, were the ghosts of his own mind. When he complains that "words do shoot back upon the understanding of the wisest and mightily entangle and pervert the judgment," it is not difficult to detect the note of self-admonition, to guess at the mental and emotional barriers which had to be overcome before he could curb his imaginative impulses and force himself into the Procrustean bed of a rigorous empiricism.[42]

I would suggest, then, that Bacon might well have addressed the critique of the Idols to the new science as well. For this reason Bacon left out of his scientific method any elements of the teleological myth that energized it. Nevertheless, the demand for satis-

[42] Harold Fisch, *Jerusalem and Albion: The Hebraic Factor in Seventeenth-Century Literature* (New York: Schocken Books, 1964), pp. 82–83.

faction sporadically emerges at just those points where rigorous logical method cannot harmonize various incompatible elements of that projected satisfaction.

Statements of purposes can be found at several levels in Bacon's scientific writings. The first level includes formulations of ultimate purposes clearly so intended. Such would be the statement in *The Advancement of Learning* that "the last or furthest end of knowledge" is "the glory of the Creator and the relief of man's estate." In another direction he says in *The New Organon* that "the end which this science of mine proposes is the invention not of arguments but of arts" (SE 3:294; 4:24). These and similar passages are as far as Bacon seemed willing to go in the matter. Even *The New Atlantis,* where one would expect to find whatever teleological and anagogical dimensions Bacon conceived for his new science, does not advance beyond the above statements. The Father of Salomon's House says that "The End of Our Foundation is the knowledge of Causes, and secret motions of things; and the enlarging of the bounds of Human Empire, to the effecting of all things possible" (SE 3:156). The details of Salomon's House do not carry us any farther.

Granted that Bacon could not have foreseen man's conquest over nature as we know it now, we may still wonder about just how Bacon conceived this "relief of man's estate." Was man's future to be one wherein "man's moral responsibility to society is solely that of achieving the uttermost improvement in living conditions as defined in terms of physical comforts for man," one wherein "man's vulgar wants are . . . insatiable, and applied science therefore is turned to increasing without fixed limits the material goods and sensual luxuries available to the people"? [43] Or is another interpreter closer to the truth when he quotes Bacon "against the danger of 'the debasement of arts and sciences to purposes of wickedness, luxury and the like,' " and goes on to say: "Bacon often leaves the impression that the career of science is something of a religion in its selflessness and sense of dedication. . . . And always he speaks of the pursuit

[43] E. L. Marilla, "Milton and Bacon: a Paradox," *English Studies* 36 (1955): 108; Robert P. Adams, "The Social Responsibilities of Science in *Utopia, New Atlantis* and After," *JHI* 10 (1949): 387.

of natural knowledge as though it were the noblest of human activities"? [44] Drawn from Bacon's explicit statements alone the promised relief could be either of the flesh or of the spirit. Possibly Bacon was unwilling to project the implications of the new philosophy beyond such cryptic utterances, or perhaps in fact he could not do so.

The second level of statements concerns goals which remain within the method of the new science and only equivocally project beyond science to its ultimate uses. These include the notions that the end of the new science is to restore the "commerce between the mind of man and the nature of things . . . to its perfect and original condition" again; or, that "from works and experiments to extract causes and axioms, and again from those causes and axioms new works and experiments"; or, that "I am come in very truth leading to you Nature with all her children to bind her to your service and make her your slave"; or, finally, that "he who knows the universal passions of matter and thereby knows what is possible to be, cannot help knowing likewise what has been, what is, and what will be, according to the sums of things." [45] Elsewhere, Bacon speaks of science as giving man freedom from the natural courses and processes of nature; of banishing fear through the knowledge of ultimate causes; of perfecting and exalting nature. But in these cases the goals are immanent to the new science: they concern the ends and purposes possible to the methods of science in its own realm, but they do not concern the uses of science itself for humanity at large.

But a third level in Bacon's writings discloses trajectories, partly plotted and incompletely stated, that point to and suggest goals for the new science of which Bacon seemed at best only dimly aware. On this mythic or visionary level, dreams of powers not released to man's consciousness were given their largest and

[44] Moody Prior, in *JHI* 15 (1964): 363. Symptomatic of Bacon's possible inability to focus and articulate his vision of science's ultimate goals is a list appended to the *New Atlantis, Magnalia Naturae, Praecipue Quod Usus Humanos* (SE 3:167–168). In this list such items as "The prolongation of life" and "The retardation of age" jostle such other items as "The altering of statures" and "More easy and less loathesome purgings."

[45] *The New Organon*, SE 4:7, 104; *The Masculine Birth of Time*, in Farrington, *The Philosophy of Francis Bacon*, p. 62; *Description of the Intellectual Globe*, SE 5:512.

most unbounded scope. Had Bacon ever become aware of the uses of science adumbrated on this level they would have doubtless amazed him. I am not talking about hydrogen bombs, test-tube babies, and landings on the moon: specific achievements which, however much Bacon might have wondered at their value, he could not have denied were implicit in his method. I am rather talking about patterns of image and statement that anagogically envision ultimate states of human perfection, of which the "natural divinations" of plagues in *The New Atlantis* (SE 3:166) and interplanetary travel are equally partial realizations.

All of these archetypal patterns arise in discussions of issues seemingly quite unrelated to them. They have already been suggested and partially discussed in the previous sections. The central yearning of the new science can be summed up in one word: freedom. Freedom from the distortions of human cognitive faculties, from the obfuscations of inherited categories, from the constrictions of time, space, and the human body: this is the burden of Bacon's vision of the new science that arises incrementally from all my previous discussion. Whether he was aware of it or not—and certainly he seems not to have been—the new science reached most largely toward a vision of man-as-angel, outside and beyond the natural world, whose total power over nature entails total freedom from nature. In short, Bacon's materialism, looked into deeply enough, becomes finally an antimaterialism so radical in his thought as to be almost totally obscured by the elaborate method he proposed for realizing it. The whole of the *Great Instauration*, its careful discounting and criticizing of human cognitive powers, is generated dialectically by an ultimate ideal of man the all-knowing and all-powerful. And further, the great effort and elaborate rhetoric aimed at perfecting these fallible powers really aims at an ideal of knowledgeless and actionless existence, and a humanity that has transcended knowledge and action, having already so mastered the world as to make them unnecessary. If the ultimate state of the Baconian man is such, then we can say that Bacon commits this man to much labor, much experimentation, much tilting with the natural world, precisely in order that he may issue out of the exigencies of a time-bound state into angelic mastery of his earthly life.

The picture of Bacon most often evoked by the aphoristic concision of the *Essays,* the pleader for the *lumen siccum* of reason in the *Instauratio Magna,* the cool observer of the psychology of political maneuver in *The History of Henry VII,* is an engraving done by Simon Pass in 1618, the year in which Bacon was made Lord Chancellor of England.[46] That portrait shows a man in full ruff, fashionable high-crowned hat, and furred gown of office. The fingertips of the left hand rest on a large volume, possibly the Bible. But it is the face that holds us. The eyes are open, protruding slightly, gazing just over the beholder's right shoulder with a look of unblinking and slightly cynical calm. The eyebrows are arched, and the mouth, the upper lip barely perceptible beneath the moustache, is set closed, a fine straight line, in the assurance that when it opens it will mold its subject with such perspecuity that it need not speak twice. Such is the Bacon of the method of the new science.

But there is another Bacon, seemingly quite different from the first, the Bacon of the funeral monument in St. Michael's Church of St. Albans. Here we behold a sitting figure, in smaller ruff this time, wide-brimmed hat, trunk hose, but completely oblivious to whatever effect these clothes engage for the viewer. The head leans against the back of the chair, resting on the closed hand of the left arm, chin tilted slightly upwards. The other arm hangs loosely over the side of the chair, and the knees are parted outwards in complete relaxation. The figure might be thought to be asleep, or perhaps in a state of visionary abstraction. "Sic," writes Sir Henry Wotton in the inscription, "sedebat." [47] This is the Bacon more often missed, the dreamer and visionary.

[46] SE 1:xv.   [47] Farrington, *Francis Bacon,* pp. 194–195.

Transition I

Its eruption from a mythic, visionary substratum of ends into the methodical surface concerned with scientific processes exhibits dialectic in its most rigid, straitened, unaccommodated form. I have explored the contradictions implicit in Bacon's ideals of intuition, of the return of a scientifically purged human intelligence to Edenic purity, and of a "plotless" state of total independence from natural laws. Bacon's attempts to resolve the contradictions of his vision into univocal identities and distinctions only meant that resolution became at once necessary and impossible. The ineluctably different structures of material objects and abstract concepts, which Bacon inherited from late scholastic nominalism, remain recalcitrant entities, like blocks of matter that can never copenetrate at the same point in the time-space continuum. Dialectic erupted in an only partially recognized manner at exactly those places in the new science where the marriages essential to it were to be consummated. The doctrine of forms, which was intended to build on the base of empirical experiment a pyramid of abstract laws, exhibits in its very ambiguity the dissolution of the elements Bacon sought to join. The return of man's mind to the primitive purity of an intellectual Eden generated an unaccommodated war of human thought with itself. Abstract conceptualization became at once the prime instrument and the main enemy of the new science. And finally, the goal of man-as-angel, implicit in the teleological thrust of the new science, committed man to total immersion in and enslavement to nature.

As I proceed through the next essays, the centrality of the myth of the new science in Renaissance thought should become increasingly clear. It will recur, in different avatars, in the lyrics of the metaphysicals, Milton's epic, and a group of plays from Shakespeare's middle period. In this respect, all the writers I discuss measure man in his self-division and fragmentation against an ideal plotless state wherein the antinomies of human experience are finally resolved, and find him wanting.

The lyrics of Donne, Herbert, and Marvell employ personae who envision goals similar to those of the new science: the resolutions of various antinomies. However, the poetic lyric adds another dimension in its address to the reader. Philosophical prose like Bacon's does not and cannot invite compensatory or ironic comment, in the manner of Plato's Dialogues. In attempting to encompass the whole of its subject in a logically coherent system, it aims only at effecting total acquiescence. Nevertheless, as the history of seventeenth- and eighteenth-century scientific philosophy shows, Bacon's new science did in fact invite, despite itself, "ironic" compensation from Descartes and his followers, not to mention the Cambridge Platonists, and later, Immanuel Kant. The domain of fictive discourse, on the other hand, whether it be lyric, or narrative, or dramatic, takes a qualitative leap beyond philosophical discourse, insofar as it invites only the reader's provisional, temporary acquiescence in a "let's pretend" enactment of human verbal actions. The reader is invited to react, to comment, to take ironic perspectives on the partialities of the agents within the fiction. That dialectic always invites such ironic perspectives, whether an author intended such or not, is indeed one of its main characteristics.

In the metaphysical lyric we are given just that frame of ironic invitation necessarily absent from Bacon's prose. This is even more significant because all three metaphysical poets, Donne and Marvell especially, take up similar philosophical problems. Here, we find new avatars of the Baconian man, each struggling to resolve the antinomies between concept and object, body and soul, and history and eternity in clear, univocal discourse, only to discover in the process the impossibility of such a resolution.

ESSAY two

The Dialectical Structure of the Metaphysical Lyric: Donne, Herbert, Marvell

INTRODUCTION

Paradoxes, contradictions, puns, nimble reversals of meaning and motivation are typical resources of the metaphysical poets. These devices signal that a calculus of clear and distinct concepts can encompass an apparently contradictory reality only by allowing contradictories. Such paradox expresses the farthest reach of reason into the realm of mystery, because it calls to reason's attention that to go farther is necessarily to go beyond itself. Paradox is thus itself paradoxical, in being both the consequence of reason's grounding in noncontradiction, and anti-rational.

These poems exhibit paradox in their personae's attempts to exhaust a multi-faceted reality in a single intuition or proposition. Such attempts generate sequences of perceptions and formulations, each referring to the same thing, but also apparently contradictory to one another. "The human person is made up of two distinct parts, a body and a soul"; "the human person is an undivided whole"; "the perfect gift of love is complete and static"; "the perfect gift of love is constantly growing"; "death is the result of sin"; "death is the way to salvation"; "sin ends in death"; "sin ends in salvation": these contradictory pairs reflect in discursive, sequential fashion the persona's vision broken up into discrete parts, struggling to reintegrate themselves through as sharp juxtapositions as possible.

Illuminating here is modern phenomenology's view of this tension. Edmund Husserl distinguishes between "the inadequate consciousness of givenness, the partial appearing" which characterizes human cognition *vis-à-vis* any object, and the "one and the same determinable X" to which this inadequate consciousness is always related.[1] As one of Husserl's commentators says, "a real thing may not present itself as such except by means of a series of perceptions succeeding one another." This series is the "noema," a continuum of perceptions to which the same object "may offer itself from a different side, at another distance, in a different orientation and aspect . . . when the subject goes around it." The wholeness of the object is reflected in "a synthesis of identification" into which these noemata enter, a synthesis such that "what appears successively constitutes itself, for consciousness, into this real thing which it is, one and identical as opposed to the multiple perceptions and also the multiple noemata."[2] One result of such a synthesis, as Husserl says, is "cases of the fusion or polythetic syntheses where there is disagreement or determination otherwise of that X which we are constantly aware of as one and the same. . . ." As a result of such a discovery "the whole perception *explodes,* so to speak, and breaks up into *'conflicting apprehensions of the Thing,'*" with the result that "the theses of these suppositions annul one another, and in such annulling are modified in a peculiar way," or in other cases, that "the one thesis, remaining unmodified, 'conditions' the cancelling of the 'contrary thesis.'"[3] The poems of Donne and Herbert present themselves as incomplete "noematic continua" reflecting realities around which no human mind can completely walk. For the reader, the object in itself is the poem as well as the reality

[1] Edmund Husserl, *Ideas: General Introduction to Pure Phenomenology,* trans. W. R. Boyce Gibson (London: Allen & Unwin, 1931), p. 385.

[2] Aron Gurwitsch, "Intentionality, Constitution, and Intentional Analysis," in *Phenomenology,* ed. Joseph J. Kockelmans (Garden City, N. Y.: Anchor Books, 1967), pp. 128–129.

[3] Husserl, *Ideas,* p. 385; italics in the original.

the poem points to. More precisely, he contemplates the poem-as-pointing, and showing itself as pointing inadequately. The reader must make continual adjustments as he grasps the reality through the poem—"through" in the sense both of instrument, and of a movement beyond it.

Andrew Marvell stands somewhat apart from Donne and Herbert. He explores the various consequences elicited by his platonizing tendency toward simple dichotomies, and tests with high sophistication the paths down which the dialectical logic of his position takes him. He recognizes that a state of innocence, sexual or political or moral, can be defined only negatively by fallen experience. The dialectical logic inherent in such definitions easily allows innocence to slip into its opposite, and must be countered by the recognition of this danger. The personae of Marvell's poems, unlike those of Donne and Herbert, announce their univocal stances through simplistic, visionary fusions, rather than in sharply juxtaposed statements. Practically, this creates little paradoxical language, although the reader is still called upon to supply counterstatements against this univocal partiality.

All three poets deal largely in the restlessness of attention caused by attempts to possess a complex and dynamic reality in some static, all-encompassing intuition. In the passage quoted above, Husserl called attention to the "fusions or polythetic syntheses" in the noematic continuum of consciousness "where there is disagreement or determination otherwise of that X which we are constantly aware of as one and the same." The dialectics in these poems involve constantly changing viewpoints on the same object. The personae attempt to see all sides of their subjects simultaneously, in a single intuitional vision, as distinct from the discursion of rational thought. Discursion which renders simultaneity in a way closest to the ideal of intuition is paradox. Being a sequence of contradictory statements, paradox announces that a true statement of the subject would be an intuited coexistence of opposites. These poems will show paradox resulting from the attempted denial of paradox, that is, of discursion and the contradictories it mediates.

DONNE

Donne's personae, like Bacon, are passionately engaged with the language of metaphysics, epistemology, and logic. Donne's poems, indeed, often proceed as logical arguments between a persona and himself, or an interlocutor, or even the recalcitrance of his own discourse. Unlike Bacon's method, however, the procedures of Donne's arguers sometimes lead to a kind of peripety and anagnorisis, whereby they discover the impossibility of resolving the contradictions they contend with. In this respect, then, dialectic is to some degree accommodated within the surface of the poem itself. Here, the myth of total reconciliation of opposites announces its own impossibility, and brings (some) lyrics to an overt critique of their nondialectical procedures. Donne speaks to the reader both through his personae and over their heads, detailing such accommodation of dialectic as the lyric—indigenously a nondialectical genre—can afford.

In the most acute and extensive analysis of Donne's thought to date, Robert Ellrodt has examined Donne's attempt to reduce the interrelations of objects and persons in time and space to a single moment of intuitive, transdiscursive vision. "[Such] everlasting 'movement beyond' is a way of 'transcending' unalloyed continuity, and it always strains toward a more intense moment, an absolute which escapes change, or ought to escape it." [4] He quotes a passage from the "Obsequies to the Lord Harrington," which summarizes this motif:

> As when an Angell down from heav'n doth flye,
> Our quick thought cannot keepe him company,
> Wee cannot thinke, now hee is at the Sunne,
> Now through the Moon, now he through th'aire doth run,
> Yet when he's come, we know he did repaire

[4] Robert Ellrodt, *Les Poètes Métaphysiques Anglais, Première Partie, Tome I: John Donne et Les Poètes de la Tradition Chrétienne* (Paris: Librairie José Corti, 1960), p. 92: "Le dépassement perpétuel est une façon de 'transcender' la pure continuité et de tendre toujours vers un instant plus intense, un absolu qui échappe, ou devrait échapper au changement."

To all twixt Heav'n and Earth, Sunne, Moon, and Aire;
And as this Angell in an instant knowes,
And yet wee know, this sodaine knowledge growes
By quick amassing severall formes of things,
Which he successively to order brings;
When they, whose slow-pac'd lame thoughts cannot goe
So fast as hee, thinke that he doth not so;
Just as a perfect reader doth not dwell,
On every syllable, nor stay to spell,
Yet without doubt, hee doth distinctly see
And lay together every A, and B;
So, in short liv'd good men, is'not understood
Each severall vertue, but the compound good;
For, they all vertues paths in that pace tread,
As Angells goe, and know, and as men read.[5]

On this passage Ellrodt remarks: "One grasps here exactly the link between intuition of the instant, and that intellectual quickness which is a conspicuous trait of Donne's mind." [6] The doctrine of angelic knowledge that Donne employs held that angels perceive many singulars through a single species. The movements of angels through the spheres and the movement of the eye and the mind across words suggest a similar tenor, namely, the assimilation of a discursive series in a single glance, that great "quickness" can only approximate. Ellrodt finds this aspect in much of Donne's poetry:

> Usually, the abrupt changes in rhythm and tone are the poet's customary way of disclosing different aspects of the same state of mind or consciousness. Temporal progression is rare. Dialectical development is precisely geared to conceal duration, and to substitute for it relations, perspectives, alternatives that depend on sequences that are logical, and in some respects spatial. Donne's personae may speak of the same dramatic instant divided into logi-

[5] H. J. C. Grierson, ed. *The Poems of John Donne,* 2 vols. (Oxford: Univ. Press, 1912), 1:273–274, lines 81–100.

[6] Ellrodt, *Les Poètes Métaphysiques Anglais,* 1:86: "On saisit ici sur le vif le lien entre l'intuition de l'instant et la rapidité de l'intelligence, rapidité qui est un trait marquant de l'esprit de Donne. . . ."

cal moments, developing in the fashion of a syllogism or of a demonstration dissolved into distinct propositions in order to explain a single truth.[7]

Quite often Donne's poems present a sequence of discrete, univocal perceptions which can only render a complex reality in paradox. A poem stands as the *explicatio,* the "out-folding" into many parts of a single reality which, seen as it "is in itself," would be the *complicatio* of these parts, grasped at once in a single intuition.[8]

One example of such *explicatio* is "Lovers Infinitenesse":

> If yet I have not all thy love,
> Deare, I shall never have it all,
> I cannot breath one other sigh, to move,
> Nor can intreat one other teare to fall,
> And all my treasure, which should purchase thee,
> Sighs, teares, and oathes, and letters I have spent.
> Yet no more can be due to mee,
> Then at the bargaine made was ment,
> If then thy gift of love were partiall,
> That some to mee, some should to others fall,
>   Deare, I shall never have Thee All.
>
> Or if then thou gavest mee all,
> All was but All, which thou hadst then;
> But if in thy heart, since, there be or shall,
> New love created bee, by other men,
> Which have their stocks intire, and can in teares,
> In sighs, in oathes, and letters outbid mee,

[7] *Ibid.,* pp. 86–87: "Habituellement, les brusques changements de rythme et de ton dont le poète est coutumier révèlent différentes facettes d'un même état d'esprit, d'un même moment de conscience. Il y a rarement progression temporelle. Le développement dialectique a précisément pour fonction de déguiser la durée, d'y substituer des relations, des perspectives, des alternatives qui relèvent de l'ordre logique, et, en quelque manière, de la spatialité. On dirait d'un même moment dramatique qui se morcèlerait en moments logiques, se développant à la manière d'un syllogisme ou d'une démonstration qui se décompose en propositions distinctes pour traduire une vérité unique."

[8] Cf. Edmond Vansteenberghe, *Le Cardinal Nicolas de Cues* (Frankfurt: Minerva GMBH, 1963; orig. pub., Paris: 1920), pp. 367ff.

This new love may beget new feares,
For, this love was not vowed by thee.
And yet it was, thy gift being generall,
The ground, thy heart is mine, what ever shall
   Grow there, deare, I should have it all.

Yet I would not have all yet,
Hee that hath all can have no more,
And since my love doth every day admit
New growth, thou shouldst have new rewards in store;
Thou canst not every day give me thy heart,
If thou canst give it, then thou never gavest it:
Loves riddles are, that though thy heart depart,
It stayes at home, and thou with losing savest it:
But wee will have a way more liberall,
Then changing hearts, to joyne them, so wee shall
   Be one, and one anothers All.[9]

The speaker's fears in the first two stanzas seem motivated less by jealousy than a desire to see just how far he can push an anatomy of his love founded on an economic model of buying and selling, gain and depletion. Such a model, though providing clear formulations to satisfy a mind anxious for them, demonstrates its own inadequacy in the process. The dialectical reversals signaling this inadequacy concentrate in the equivocations on "all." On the one hand, "all" refers quantitatively to a certain "amount" of love. If their love seems to be "growing" toward completion, the speaker asks how "all" can refer to love both bestowed wholly and yet continuously growing. If "all" refers to the first gift of love then the speaker would prefer not to call it "all," for he also wants the "new rewards in store" that come with increase. On the other hand, "all" refers qualitatively, or at least "nonquantitatively," to a continuously expanding totality that is complete at every point of growth. The conceptual problem arises because, quantitatively speaking, the signification of

---

[9] This and the rest of the love poems of Donne treated here are drawn from Grierson's ed.

"all" becomes equivocal at every increase, referring now to one amount, now to a greater, and if this is so then "I shall never have Thee All."

The speaker is working, obliquely and negatively, toward a conception of "all" that is both quantitative and "qualitative," that can grasp the totality of their love union at every particular point of growth (the static completeness of love totally given and received), while allowing the possibility for growth as well. The best way to approach this resolution is to start at the end and work backwards, for the last five lines state, not so much an answer to "Loves riddles," as rather the achieved recognition of why they are so. The answer to the riddle is that the lovers are both "one" and "two": from the viewpoint of duality the heart departs, from that of unity "It stayes at home." Insofar as the lovers are "one" being, there is no place for the language of addition and depletion, because each gives his love to himself. Therefore, because they remain always separate persons, a condition yielding ever-closer union, their love remains the same not despite but because of this growth.

The speaker realizes that defining their love as either static or growing requires the affirmation of its opposite. Both sides of the conflict generate each other, thereby showing themselves as partial views of the unity-plus-separation and growth-plus-completeness of the love union. The conclusion asks both the persona and the reader to hold in their minds simultaneously all of these terms, for in joining their hearts the lovers will "Be one" as well as "one anothers All." This puzzling last line imitates their paradoxical identity: "Be one" suggests the unequivocal meaning of "unity" until we come to "one anothers All," which then takes up the meaning of mutual exchange, and in retrospect the first "one" identifies the lovers as separate individuals. The poem requires the reader at the end to grasp in an instant what up to that point has been set forth in sequence: the interpenetration of union and separation, growth and completeness.

Another poem on a similar issue, in which the speaker less happily encompasses its paradoxes, is "A Lecture upon the Shadow":

Stand still, and I will read to thee
A Lecture, Love, in loves philosophy.
    These three houres that we have spent,
    Walking here, Two shadowes went
Along with us, which we our selves produc'd;
But, now the Sunne is just above our head,
    We doe those shadowes tread;
    And to brave clearnesse all things are reduc'd.
So whilst our infant loves did grow,
Disguises did, and shadowes, flow,
From us, and our cares; but, now 'tis not so.

That love hath not attain'd the high'st degree,
Which is still diligent lest others see.

Except our loves at this noone stay,
We shall new shadowes make the other way.
    As the first were made to blinde
    Others; these which come behinde
Will worke upon ourselves, and blind our eyes.
If our loves faint, and westwardly decline;
    To me thou, falsly, thine,
    And I to thee mine actions shall disguise.
The morning shadowes weare away,
But these grow longer all the day,
But oh, loves day is short, if love decay.

Love is a growing, or full constant light;
And his first minute, after noone, is night.

Citing the last line of this poem, Ellrodt notes that the relation between change and permanence in Donne's poetry is reciprocal. His personae desire either a continuously changing and renewed love experience (for example, "The Indifferent"), or they attempt "l'arrêter, la fixer, l'eterniser" (for example, "The Good-Morrow" and "The Canonization").[10] From a dialectical viewpoint we might wonder if both goals are not identical. In "A Lecture

---

[10] Ellrodt, *Les Poètes Métaphysiques Anglais*, 1:91.

upon the Shadow" the persona reduces love to two antithetical possibilities: either complete union or complete separation, either permanent love or the death of love. The reader perceives the persona violating his metaphor in order to force his point— "his first minute, after noone, is night." The movement of time and the sun does not necessarily signal the death of love. But the possibility that love may decay through time drives the persona toward demanding absolute certainty one way or the other. He refuses the possibility that their love may decay through the same diurnal process by which it grew, and attempts to remove it from time. The reader silently admonishes the persona that, in removing his love from decay through time, he is implicitly rejecting the love that time has brought him.

The difficulties in defining love against its potential destroyers is taken up by Donne again in "The Canonization," with a conclusion more genial, if just as uncertain.

> For Godsake hold your tongue, and let me love,
>   Or chide my palsie, or my gout,
> My five gray haires, or ruin'd fortune flout,
>   With wealth your state, your minde with Arts improve,
>   Take you a course, get you a place,
>   Observe his honour, or his grace,
> Or the Kings reall, or his stamped face
>   Contemplate, what you will approve,
>   So you will let me love.
>
> Alas, alas, who's injur'd by my love?
>   What merchants ships have my sighs drown'd?
> Who saies my teares have overflow'd his ground?
>   When did my colds a forward spring remove?
>   When did the heats which my veines fill
>   Adde one more to the plaguie Bill?
> Soldiers finde warres, and Lawyers finde out still
>   Litigious men, which quarrels move,
>   Though she and I do love.

The poem begins with the lovers as social outcasts and ends with them as saints. Both roles are alien to the world of busyness—"Countries, Townes, Courts"—the one in its reprehensible idleness, the other by its transcendent purity. The plot of the poem reverses itself neatly in the third stanza, where the persona, like Erasmus's Stultitia, first accepts his critic's categories of dispraise in order to turn them into categories of approbation:

> Call us what you will, wee are made such by love;
>   Call her one, mee another flye,
> We'are Tapers too, and at our owne cost die,
>   And wee in us finde the' Eagle and the Dove.
>   The Phoenix ridle hath more wit
>   By us, we two being one, are it.
> So to one neutrall thing both sexes fit,
>   Wee dye and rise the same, and prove
>   Mysterious by this love.

Donne exploits to witty effect an ambiguity which nineteenth-century novelists, such as Dickens, Dostoevsky, and Twain, treat in a rather more sentimental fashion: the saintly fool or outcast, the good-hearted prostitute, and similar characters indicate the ways in which both valences can coincide. The persona's interlocutor deserves his comeuppance, in that his smug contempt for the profligate can be depended upon to include a sedulous respect for religion. Justice is fulfilled when, after being lectured in the language of virtue, the persona ends by projecting the lovers-saints invoked by the devotees of religion.

> We can dye by it, if not live by love,
>   And if unfit for tombes and hearse
> Our legend bee, it will be fit for verse;
>   And if no peece of Chronicle wee prove,
>   We'll build in sonnets pretty roomes;
>   As well a well wrought urne becomes
> The greatest ashes, as halfe-acre tombes,
>   And by these hymnes, all shall approve
>   Us *Canoniz'd* for Love:
>
> And thus invoke us; You whom reverend love
>   Made one anothers hermitage;

You, to whom love was peace, that now is rage;
  Who did the whole worlds soule contract, and drove
    Into the glasses of your eyes
    (So made such mirrors, and such spies,
  That they did all to you epitomize,)
    Countries, Townes, Courts: Beg from above
    A patterne of your love!

To begin with, the speaker reminds his critic that he has, indeed, neglected some of the standard *topoi* of outraged self-righteousness: in addition to the illicit sex, he might have noted the persona's age as well as his lechery, his gout (the appropriate disability of profligates), his wasted money, and neglect of advancement. In the second stanza, the persona dramatizes hyperbolically the discrepancy between his private world of love and the larger commonwealth. His sighs have destroyed no commerce, his tears have not trespassed on private property, his passion's heat has violated no canons of public hygiene, and so on. The interlocutor's squint-eyed explosion of sexuality into a destructive force of national proportions reminds one of the current popular fantasy that the Roman Empire "fell" because of its total dedication to sexual orgy. Thus the first two stanzas at once establish the critic's norms of gain and loss, and extend them to absurd and self-deflating proportions.

In the third stanza the persona achieves the crucial reversal whereby the critic's arguments are both accommodated and defeated. The getting and spending of taking a "course" and securing a "place" are metamorphosed into another economy, by which the lovers "at our owne cost" gain themselves in dying, thereby proving "Mysterious" to the balance-sheet mentality of the critic. In the fifth stanza, "The whole worlds soule" which the lovers "did . . . contract, and drove / Into the glasses of [their] eyes" becomes a tiny world encompassed by, rather than encompassing, the lovers. The speaker's conversion of his love into religion turns on identifying sexual orgasm with martyrdom. Nevertheless, his attempt only succeeds in eliciting from the reader the realization that this identification moves on a two-way street. The speaker's forcing the religious sense of "die" exclu-

sively likewise forces the reader into the compensatory realization
that this dying is only sexual. At the same time, we cannot wholly
disallow the speaker's metaphorical transformation of his love
because, for one thing, he accrues a few points for the wittiness
of his put-down. Second, this transformation calls attention to
elements in his love to which the critic remains blind. The
speaker's description of "the' Eagle and the Dove," and the
Phoenix to which "neutrall thing both sexes fit" names a relationship intense and valuable. Nevertheless, the lovers' "death"
points us in two different directions, for it is at once sexual inter-
course and something more than that. Discounting the lover's conversion of his love into religious martyrdom does not reaffirm the
critic's position, however. Rather, the poem stresses the depen-
dence of both positions on each other for their definition.

In a sense, the answer to these two poems is "The Anniversarie," wherein acceptance of time and inevitable death frees the
two lovers to enjoy their love in the present.

> Let us love nobly, and live, and adde againe
> Yeares and yeares unto yeares, till we attaine
> To write threescore: this is the second of our raigne.
>
> [28–30]

The poem begins with the fact of aging and decay, summed up
in references to all those who are subject to time:

> All Kings, and all their favorites,
>   All glory of honors, beauties, wits,
> The Sun it selfe, which makes times, as they passe,
> Is elder by a yeare, now, then it was
> When thou and I first one another saw:
> All other things, to their destruction draw. . . .
>
> [1–6]

Against decay, however, the speaker asserts that, paradoxically,
only their love "hath no decay;/ . . . Running it never runs
from us away, / But truly keepes his first, last, everlasting day"
(7–10). The answer, which does not unravel this paradox but
only asserts why and how this paradox is true, lies in the second
stanza:

But soules where nothing dwells but love
(All other thoughts being inmates) then shall prove
This, or a love increased there above,
When bodies to their graves, soules from their graves
    remove.

[17–20]

The primordial, conflicting terms of love and death, when ap-
propriated by the lovers, become complementary rather than mutually destructive. Love's transcendence over death requires not
the platonist's rejection of the body, but an acceptance of it.
Rather than define their love against the destruction of time,
the lovers overtly acquiesce in their own deaths, thereby freeing
themselves from their concern with it:

Alas, as well as other Princes, wee,
(Who Prince enough in one another bee,)
Must leave at last in death, these eyes, and eares,
Oft fed with true oathes, and with sweet salt teares; . . .

[13–16]

In the first three of these poems, as Leonard Unger says, Donne
explores "the process by which the speaker arrives at a consciousness of rival attitudes." [11] The personae are coerced into
accommodating a more complex reality than their insistence on
partial visions had allowed for. The reader is invited to qualify
the personae's discourses until both—poem's discourse and
reader's corrective cross-biasing of this discourse—become "noematic continua," dynamic shifts of viewpoint around an apparently contradictory reality. Poems like "The Anniversarie,"
however, or "The Extasie," do not fit into this category. In both
cases, the speakers' confident and serene tone shows none of the
self-defeating anxiety for univocal completeness that appears in
"Love's Infinitenesse," "A Lecture upon the Shadow," or "The
Canonization."

I take "The Extasie" as a serious poem, in that I find in it no
ironic comment on the rhetoric of the spirit used as a means to

11 *Donne's Poetry and Modern Criticism* (Chicago: Regnery, 1950), p. 75.

fleshly persuasions.[12] The poem's argument is governed by the
conceptual difficulties of formulating a body-soul relation which
avoids the platonic split between "evil" flesh and "pure" spirit.
Donne's sardonic wit on the conflict between bitter sensualist and
doting platonic lover appears in "Love's Alchemy": there the
question of tone makes the poet's intention impossible to mistake.
To take "The Extasie" as a similar piece of sardonic unmasking
misses the fact that the movement in this poem is not from the
spirit to the body, but from the body-soul split to a body-soul
union.

The notion of ecstasy, derived as Professor Hughes shows
from neoplatonic sources,[13] expresses in the poem a body-soul
relation quite foreign to that which neoplatonic ecstasy implies.
Donne's conception of body-soul union went beyond the platonic
split, as seems evident from a passage in the *Devotions Upon
Emergent Occasions*. Speaking of sin invading both, he exclaims,
"It is the union of the body and soul, and, O my God, could I
prevent that, or can I dissolve that?" [14] The dissolution in the
poem derives from the lovers' demand for clear conceptualization
"Of what we are composed, and made." The fiction of ecstasy is
employed to make intelligible, not the lovers' grasp of the doctrine, but rather their confrontation with a mystery of human
love.

The union itself escapes complete grasp in unequivocal conception and language. At best, the law of noncontradiction breaks
it down into distinct parts, and this exigency governs the structure
of the poem. The central metaphor which reintegrates body and
soul is a common contemporary physiological explanation of that
union itself, the notion of "animal spirits":

> As our blood labours to beget
> Spirits, as like soules as it can,

---

[12] Cf. Pierre Legouis, *Donne the Craftsman* (Paris, 1928), p. 64; N. J. C. Andreasen, *John Donne: Conservative Revolutionary* (Princeton: Princeton Univ. Press, 1967), p. 168.

[13] Merritt Y. Hughes, "Some of Donne's 'Ecstasies,'" *PMLA* 75 (1960): 509–518.

[14] John Donne, *Devotions Upon Emergent Occasions* (Ann Arbor: Ann Arbor Paperbacks, 1959), p. 148.

    Because such fingers need to knit
      That subtile knot, which makes us man:
    So must pure lovers soules descend
      T'affections, and to faculties,
    That sense may reach and apprehend,
      Else a great Prince in prison lies.

[61–68]

During the ecstasy the lovers' two souls become a single "new soule" (45), as well they might, once the division interposed by bodies is removed. In "unperplexing" their love, the two lovers can see clearly "what we love" (30). Unperplexing this subtle knot releases reader as well as speaker from paradox and the perplexity of contradiction. But this split becomes possible only by assuming a body-soul union. The lovers move, not from neoplatonic ecstasy to copulation, but from part-by-part examination of the copenetration of human faculties, to a reaffirmation of that copenetration itself.[15]

In "The Extasie" as in "The Anniversarie" conflict is abrogated, because the fragmentation of the poem's vision into different perceptions in the noematic continuum is allowed fullest range for development. The speaker has earned the right to reunite body and soul, because he has fully allowed and explored the other side of the mystery, the body-soul split. Whereas the poems discussed earlier manifested the inadequacy of their visions through attempts to make a univocal, partial view stand for a total one, "The Extasie" overtly allows the sequence of univocal noemata and proceeds to the opposite conclusion: a totality that the various parts of the poem can only reflect partially.

The dialectical logic controlling Donne's religious poetry works in the same manner. However, as Arno Esch acutely notes, the separation between lover and lover is not an adequate model for the much greater gulf that Donne strives to bridge between God and sinner, one which is infinite.[16] The poles between which the dialectic in these poems moves—sin and salvation, despair

---

[15] For a fuller explication of this poem along these lines, see Michael McCanles, "Distinguish in Order to Unite: Donne's 'The Extasie,' " *SEL* 6 (1966): 59–75.

[16] Arno Esch, *Englische Religiöse Lyrik des 17. Jahrhunderts. Studien zu Donne, Herbert, Crashaw, Vaughan* (Tübingen: Niemeyer, 1955), pp. 37–38.

and hope—interpenetrate at only the highest reaches of human intuitive experience, an experience that even more radically discounts human finiteness than do the love poems.

One of the "Holy Sonnets," "Oh, to vex me," and the "Hymne to God my God, in my sicknesse," illustrate Donne confronting similar paradoxes of faith in two different ways.

> Oh, to vex me, contraryes meete in one:
> Inconstancy unnaturally hath begott
> A constant habit; that when I would not
> I change in vowes, and in devotione.
> As humourous is my contritione
> As my prophane love, and as soon forgott:
> As ridlingly distemperd, cold and hott,
> As praying, as mute; as infinite, as none.
> I durst not view heaven yesterday; and to day
> In prayers, and flattering speaches I court God:
> To morrow I quake with true feare of his rod.
> So my devout fitts come and go away
> Like a fantastique Ague: save that here
> Those are my best dayes, when I shake with feare.[17]

The oscillating paradoxes of this poem record the manic-depressive cycle of a soul too eager for resolution and certainty. Neither state can escape turning into its opposite, because his "flattering speaches" suggest to him the possibility of presumption, and the despair consequent upon this realization likewise calls for a renewed faith in God's mercy. In searching for the safest point of irresolution, the speaker chooses the trough of "feare" over the crest of "flattering speaches." At this point his confrontation with God is least clouded by second guessing. The conclusion, that "Those are my best days, when I shake with feare," designates a point of tenuous psychological repose, which the speaker has presumably earned because he has gone through and exhausted the possibilities of "As praying, as mute; as infinite, as none." There is no resolution in the poem, because the speaker tries too hard to attain resolution. The alternation be-

[17] John Donne, *The Divine Poems,* ed. Helen Gardner (Oxford: Clarendon Press, 1952); the texts of this and the next poem are both from this ed.

tween suspected presumption and consequent despair becomes a "constant habit," and no escape from this vicious circle seems possible. The reader can only assent to the poem's dialectic, because the speaker's drive for certitude can entail nothing else but this. Dialectic, in other words, shows itself inevitable here precisely because the speaker has refused it.

But if enslavement to dialectical oscillation follows upon refusing it, the reverse becomes possible once the speaker accepts the paradoxes of faith. One of the few poems wherein Donne achieves such an acceptance is the "Hymne to God my God, in my sicknesse." Here a similar conflict creates paradoxes whereby the speaker transcends the partial vision that gives rise to them.

> Since I am comming to that Holy roome,
>   Where, with thy Quire of Saints for evermore,
> I shall be made thy Musique; As I come
>   I tune the Instrument here at the dore,
>   And what I must doe then, thinke now before.
>
> Whilst my Physitians by their love are growne
>   Cosmographers, and I their Mapp, who lie
> Flat on this bed, that by them may be showne
>   That this is my South-west discoverie
>   *Per fretum febris,* by these streights to die.
>
> I joy, that in these straits, I see my West;
>   For, though theire currants yeeld returne to none,
> What shall my West hurt me? As West and East
>   In all flatt Maps (and I am one) are one,
>   So death doth touch the Resurrection.

The joy of the poem, together with amusement at the sedulous physicians, expresses an air of detachment. The speaker surveys himself from a viewpoint beyond death that affords an easy prospect of just how "death doth touch the Resurrection," how "both *Adams*" are "met in me" (fifth stanza), and how "that he may raise the Lord throws down" (sixth stanza). And yet this transcendence is projected from a supine position, in which the speaker is still a flat map wherein West and East have not yet touched. The poem expresses an act of faith so perfect as to allow serene jokes at the paradoxes it must encompass; and this serenity, far from diluting the paradoxes, makes them stand as the final act of a man about to take leave of paradoxes forever. From a perspective in which the speaker is already "made thy Musique" the death-resurrection paradox can be allowed and accepted because already resolved. Nevertheless, that this poem records an act, rather than a fulfillment, of faith is signaled by the speaker's distinguishing the components of the death-resurrection theme, while also stressing their identity to the eyes of faith. The flat map, whereon East and West are opposite points, invites the reader to join with the speaker in discounting the metaphor itself, for such projections violate the true structure of the earth, on which East and West "are one." Further, he prays (fifth stanza) that the second Adam's blood may redeem him because he is already suffering the final effects of the first Adam's sin. He admits that we only "thinke" that *"Paradise* and *Calvarie,* / *Christs* Crosse, and *Adams* tree, stood in one place." In doing so, he affirms the reality of that identification ("Looke Lord, and finde both *Adams* met in me"), for Christ's redemption of Adam was conditioned by his own identification with Adam. Thus the causal relation of death and redemption is asserted primarily through their first having been sundered.

In both sacred and profane poems Donne engages to best purpose the intimate confrontation between demands for unchanging certitude, and a human or divine reality that can be seen only in continually modified perceptions. In the love poems dialectic concludes in various approximations to intuition; in the divine poems dialectic demonstrates the need for its own cessation. The interpenetration of dynamism and stasis in the best of his poetry is summed up by Donne himself in one of his sermons, where his description of the beatific vision makes it an archetype of those partial visions rendered in his poetry:

I shall have an un-interrupted, an un-intermitted, an un-discontinued sight of God; I shall looke, and never looke off; not looke, and looke againe, as here, but looke, and looke still, for that is *Continuitas intuendi.* There my soule shall have *Inconcussam quietem;* we need owe *Plato* nothing; but we may thank *Plato* for this expression, if he meant so much by *Inconcussa quies,* That in heaven my soule shall sleep, not onely without trouble, and startling, but without rocking, without any other help, then that peace, which is in it selfe; My soule shall be thoroughly awake, and thoroughly asleep too; still busie, active, diligent, and yet still at rest.[18]

In Donne's lyrics dialectic makes its appearance through and despite his personae's attempts to deny it. In this respect, they foreshadow not only similar procedures in the poetry of Herbert and Marvell, but the more complex incorporations of dialectic in *Paradise Lost* and Shakespeare's plays. Donne's poems stand at an ironic distance from author and reader alike, a distance filled by precisely those compensatory dialectical realizations that the personae have overtly refused. This is the main result of his exploiting equivocal verbal and logical situations of a Baconian cast in a fictive genre that can overtly invite such compensations. A poem's plot progresses from initial attempts to resolve contradictions into univocal distinctions and identities to concluding stances of "transcendence," which announce the inadequacy of these attempts. Even in such poems as "A Lecture upon the Shadow," where transcendence does not occur, the trajectory of the poem's argument—as distinguished from the persona's—is completed by the reader's own ironic reactions. And this raises another point, which will become increasingly important as I proceed. Between arguments made and actions taken within the frame of the fiction, and the total significance of these as the whole fiction conveys it to the reader, there is a dialectic that parallels and controls the dialectic within the fiction itself.

Herbert's personae, like Donne's, initiate their lyric discourse with the intention of resolving an antinomy. They attempt to incorporate in language rationally apprehensible the central paradox of salvation. And like Donne, Herbert also directs his personae's speeches so that they become critiques of themselves. It

[18] Quoted in Arnold Stein, *George Herbert's Lyrics* (Baltimore: Johns Hopkins Press, 1968), p. 190.

might be said by now in this discussion that these critiques concern not any specific antinomy, but rather a basic set of the human mind as it confronts antinomy in general. The basis of this set is, of course, the law of noncontradiction. This law, which as Aristotle saw is a proposition we rather reason by than reason from, requires the human mind to grasp antinomies according to either simple identities or distinctions. And for this reason, the law of noncontradiction is itself paradoxical: it does nothing so much as generate more contradiction to the degree men seek to impose on antinomical realities the demand for noncontradiction. All of which is another way of saying that the demand for noncontradiction is the radical cause of dialectic. In a very real sense, then, this conflict between antinomical realities on the one hand, and the demand for noncontradictory intelligibility—the necessities, pressures, and irreducibilities of this conflict—are what Donne, Herbert, as well as Marvell, seek to communicate.

HERBERT

One finds few verbal paradoxes in the surfaces of Herbert's poetry because, as Ellrodt noted, paradox is the typical situation that Herbert describes—Herbert does not need them because he speaks of them all the time.[19] The difference between Herbert and Donne can be seen in the ways their personae elicit complementary realizations from the reader to counterbalance their own partiality. Donne pushes the resources of discursion to the point where it breaks down, or rather breaks open to reveal, as best it can, the reality it masks in the process of conveying it. Unlike Donne's personae, Herbert's persona uses a language deceptively simple. By eschewing the complexities of paradox, Herbert's poetry allows the persona's impurity of motives to appear with disheartening explicitness. His drive toward perfect repose of confidence in his salvation is countered dialectically by continually renewed awareness of this impurity, and of grudging at the overwhelming simplicity of God's mercy. The persona's continual oscillation between spiritual exaltation and depression

[19] Ellrodt, *Les Poètes Métaphysiques Anglais*, 1:317.

becomes itself the necessary condition of his salvation, a crooked and indirect way to Christ's banquet.[20]

The second of *The Temple's* three parts, "The Church," traces the dialectic of the persona's spiritual life from the simplistic moral categories of "The Church-Porch," to its becoming a type of the history of the whole Church seen from a God's-eye viewpoint in "The Church Militant." The final poem of "The Church" records the goal toward which that part has been moving, and the subtlest temptation that the persona faces:

Love III

Love bade me welcome: yet my soul drew back,
        Guiltie of dust and sinne.
But quick-ey'd Love, observing me grow slack
        From my first entrance in,
Drew nearer to me, sweetly questioning,
        If I lack'd any thing.

A guest, I answer'd, worthy to be here:
        Love said, You shall be he.
I the unkinde, ungratefull? Ah my deare,
        I cannot look on thee.
Love took my hand, and smiling did reply,
        Who made the eyes but I?

Truth Lord, but I have marr'd them: let my shame
        Go where it doth deserve.
And know you not, sayes Love, who bore the blame?
        My deare, then I will serve.
You must sit down, sayes Love, and taste my meat:
        So I did sit and eat.[21]

This poem epitomizes a spiritual struggle informing most of "The Church." As Herbert saw, the subtlest temptations wait

[20] Cf. Stanley Stewart, *The Enclosed Garden: The Tradition and the Image in Seventeenth-Century Poetry* (Madison, Milwaukee, and London: Univ. of Wisconsin Press, 1966) for a perceptive summary statement on exactly this point, pp. 56–57.

[21] *The Works of George Herbert*, ed. F. E. Hutchinson (Oxford: Clarendon Press, 1964); all poems of Herbert are quoted from this ed.

for those souls already committed to the spiritual life. They manifest themselves in the persona's presumption and despair— in a word, his pride. In this poem the speaker's humility before the simplicity and tact of Love is double-valent, and for this reason he almost fails of salvation when God invites him to partake of it. The speaker's sharp feeling of unworthiness is half genuine and half the mask of pride. He is frightened here, as elsewhere, by the imperturbability of Love's answers: "If I lack'd anything," "You shall be he," "You must sit down, . . . and taste my meat." It is the sheer simplicity of God's generosity, a generosity that encompasses rather than answers the persona's ambiguous humility, that the persona finds most difficult to accept. Because this generosity—so completely beyond the persona's comprehension—refuses to chastise his reluctance, he feels all the more reluctant. Here the persona's latent presumption and despair meet in a single act. And whereas through many of the previous poems the persona has had to wind and twist himself up to accepting God's mercy through much verbal agony, here final victory is signaled by one of the most powerful understated climaxes in English poetry: "So I did sit and eat."

As with some of Donne's religious poems, the goal of Herbert's poetry is silence, the "earned" silence of the soul who no longer needs to worry, because he has realized and begged forgiveness for all the possible perversions of his own motives. For Herbert, as for Donne on occasion, those are his best days when he shakes with fear. He can stand God's condemnation perhaps better than God's mercy, because in the first case he at least knows that the only other way is up. Those moments of exaltation, of temporary joy at the intimations of salvation are most dangerous, and precipitate a plunge back into spiritual depression:

> Oh, what a thing is man! how farre from power,
> > From setled peace and rest!
> He is some twentie sev'rall men at least
> > Each sev'rall houre.
>
> One while he counts of heav'n, as of his treasure:
> > But then a thought creeps in,

And calls him coward, who for fear of sinne
    Will lose a pleasure.

Now he will fight it out, and to the warres;
    Now eat his bread in peace,
And snudge in quiet: now he scorns increase;
    Now all day spares.
                    ["Giddinesse," 1–12]

This inconstancy is also an essential theme of *The Temple*
itself. Several attempts have been made to perceive an order in
the book as a whole, which in most editions, including Hutchinson's, follows the final order given by Herbert before his death.[22]
Hutchinson himself holds that in the original order "though it
may sometimes be accidental, there are many instances of purpose" (p. lxix), while Fredson Bowers has, more recently, asserted roundly that "the order of the poems in George Herbert's
Temple is not random but is planned according to developing
sequences that work out major themes." [23] However, none has
noticed that the poems are arranged according to a sine wave of
heights and depths which many of the individual poems take as
their subject. Beginning with "The Church-Porch" and moving
through the first dozen or so poems of "The Church," one is
given a representative cross-section of the vicissitudes of the
persona's spiritual life.

"The Church-Porch" addresses a "Gallant" who cares more
for clothes, manners, and camaraderie than the spiritual life.
Therefore the poem makes pleasure a bait to lure the gallant to
religion. Compared with the poems of "The Church" and the
profoundly complex vision of the spiritual life they mediate,
"The Church-Porch" shows itself as ironically simplistic. Its
moral exhortation is the counsel of prudence, sounding more than
a few times like Polonius:

[22] Cf. introductory material in Hutchinson, *ibid.*, pp. l–lxxvii.

[23] Fredson Bowers, "Herbert's Sequential Imagery: The Temper," *MP* 59
(1962): 202. There have been other attempts to establish some kind of structural
unity in *The Temple,* including Elizabeth Stambler, "The Unity of Herbert's
'Temple,'" *Cross Currents* 10 (1960): 251–266; John David Walker, "The Archi-
tectonics of George Herbert's *The Temple,*" *ELH* 29 (1962): 289–305.

Play not away the vertue of that name,
Which is thy best stake, when griefs make thee tame.
[65–66]

Mark what another sayes: for many are
Full of themselves, and answer their own notion.
Take all into thee; then with equall care
Ballance each dramme of reason, like a potion.
   If truth be with thy friend, be with them both:
   Share in the conquest, and confesse a troth.
[319–324]

These counsels presuppose a simple opposition between the sin
to be shunned and the virtue to be embraced. The balance of the
final couplet sums up this moral vision nicely:

If thou do ill; the joy fades, not the pains:
If well; the pain doth fade, the joy remains.
[461–462]

"The Church-Porch" thus stands as a prelude to the main
body of poems in several ways. On the one hand, it offers counsel to a soul quite obviously incapable of any notion of spiritu-
ality beyond the hortatory relaying of moral precepts, with all the
simplistically narrow vision of the moral life these imply. But this
poem on the other hand leads the reader *through* itself to the
poems of "The Church"—"through" in the senses both of instrumentality, and of something that is only temporary, something to be left behind when the goal is reached.

Viewed with hindsight from within the perspective of "The
Church," "The Church-Porch" must be seen ironically, in that
what it preaches is good as far as it goes, but is not good enough.
It gives us the carefully simple diction of the later poems, but
here serving a moral vision without depth and circumscribed. It
exhorts, whereas the poems of "The Church" employ a much
more sophisticated rhetoric, insisting that no single experience
in the spiritual life is absolutely the right one. One could say that
just this sort of simplistic moralism generates the dialectic of the
later poems. Against this moral vision the poems of "The
Church" stand out, demonstrating the well-nigh interminable

spiritual labyrinths a soul must follow if it begins with the ideal of easy victory which this moral vision promises. Certainly its optimism leads on the unconverted; but as Herbert shows in "Affliction I," "When first thou didst entice to thee my heart, / I thought the service brave" (p. 46:1–2), the early ease of devotion is soon lost as the soul travels into more ambiguous regions of motivation and understanding. And so we can say that "The Church-Porch" leads into the moral dialectic of "The Church" precisely in being itself so univocally nondialectical.

"Superliminare," the inscription over the door into the Church itself, bridges the gap between the "former precepts" (1) and "The churches mysticall repast" (4), which will not occur until the last poem of "The Church," namely "Love III" already quoted. What lies between these two points is also indicated:

> Nothing but holy, pure, and cleare,
> Or that which groneth to be so,
> May at his perill further go.
> [6–8]

The note of "groneth" is new, not found in "The Church-Porch," and implies a moral context of yearning and struggle that the previous poem does not suggest, but which sums up exactly the spiritual landscape of "The Church."

The first sixteen poems of "The Church," from "The Altar" through "Affliction I," both in themselves and in relation to one another, establish a pattern of spiritual experience which the rest of the sequence will only refine but never escape. "The Altar," "The Sacrifice," "The Thanksgiving," "The Reprisall," "The Agonie," and "The Sinner" record a psychological curve that begins with the speaker's overt humility, and moves on through a meditation on Christ's death starting in joy, only to end in "The Sinner" with a renewed sense of the speaker's sinfulness. The first poem exemplifies one of the essential spiritual experiences of the whole book. As Joseph Summers says about "The Altar," "Herbert's conceptions that the broken and purged heart is the proper basis for the sacrifice of praise and that even stones may participate in and continue that praise were firmly biblical." Herbert directs the metaphor of the heart made stone by sin, so that through its stoniness it can be made part of an altar. Summers says further on, "God has commanded a continual sacrifice of praise and thanksgiving made from the broken and contrite heart," [24] and as the reader will discover, the speaker's worthiness to give praise and thanksgiving primarily depends on his continual awareness of his unworthiness for doing so. The altar in this poem can only be made of stony hearts that recognize themselves as such.[25]

The next poem, "The Sacrifice," I will analyze in detail later on. It calls attention to the speaker's incapacity for encompassing the paradoxes of Christ's crucifixion, a fact made palpable in the succeeding poem, "The Thanksgiving." Here the speaker is struck by a realization that will continually in the later poems silence him in the midst of his confident verbalizing of the mysterious economy of salvation. He discovers, quite simply, that no actions of thanksgiving that he can perform will in any way achieve parity with Christ's sacrifices:

> But how then shall I imitate thee, and
>   Copie thy fair, though bloudie hand?
> Surely I will revenge me on thy love,
>   And trie who shall victorious prove.
>   [15–18]

Then follows a catalogue of the things the speaker will give up and spend to match Christ, which is touching in being at the same time jauntily smug and piously joyful:

> If thou dost give me wealth, I will restore
>   All back unto thee by the poore.
> If thou dost give me honour, men shall see,

[24] Joseph H. Summers, "The Poem as Hieroglyph," in *George Herbert: His Religion and Art* (Cambridge: Harvard Univ. Press, 1954); reprinted in *Seventeenth-Century English Poetry*, ed. William R. Keast (New York: Oxford Univ. Press, 1962), p. 231.

[25] Chapter 3, "Letting Go: The Dialectic of the Self in Herbert's Poetry," in Stanley Fish, *Self-Consuming Artifacts* (Berkeley and Los Angeles: Univ. of California Press, 1972) complements this section on Herbert, in its concern with how Herbert's poetry invites the reader to discount itself. Prof. Fish's book was in the process of being published at the time my section on Herbert was being completed.

> The honour doth belong to thee.
> I will not marry; or, if she be mine,
>   She and her children shall be thine.
>
> For thy predestination I'le contrive,
>   That three yeares hence, if I survive,
> I'le build a spittle, or mend common wayes,
>   But mend mine own without delayes.
> Then I will use the works of thy creation,
>   As if I us'd them but for fashion.
> The world and I will quarrell; and the yeare
>   Shall not perceive, that I am here.
>   [19–24, 31–38]

Here Herbert reproduces the slightly breezy manner of the speaker's self-sacrifice, a breeziness at least three-quarters sincere, though still somewhat shallow for all that. At the end, at the moment of exaltation, we discover with the speaker that this exaltation requires some deepening of its shallowness:

> O my deare Saviour, Victorie!
> Then for thy passion—I will do for that—
>   Alas, my God, I know not what.
>   [48–50]

The sudden silence at the end of "The Thanksgiving" leads into more ambiguous realizations in "The Reprisall," where the speaker discovers that his desire to match Christ's sacrifice contains not a little pride. The poem begins with the speaker's slightly nettled and irritable statement that "I have consider'd it, and finde / There is no dealing with thy mighty passion," for even if he dies for Christ, his sins still deserve condemnation. In the third stanza the speaker's impurity of motive surfaces to the point where even he almost recognizes it:

> Ah! was it not enough that thou
> By thy eternall glorie didst outgo me?
> Couldst thou not griefs sad conquests me allow,
>   But in all vict'ries overthrow me?
>   [9–12]

The speaker quarrels with Christ's taking away not only the achievement of glory (a sector of the battle duly allotted to God) but the conquest of grief as well. In the ambiguous syntax of the eleventh line the speaker hopes to conquer the grief of repentance by overtly encouraging its conquest of him. The last stanza records an incomplete resolution at best:

> Yet by confession will I come
> Into thy conquest: though I can do nought
> Against thee, in thee I will overcome
> The man, who once against thee fought.

The mixture of motives here is almost beyond disentangling. We do not question the speaker's desire to perform Christ's will and make His sacrifice his own. We do question the speaker's grudging assertion of his own part in the matter in the midst of his acquiescing in Christ's having done all. By "confessing" Christ's transcendent redemption he may conquer the "man, who once against thee fought"; but he may also become Christ's secret enemy in still hoping to make his own part something to be valued, to "come / Into thy conquest" in a way that would "conquer" God by the very act of flourishing his humility before Him.

In "The Agonie" the speaker agrees that Christ's suffering as well as the love that that suffering made possible are beyond his comprehension; and "The Sinner" concerns the speaker's realization of his own small worth, with his "shreds of holinesse" amid "quarries of pil'd vanities" (5–6). This cycle of spiritual experience returns to its starting place in the last lines: "Yet Lord restore thine image, heare my call: / And though my hard heart scarce to thee can grone, / Remember that thou once didst write in stone" (12–14). A similar sine wave is charted in the next group of poems. "Good Friday" applies Christ's death to the speaker; then the sequence moves through the increasing joy of "Redemption," "Sepulchre," "Easter," "Easter-wings," "H. Baptisme I," and "H. Baptisme II," only to founder again with "Nature," "Sinne I," and "Affliction I."

The key to the rise and fall of the speaker's spiritual state, or more precisely, his attitudes toward this state, are two lines from "The Temper I":

> If what my soul doth feel sometimes,
>   My soul might ever feel!
>
> [3–4]

A similar wish is expressed, significantly, in the last poem of the second sequence before the speaker's descent into spiritual depression, "H. Baptisme II." Here the speaker wishes to conform himself to God's will with all the pliability of a child

> O let me still
> Write thee great God, and me a childe:
> Let me be soft and supple to thy will,
>   Small to my self, to others milde,
>   Behither ill.
>
> [6–10]

The expansion and matching contraction of the lines imitates the "narrow way and little gate" (2) by which, through baptism, Christ did "antedate / My faith in me" (4–5), a "narrowness" expanding in each stanza with prayers to continue this faith, and contracting finally with the affirmation that

> The growth of flesh is but a blister;
>   Childhood is health.
>
> [14–15]

In both these poems, the speaker desires overtly to maintain a state of simple and uncomplicated presence to God. The impossibility of such appears both in the speaker's continual oscillation of attitude, and in his restlessness when confronted with the overwhelming gratuitousness of Christ's invitation to rest in that presence. As in "Love III," the speaker hangs back through motives that would appear to prepare him for it—his humility and consciousness of his own sinfulness.

One poem that expresses most sharply this inner contradiction is "Dialogue." The speaker's awareness of God's infinite goodness so heightens his sense of sin that he completely neglects any sense of how that goodness issues in mercy. In this poem Herbert shows his mastery of speech that subtly betrays impure motives:

> Sweetest Saviour, if my soul
>   Were but worth the having,

> Quickly should I then controll
>   Any thought of waving.
> But when all my care and pains
> Cannot give the name of gains
> To thy wretch so full of stains,
> What delight or hope remains?
>   [1–8]

Luther would have recognized immediately the speaker's problem: he gives too much weight to his own efforts, the failure of which should signal to the speaker the pride hidden beneath such Pelagian confidence. But there is something more here. The counsel of this first stanza is implicitly that of despair, and we recognize the speaker's yearning for rest in God here perverted malignly into a slothful desire simply to give up. The complaint to Christ is both a petition for salvation and an argument that such is impossible.

> *What, Child, is the ballance thine,*
>   *Thine the poise and measure?*
> *If I say, Thou shalt be mine;*
>   *Finger not my treasure.*
> *What the gains in having thee*
> *Do amount to, onely he,*
> *Who for man was sold, can see;*
> *That transferr'd th' accounts to me.*
>   [9–16]

This is not so much an answer as an attempt to undercut the presuppositions of the speaker's argument. Christ chides the speaker for his attempt to measure the "cost" of saving him by a finite standard. And we can notice here again Herbert's superb mastery of tone of voice. He conveys Christ's appropriation of salvation to Himself as something so far beyond the speaker's understanding that his anxieties become suddenly reduced to fussiness and impertinent meddling. Here, the line "Finger not my treasure" plays a large part, suggesting that the speaker's spiritual agony is really a kind of sleazy curiosity, superimposed on and fused with Christ's irritated assertion of absolute possession of a soul saved. Not only is the speaker saved, but his sal-

vation is already safely written up in the account book; all that
remains is to slap his hand. The speaker yearns for reasons for
his salvation, a formulation of parity between cost and goods
which Christ parodies in his balance-treasure-accounts metaphors.
In short, he wants salvation on terms that he can feel justified
in accepting because they are accommodated to his own vision of
the matter. It is the purely gratuitous gift that he cannot stand:

> But as I can see no merit,
>   Leading to this favour:
> So the way to fit me for it
>   Is beyond my savour.
> As the reason then is thine;
> So the way is none of mine:
> I disclaim the whole designe:
> Sinne disclaims and I resigne.
>
> *That is all, if that I could*
>   *Get without repining;*
> *And my clay, my creature, would*
>   *Follow my resigning:*
> *That as I did freely part*
> *With my glorie and desert,*
> *Left all joyes to feel all smart—*
>   Ah! no more: thou break'st my heart.
>
> [17–32]

When the speaker disclaims "the whole designe" because it originates in Christ's gift of salvation rather than in his own merit,
Christ turns the argument back on him and points out that this
"resigning" is all he asks of him. It is just the breaking of his
own heart at Christ's resignation that the speaker has been resist-
ing. Suddenly, at the end, the poem breaks loose from the malign dialectic between false humility and false pride, and opens
into the infinite space of Christ's gift of salvation, a space that
no words can encompass: the speaker has, at least momentarily,
earned the right to silence.

These poems mediate two different perspectives on salvation,
infinitely separated from each other. The speaker's effort to

purify himself becomes the very obstacle to that goal for it places
him in the false position of interpreting the divine necessities
governing this purification. Herbert has thus neatly rendered one
of the acutest paradoxes of the spiritual life. In either acting or
ceasing to act the speaker runs the risk of falling, and this dialectic gains its logical rigor from the demand for perfect rest in
Christ that underlies both extremes. The dialectical logic that
frustrates the impulses of the speaker likewise propels him
through itself ("by means of," "beyond") to moments of transdiscursive quiet in which all dialectic is stilled. The most famous rendering of these moments is in "The Flower":

> These are thy wonders, Lord of power,
> Killing and quickning, bringing down to hell
>   And up to heaven in an houre;
> Making a chiming of a passing-bell.
>   We say amisse,
>   This or that is:
> Thy word is all, if we could spell.
>   [15–21]

The most extended attempt to transcend dialectic by means
of dialectic occurs in "The Sacrifice." William Empson isolates
the paradox of the poem's theme in lines where Christ associates
the Jews' spitting on Him, and His healing the blind man:

> Behold, they spit on me in scornfull wise,
> Who by my spittle gave the blinde man eies,
> Leaving his blindnesse to my enemies:
>   Was ever grief like mine?
>   [133–136]

"These two events are contrasted, but that they should spit
upon me is itself a healing; by it they distinguish me as scapegoat,
and assure my triumph and their redemption; and spitting, in
both cases, was to mark my unity with man." [26] Also, as Empson says later,

26 William Empson, *Seven Types of Ambiguity* (New York: Meridian Books,
1957), pp. 260–261.

in the person of the Christ the supreme act of sin is com-
bined with the supreme act of virtue. Thus in two ways,
one behind the other, the Christ becomes guilty; and we
reach the final contradiction: . . . scapegoat and tragic
hero; loved because hated; hated because godlike; freeing
from torture because tortured; torturing his torturers because all-merciful; source of all strength to men because
by accepting he exaggerates their weakness; and, because
outcast, creating the possibility of society.[27]

These paradoxes both juxtapose and separate human and
divine perspectives. In so doing, they lead to a recognition of how
the two are joined through actions which, on the part of the Jews,
assume their separation. Thus the Jews kill Christ for motives
that presuppose a narrow, pharisaical, human perspective, which
killing has divine effects. And because the Jews separate the divine
and human in their treatment of Christ, and since Christ as
sufferer and redeemer confers benefits that bridge this gulf, we
might say that actions under the overt sign of "separation" end
in results under the sign of "union." The bridge between divine
and human—the incarnate Christ—which allows them to attack
the divine order through the human, also makes possible the
redemption of the human order by the divine. Thus the Jews
both "condemn" and "save" themselves by the same act.

The poem takes Christ from the Garden of Gethsemene to
the Crucifixion, and this progression provides a substructure for
the separate three-line comments, concluding each time with the
constant refrain. The persona's viewpoint is "naive." Such paradoxes as "yet at their commands / I suffer binding, who have
loos'd their bands" (46–47), and "I him obey, who all things
else command" (83), attempt no elucidation. Rather, Christ's
agony at the dialectical attributes of his death is analogous to the
"strain" the reader suffers in the logical realm at having to
unravel this dialectic. For example:

> Yet still they shout, and crie, and stop their eares,
> Putting my life among their sinnes and fears,

[27] *Ibid.*, pp. 262–263.

> And therefore wish *my bloud on them and theirs:*
> > Was ever grief like mine?

> See how spite cankers things. These words aright
> Used, and wished, are the whole worlds light:
> But hony is their gall, brightnesse their night:
> > Was ever grief, &c.
> > > [105–112]

The persona's and the reader's perspective encompasses more than does that of the Jews, and the reader is invited to realize anew this import through Christ's comments on the Jews' ignorance of it.

Another version of the same irony is that the Jews unknowingly enact, through their mockery of Him, obeisance to their king. At one point Christ says:

> Then from one ruler to another bound
> They leade me; urging, that it was not sound
> What I taught: Comments would the text confound.
> > [53–55]

And again:

> Yet since mans scepters are as frail as reeds,
> And thorny all their crowns, bloudie their weeds;
> I, who am Truth, turn into truth their deeds:
> > [177–179]

In the first case Christ calls attention to the overtly "religious" norms held forth by the Jews in condemning Him ("Then they accuse me of great blasphemie, / That I did thrust into the Deitie, / Who never thought that any robberie" [61–63]), and points out thereby how their sense of theological decorum becomes inadvertently trivial in the face of a divine-human interpenetration which that decorum ignores. In the second passage, Christ reinterprets his crown, reed, and robe as an ironic epiphany of the frailty of earthly kingship. When we put these together—the Jews' theological "decorum" and their insistence that Christ was really pursuing a political crown—we begin to see where the narrowness of the Jews' religious vision becomes the paradoxical instrument for engendering a new vision that is to sweep away the old. We could say indifferently that the Jews crucified Christ either because He was too large for their comprehension or because He was not large enough. Since these paradoxes affirm the interpenetration of the divine and the human, we can only deduce that it is precisely this interpenetration that the Jews cannot understand—at least as they enact this non-understanding in killing Christ. They act out their assumptions of divine-human split in accusing Christ of arrogating to Himself divine powers, and thereby "objectively" make true all that they say in jest: overt irony conveys, ultimately, direct vision.

There are a few poems in *The Temple,* "Sunday" and "The Flower" among them, where the persona is serenely at one with God, poems the tone of which is celebration rather than cerebration. Among these, the longest and one of the most impressive is "Providence." The best way into the richness of its serenity is to note that it stands out among the many poems in complex and varied stanza forms as one of the few to employ the simple pentameter quatrain, rhymed a-b-a-b. Counterpointed against this regularity, thereby imitating the natural world's assymetry under God's mastering it in total harmony, are continual shifts in caesura, enjambment, and the subtle cross-patterning of syntactical group and line measurement. All of these qualities are announced in the opening stanzas:

> O Sacred Providence, who from end to end
> Strongly and sweetly movest, shall I write,
> And not of thee, through whom my fingers bend
> To hold my quill? Shall they not do thee right?
>
> Of all the creatures both in sea and land
> Onely to Man thou hast made known thy wayes,
> And put the penne alone into his hand,
> And made him Secretarie of thy praise.
>
> Beasts fain would sing; birds dittie to their notes;
> Trees would be tuning on their native lute
> To thy renown: but all their hands and throats

> Are brought to Man, while they are lame and mute.
>
> [1–12]

The subject of this music is an interpenetration of God and nature, and of the divine and human perspectives, which Herbert
can only hectically grasp at in many other poems. The Providence
that moves both "strongly" and "sweetly" through all of creation
likewise moves throughout the poem in statement and rhythm.
The subtle tension between power and calm, between the transcendence of the Deity and the intimate detail of an orderly
nature, and ultimately between the Divine will and the autonomy
of the natural world all parallel the delicate balance between
coalescence and distinction Herbert strives through so many
poems to achieve for his own soul. And so the persona is led to
say:

> We all acknowledge both thy power and love
> To be exact, transcendent, and divine;
> Who dost so strongly and so sweetly move,
> While all things have their will, yet none but thine.
>
> For either thy command or thy permission
> Lay hands on all: they are thy right and left. . . .
>
> [29–34]

Mute nature's praise of God through articulate man joins with
Providence in such a way that creation and praise, emanation
and return become two reciprocal parts of a single action:

> Thou art in small things great, not small in any:
> Thy even praise can neither rise, nor fall.
> Thou art in all things one, in each thing many:
> For thou art infinite in one and all.
>
> [41–44]

> All things that are, though they have sev'rall wayes,
> Yet in their being joyn with one advise
> To honour thee: and so I give thee praise
> In all my other hymnes, but in this twice.
>
> Each thing that is, although in use and name
> It go for one, hath many wayes in store

To honour thee; and so each hymne thy fame
Extolleth many wayes, yet this one more.

[145–152]

These last two stanzas, which end the poem, are possibly alternative versions, though Hutchinson notes (p. 520) there is no indication of this in the MS. Close attention will disclose that they
envision the interpenetration of unity and diversity from the
viewpoints of each consecutively, and are carefully correlated.
"All things" of the first matches "Each thing" of the second
stanza, just as the "twice" of the first becomes "one more" of
the second. All the creatures of nature, though they are distinct
and "have sev'rall wayes," nevertheless "joyn with one advise"
in praising God: here the perspective within a "synoptic" view
of nature emphasizes diversity merging into a unity. Then reversing the perspective, we begin with "each thing" peculiarly at
one with itself "in use and name" yet having "many wayes in
store" of praising God. Likewise, in the first stanza the persona
finds that all of his other poems praise God only for himself, while
this one does so for both himself and all of nature. And in the
second stanza, like each individual creature, each poem praises
God in many ways, and from that viewpoint this present one
merely adds to the number. These two stanzas in conjunction
sum up a theme which the poem has continually illustrated in
a plenitude of precise detail, namely, that nature becomes one in
praising God because each part of it stands by itself praising God
in its own way.

It is easily seen why, in this poem, the speaker avoids his
usual dialectic between exaltation and depression. Here, God's
simultaneous transcendence and immanence, and correspondingly,
the creature's simultaneous subsumption under and autonomy
within providence, are all overtly celebrated in the poem. Herbert,
in the excellent formulation of Erich Przywara, has realized that
God is "immanent within all the creaturely because it is creaturely, and transcendent to all the creaturely because it is creaturely." [28] What might be in other contexts competing opposites

---

[28] P. Erich Przywara, S.J., *Polarity: A German Catholic's Interpretation of
Religion,* trans. A. C. Bouquet (London: Oxford Univ. Press, 1935), p. 70.

can each be given lovingly its due because *all* of them are given
their due.

Illustrative of this strategy is the large space given over to
what, outside of its providential context, would appear a mere
catalogue of the natural world's beauties and commodiousness:

> Sheep eat the grasse, and dung the ground for more:
> Trees after bearing drop their leaves for soil:
> Springs vent their streams, and by expense get store:
> Clouds cool by heat, and baths by cooling boil.
>
> [69–72]

> Hard things are glorious; easie things good cheap.
> The common all men have; that which is rare
> Men therefore seek to have, and care to keep.
> The healthy frosts with summer-fruits compare.

> Light without winde is glasse: warm without weight
> Is wooll and furre: cool without closenesse, shade:
> Speed without pains, a horse: tall without height,
> A servile hawk: low without losse, a spade.
>
> [97–104]

The circumscribing providence which produces them and which
they praise has already, from the poem's beginning, been taken
into account. Therefore the persona can afford, within the economy of his vision, the rich expansiveness of the catalogue, of item
piled on item, without any suggestion of materialism or naturalism
creeping in around the edges, for the joy in this richness has
already been properly credited. The interpenetration of providence and nature appears analogously in nature itself, where the
plenitude of creatures imitates that divine plenitude which they
unite in mirroring so diversely. That "Thy even praise can neither
rise, nor fall" is a function of nature's wide potentiality for
change and a diversity wherein, like Herbert's four-line stanzas,
assymetries coalesce in perfect wholes.[29]

[29] Herbert achieves here a perfect example of what William F. Lynch, *Christ
and Apollo: The Dimensions of the Literary Imagination* (New York: Sheed and
Ward, 1960), p. 133, calls the "analogical imagination": ". . . [which] insists on
keeping the same and the different, the idea and the detail, tightly interlocked in

"Providence" is, in a sense, the kind of poem the persona of *The Temple* aspired to write all the time, a poem in which God and self are serenely at one in a total vision reflecting the interpenetration of God's will and man's. Poems like "Providence" by their rarity in "The Church" demonstrate where they stand in the ongoing dialectical progress of the whole. Herbert's fidelity to all the pressures of his experience, especially at those points where these tend to change direction under his very eyes, allows him to "rest" in such poems only after much spiritual travail. "Providence" follows "Vanitie II," "The Dawning," "Business," "Dialogue" (already discussed), and "Dullnesse": all poems which lament the speaker's sluggishness in the face of God's proddings. In this context "Providence" signals a re-awakening to the mysterious coalescence of God's will with his own. But when the eight-line poem "Hope" immediately follows, we realize anew the frailty and evanescence of even such sustained music as "Providence" achieves. The conclusion is petulance:

> I Gave to Hope a watch of mine: but he
>   An anchor gave to me.
> Then an old prayer-book I did present:
>   And he an optick sent.
> With that I gave a viall full of tears:
>   But he a few green eares.
> Ah Loyterer! I'le no more, no more I'le bring:
>   I did expect a ring.

We have moved rapidly and far from the previous poem's praise of "Sacred Providence, who from end to end / Strongly and sweetly movest," and whose "even praise can neither rise, nor fall." Distinguishing between what he can and cannot expect is the speaker's continual burden and concern.

Though Herbert's poetry could in no way be called mystical, there is some usefulness in looking at it as such. The persona's

---

the one imaginative act. As its idea or pattern descends into the images of reality, it adapts itself perfectly to every detail of difference, without ever suffering the loss of its own identity. And the theme is always on the inside of the images. It is always eminently positive and is always creating difference and autonomy."

highest vision reaches to the salvific copenetration of his will and God's; however, his language and thought cannot totally apprehend it. Herbert never leaps into the abyss, the "dark night of the soul" as St. John of the Cross calls it, wherein all words, thoughts, images, and sense experiences are left behind in the vacancy of being, waiting to be filled by a divine presence wholly beyond human comprehension. On the contrary, Herbert announces the ineffability of the divine salvific economy through his persona's manifestly inadequate attempts to reduce it to clear thought and speech. Language and thought fail at the very threshold of the divine, pointing through and by means of this failure to a divine reality thereby defined specifically as transverbal and transconceptual (as per Wittgenstein's dictum, "There are indeed things that cannot be put into words. They *make themselves manifest*. They are what is mystical"). Dialectic, as Herbert's poetry shows, comments finally neither upon the realms of history and of the divine, nor upon the ineluctable structures of human thought, but upon the confrontation between the two.

Dialectic for Marvell is also a consequence of human ways of thinking and speaking. His best poems, including "The Garden" and "Upon Appleton House," develop this aspect of dialectic in an even more sophisticated critique. Like much of the poetry of Donne and Herbert, these poems are at once statements seeking to deny dialectic, and critiques of these denials. They open through their rich allusiveness almost infinite vistas on the dialectical antinomies that Western culture has incessantly rehearsed over the two millenia from the Greek period down to the Renaissance. Marvell's critique of dialectic, like Milton's, is also a critique of human culture; and this dimension distinguishes them from Donne's and Herbert's. Marvell's personae, particularly in these two poems, are from the beginning aware of the ambiguities in things, in words, and in the *rapprochement* between the two. The reader does not simply supply counterarguments to the personae's assertions. Rather, he is invited to contemplate continual transformations of metaphor, statement, tone, and reference, while cooperating in Marvell's own attempt to bend his language into conformity with the dialectics that this language creates but cannot finally encompass. In this regard, Marvell, at least in "The Garden" and "Upon Appleton House," stands nearer to Milton than does either Donne or Herbert. Dialectic is already present on these poems' surfaces, and is to that extent accommodated. Its presence, however, still bears the marks of more simplistic, nondialectical demands lying in the strata beneath the persona's language, and in this Marvell's poetry forms part of a single lyric tradition with that of Herbert and Donne.

MARVELL

Most recent criticism has tended, I think rightly, to view the whole corpus of Marvell's poetry, the post-Restoration satires excluded, as a composite commentary on a set of parallel themes or, as Professor Rosalie Colie puts it, problematics. She says at the beginning of *"My Ecchoing Song":*

> From his flexible use of themes, his distribution of thematic elements, his combinations of rhetorical techniques, one can only conclude that Marvell's chief reason for writing lyric poetry was an overriding interest in the problems of lyric poetry.
>
> He was certainly much interested in particular themes, but not, I think, committed to any particular theme or obsessed by it. Indeed, the variety of the uses to which he subjects his themes . . . argues for his preoccupation rather with their problematics than with their conventional or single message.[30]

Marvell surveys a wide variety of Renaissance poetic genres and their accompanying themes to formulate a detached criticism of the strengths and limitations of the particular visions that each mediates. Thus Marvell often deals with the traditional antinomies of spirit and flesh, eternity and time, contemplation and action, innocence and fallenness, by employing the various genres and conventions that had traditionally mediated these antinomies up to his own time.[31] Most critics agree that Marvell

[30] Rosalie L. Colie, *"My Ecchoing Song": Andrew Marvell's Poetry of Criticism* (Princeton: Princeton Univ. Press, 1970), p. 13.

[31] *Ibid.*, pp. 51, 57, and *passim*.

set the issues of his poems in antinomical terms.[32] Not so obvious in his poetry is what I call the ambiguity of definition: the logic inherent in antinomical problematics by which each antinomy can only be defined in terms of its opposite, and can maintain its identity only at the expense possibly of turning into its opposite.

In general, the various antinomies that I listed above are reducible to an underlying pattern, roughly platonic, which sets off the timeless innocence of the spirit against the fallen historicity of the flesh. For efficiency's sake, one might say that Marvell faced the essential problem, no matter what version might appear in any given poem, of "primitivism." This term covers a disconcertingly large number of versions, a fact that led A. O. Lovejoy and George Boas to ferret out the various meanings primitivism has had in Western culture. In *Primitivism and Related Ideas in Antiquity* (1935), the only volume ever to appear of a projected series, they list several varieties of primitivism that are specifically found in Marvell's poetry:

(f) The "natural" state of any being as its congenital or original condition; hence, in the case of mankind, or of a given people, its primeval state, in contrast with subsequent historic alterations or accretions.

(g) "Nature" as that which exists apart from man and without human effort or contrivance, in contrast with "art," i.e., with all that is artificial or man-made.

(h) "Nature" as that *in* man which is not due to taking thought or to deliberate choice: hence, those modes of human desire, emotion, or behavior which are instinctive or spontaneous, in contrast with those which are due to

[32] I am particularly indebted to Harold E. Toliver, *Marvell's Ironic Vision* (New Haven and London: Yale Univ. Press, 1965); Lawrence W. Hyman, *Andrew Marvell* (New York: Twayne Publishers, 1964); Harry Berger, Jr., "Marvell's 'Garden': Still Another Interpretation," *MLQ* 28 (1967): 285–304; John M. Wallace, *Destiny His Choice: The Loyalism of Andrew Marvell* (Cambridge: University Press, 1968); M. J. K. O'Loughlin, "This Sober Frame: A Reading of 'Upon Appleton House,'" in *Andrew Marvell: A Collection of Critical Essays*, ed. George deF. Lord (Englewood Cliffs, N.J.: Prentice-Hall, 1968), pp. 120–142, an essay that takes a viewpoint on this poem close to my own.

the laboring intellect, to premeditation, to self-consciousness, or to instruction.[33]

All of these versions are defined against some facet of man's
present, historical existence. This often-noted aspect of primitivism is summarized by Harry Levin:

> Undetachably our lives stand rooted in the firm realities
> of here and now. Restlessness may project our thoughts
> in unspecified directions: "Anywhere out of the world,"
> to echo the phrase that Baudelaire echoed from Thomas
> Hood. But if our longing to escape—or, more positively,
> better our condition—has any goal, however dimly en-
> visioned, it must be located elsewhere or otherwhile.
> Standing here and wishing to be there, we are given a
> choice, at least by imagination; we may opt for some
> distant part of the world, a terrestrial paradise, or for an
> otherworld, a celestial paradise. . . .
>
> Any enumeration of those ills whose absence was the
> precondition of bliss, obviously, reflects back again from
> the illusory past to the less than satisfactory present and,
> more immediately, to the beholder who is less than satis-
> fied with what he beholds. Roughly speaking, the golden
> age is all that the contemporary age is not.[34]

The close connection between primitivistic ideals and pastoral
literature has allowed the pastoral also to function as a satirical
standpoint projected against the complexities of sophisticated
urban society.[35] Such uses of the pastoral standpoint can range
from simplistically dichotomistic examples, such as Spenser's
The Shepheardes Calender and Twain's *Huckleberry Finn,* to
multivalent treatments such as Shakespeare's *As You Like It*
and Golding's *The Lord of the Flies.*

Because a primitivistic ideal is necessarily projected by a
nonprimitive imagination (tribes at the headwaters of the Ama-

---

[33] New York: Octagon Books, 1965 (repr.), p. 13; italics in orig.

[34] Harry Levin, *The Myth of the Golden Age in the Renaissance* (Bloomington
and London: Indiana Univ. Press, 1969), pp. 8, 11.

[35] Cf. Chapter 1, "Pastoral Poetry," in Hallett Smith, *Elizabethan Poetry*
(Cambridge: Harvard Univ. Press, 1952), pp. 1–63.

zon can hardly cultivate the primitivistic because they are already primitive), it contains a radical ambiguity. The primitivistic ideal is at once the reverse of the *status quo* and its dialectical
mirror image. Marvell's lyrics aim not so much at a solution of
this anomaly, as at a criticism of the self-cancelling dialectic implicit in this way of setting the issues. Marvell's insight into
the ambiguous dialectical definition of primitivism appears similar
to that of another recent student of the subject. In a perceptive
analysis of this ambiguity, Karl Mannheim distinguishes between
the ideology of a given society, its overtly formulated rationalizations of the *status quo,* and that society's utopia, its ideals
projected as states of being yet to be striven for:

> We wish to single out the living principle which links the
> development of utopia with the development of an existing
> order. In this sense, the relationship between utopia and
> the existing order turns out to be a "dialectical" one. By
> this is meant that every age allows to arise (in differently
> located social groups) those ideas and values in which are
> contained in condensed form the unrealized and unfulfilled
> tendencies which represent the needs of each age. These
> intellectual elements then become the explosive material
> for bursting the limits of the existing order. The existing
> order gives birth to utopias which in turn break the bonds
> of the existing order, leaving it free to develop in the
> direction of the next order of existence.[36]

Though the utopias Mannheim considers include types of social
and political reform and revolution other than those motivated
by primitivistic ideals, his discussion of Reformation chiliastic
sects such as the Anabaptists shows the immediate relevance of
his distinction to the logic that generates primitivism. Further,
he states the paradox implicit in this logic:

> Whenever an idea is labelled utopian it is usually by a
> representative of an epoch that has already passed. On
> the other hand, the exposure of ideologies as illusory ideas,

---

[36] Karl Mannheim, *Ideology and Utopia,* trans. Louis Wirth and Edward Shils
(New York: Harcourt, Brace, n.d.), p. 199.

adapted to the present order, is the work generally of representatives of an order of existence which is still in process of emergence. It is always the dominant group which
is in full accord with the existing order that determines
what is to be regarded as utopian, while the ascendant
group which is in conflict with things as they are is the
one that determines what is regarded as ideological.[37]

Though Mannheim speaks primarily of his own concern,
namely, economic and social change, nevertheless the same paradox occurs in any other projection of a utopia against a present
ideology. Utopias depend radically for their themes and structures on the state of things "as they are," because such utopias
always derive their categories of melioration from the state of
things against which they are projected. A utopian standpoint
criticizes the adherent of the *status quo* as a victim of illusion, as
the creator of ideologies that pretend to some absolute validity,
but which are really rationalizations, myths, propaganda. For
this reason Mannheim states that utopias become visible from
viewpoints identified with the *status quo,* and in reverse, ideologies are named from utopian perspectives.

Marvell's lyrics embody a similar insight. The great good
place can only be envisioned from within a perspective outside
of it, a standpoint in the fallen world. It depends upon that
world's language, categories, and most importantly, its fallenness
as a springboard. To project such a vision as simply the reverse
of a fallen state connoting the flesh, sexuality, enslavement to
time and to the complexities of civilization is thus to tie it firmly
to its opposite. The primitivistic stance in Marvell's poetry idealizes
the spirit at the expense of history, and spontaneous naturalness
at the expense of art. In doing so, it attempts to break down the
dialectical correlation of these antinomies in the interest of a
(necessarily partial) resolution in favor of the first of these. The
danger is, as Marvell saw it, that such idealizing may in turn
generate compensatory (and likewise partial) emphases on the
flesh, unmoralized action, and meretricious "artfulness." Marvell's problem lay in giving his ideal garden state a positive, not

37 *Ibid.,* p. 203.

merely a negative, definition. As I will show, Marvell signals his escape from between the horns of this dilemma not by his succeeding, but rather by his poised recognition of the necessities that prevent an escape.

I am going to discuss in detail "The Garden" and "Upon Appleton House," but only as much of these poems as will indicate how Marvell dealt with the similar dialectical issues he sets in both of them. Poems such as "On a Drop of Dew," "A Dialogue Between The Resolved Soul, and Created Pleasure," and "Clorinda and Damon" mediate a platonic view of man's aspirations, affirming with little tension a transcendence of spirit over flesh, and eternity over time. Others, including "To His Coy Mistress," "Daphnis and Chloe," and "The Unfortunate Lover" present a cynical view of man's enslavement to the flesh and passion, the correlative opposite of platonic yearning. Both groups follow out dichotomistic platonic thought structures to their logical conclusions. For the vision out of which both groups issue allows only two, mutually exclusive, possibilities—death to time, or death in time. A third group overtly and ironically confronts this dialectical correlation, and includes "A Dialogue Between the Soul and Body," "The Nymph complaining for the death of her Faun," "A Definition of Love," "Young Love," "A Picture of Little T. C. in a Prospect of Flowers," and the four Mower poems. Classifying these poems together and ignoring their different tones and conclusions, we can see that in all of them Marvell comments on the impasse that results when platonic antinomies confront one another on a common ground allowing them neither separation nor mutual harmony. "A Dialogue" explores how the Body and the Soul, both arguing within a platonic framework that would separate them, inadvertently deliver the message that they are inextricably entangled. "A Definition of Love," "The Nymph," and the Mower poems all elaborate the impossibility of living in a mixed world, while demanding platonic innocence and denying passion and man's fallenness. "Young Love" and "A Picture of Little T.C." present examples of human love idealized precisely because the love objects are prepubertal children incapable of offering sexual temptation.

This last group approaches in the sophistication of their accommodations the attitudes worked out in "The Garden" and "Upon Appleton House." They demonstrate the need for a conceptual framework that somehow goes beyond the either-or categories of platonism and primitivism. The three groups of poems exhibit the impossibility of making a dichotomistic view of the human condition adequate to all the pressures and claims thereof. The poems of the first group achieve their ideal consummations by ignoring much of the human life they claim to represent. Had we only these and similar poems we could rank Marvell among the minor platonizing poets of the seventeenth century, such as Drummond of Hawthornden and Lord Herbert of Cherbury, poets who claim little of our attention because they say so much in one direction while ignoring so much in many others.

Just as in homeopathic medicine one is made immune to a disease by being given it (a medical version of the *felix culpa*), so in "The Garden" the violent intrusion of history and sexuality is avoided by its being willingly allowed, but in an attenuated form. Inoculation against the dangers of dialectical definition involves a further criticism of the very pastoral conventions the poet is employing. Rosalie Colie has articulated clearly the relation in the poem of its main thematic concerns to Marvell's use of the *hortus* convention itself: "This poem sets problems of the relation of experience to thought, and problems of thinking itself; it illustrates its critical nature by its peculiar comment on its own, or the poetic, activity; that is, it comments on its own creation and its own meaning even as it undergoes that creation and establishes that meaning." [38] Marvell here tests the dialectical exigencies in the twin motives of retirement from and engagement with history, by exploring how these have been articulated within the conventions and genres traditionally assigned to them. "The Garden" tests the retirement *topos* by showing not only what it must achieve but also what it must avoid, since the dialectical nature of the *topos* carries with it the pressures of time and the flesh it seeks to deny. "The Garden" tells us that retirement as a denial of time and the flesh can be achieved, if at all, only at the expense of being inoculated with that time and flesh.

[38] Colie, *"My Ecchoing Song,"* p. 151.

"The Garden" moves through successive rejections of the world enumerated as variations of each other. Worldly action and sensuous love are left behind in the first four stanzas, and in stanzas six and seven the body itself is shed. "The Palm, the Oke, or Bayes" are metamorphosed into "the Garlands of repose" (2, 8).[39] In turn, Daphne and Syrinx, the objects of rape, are translated into plants, and Marvell finds the gods really happier with them in that state. The farthest point of withdrawal is reached in the famous sixth stanza, where "The Mind, from pleasure less, / Withdraws into its happiness" (41–42), and we are given that still, timeless, unmoving point of pure contemplation, so mysterious because it transcends discursive thought and brings us to that grasp of all things in a single concept:

> Yet it creates, transcending these,
> Far other Worlds, and other Seas;
> Annihilating all that's made
> To a green Thought in a green Shade.
> [45–48]

But the act of withdrawal is not perfect. Or rather, we might say that Marvell has reached the height of his sophisticated vision when he shows us that the withdrawal can be perfect only if it is allowed to be imperfect. As Lawrence W. Hyman points out, "If Daphne turns into laurel, then the laurel becomes more and more like Daphne. That is, the pleasures which the androgynous Adam enjoyed, although at all times perfectly innocent, seem to resemble the sexual pleasures of mortal men."[40] A similar coalescence and reversal holds true, as he points out, for the fifth stanza:

> What wond'rous Life in this I lead!
> Ripe Apples drop about my head;
> The Luscious Clusters of the Vine
> Upon my Mouth do crush their Wine;
> The Nectaren, and curious Peach,

[39] All quotations from Marvell's poetry are from *The Poems and Letters of Andrew Marvell,* ed. H. M. Margoliouth, 2 vols. (Oxford: Clarendon Press, 1952; 2nd ed.), 1:20–21.

[40] Hyman, *Andrew Marvell,* p. 67.

Into my hands themselves do reach;
Stumbling on Melons, as I pass,
Insnar'd with Flow'rs, I fall on Grass.

[33–40]

The sensuality here is an inoculated sensuality, and the fall harmless. Its harmlessness, and the carefully contrived conditions that make it so, have not been obvious to all. Professor Colie's setting of the problem of interpreting this passage, with which I agree while disagreeing with her solution, provides the best way into Marvell's formulations here:

> But one cannot have it both ways: if the poet "falls" in the Christian sense, then his ecstasy can hardly be so transcendent as it is [by some] felt to be; if he simply falls "on Grass," thereby affirming his own mortality and acting out his own death to come, then what are we to make of the genuine joy of the ecstatic experience? One way or another, the stern Biblical meanings of the "fall" seem irrelevant here.[41]

My answer to this is that, simply, not only can Marvell have it both ways, but also that he does and must; the whole point of the poem is that we can only have a fall that avoids the malign effects of an earlier, more devastating fall, if that latter fall is somehow included in the *hortus* world of innocence, taken account of by it, and accommodated. Marvell has avoided the ambiguities of dialectical definition, which occur as long as the two opposites remain simply negations of each other, by allowing the fallen nature of man admittance into the *hortus* world. Having been allowed in the multivalent reference to the "fall on Grass," man's fallenness can now be, if not dismissed, at least temporarily ignored in affirming the quite univocal meaning of "Fall" as harmless play. I would therefore take the often-recognized multiplicity of references in this poem one step further, and say that Marvell's ultimate vision is not of complexity but of simplicity. "The Garden" wondrously achieves this simplicity by first inoculating the literal level with far-reaching references to all those pressures

[41] Colie, *"My Ecchoing Song,"* pp. 162–163.

in the historical world of fallen man that withdrawal seeks to negate. Thus dialectic is avoided by making dialectic the norm.

Obviously, one can achieve such a state only by descending to the vegetative level ("Upon Appleton House" will give us a bemused Andrew Marvell turning into a plant). Like Daphne and Syrinx, the speaker experiences sexual love without sensuality, because sensuality overtly suffuses the language that mediates these amorous fruits. Literally, this garden does not and cannot exist separate from the poem's language, for Marvell purposely articulates and criticizes the traditional verbal means through which men have for centuries expressed their yearning for the golden age. The "Ripe Apples," "Luscious Clusters of the Vine," the traps of Melons and insnaring flowers of stanza five fuse sexuality and vegetative innocence, making possible a separation of these two states with some safety. I say "with some safety," because they are freed, if only ambiguously, from the equally ambiguous fusions consequent on attempts to keep them unequivocally apart. The language not only mediates the speaker's vision here, it also, and primarily, demonstrates that vision. Adjective, participle, and substantive fuse in metaphor the very dialectic to be exorcised.

As the speaker withdraws further, he enacts a similar accommodation of dialectic by suggesting a countermovement. The "green Thought in a green Shade" moves farthest from the material world, and also faces toward the world, assimilating it. Here, extremes meet. "The Mind, that Ocean where each kind / Does streight its own resemblance find" (43–44), retreats both toward a vanishing point ("Annihilating all that's made" [47]), and through this vanishing point, past which mind and matter no longer diverge, but fuse. In the next stanza (seven), the soul as a bird casts "the Bodies Vest aside" (51), to fly into the boughs of a tree, but it does so only "till prepar'd for longer flight." The final divesting is deferred, and the poem reminds us once again that, however much this garden looks anagogically forward to the actual removal from time and the flesh, it remains still a garden of the human mind, constructed wholly out of and by the instruments of that mind, human language. Ruth Wallerstein's interpretation of the "various light" which the soul

"Waves in its Plumes" (56), is extremely suggestive: "The meditation on values and the definition completed, Marvell gives us in the next stanza an actual experience of transcendence, of which the meditation itself is a part. For is not the *various light* the multifold reflection in nature of the one essential light from which nature springs?" [42] The soul's plumes are the "silver Wings" of line 54; does this mean that the soul reflects the various light of nature, itself reflecting variously the light of God? Or do the plumes, like Shelley's dome of many colored glass, make this light "various" because the soul cannot yet reflect without sundering the light into many diverse colors? In either case, or rather by taking both together, we discover that divesting the soul from the body and the material world turns it back to this world.

In the next stanza, Marvell creates a complex fusion-plus-separation of his own garden with the garden of Eden, not only before the Fall but before the creation of Eve. First, this garden is described as indeed like "that happy Garden-state / While Man there walk'd without a Mate" (57–58); but the second half of the stanza remembers that " 'twas beyond a Mortal's share / To wander solitary there" (61–62). In short, *this* is a "Mortal's share": a garden which is a type of that original garden, but in being only a type, is also at best a projection of that garden from a perspective within the fallen world.

Finally, the farthest recognition of the dialectical exigencies preventing his escape from type into anagogical anti-type is given in the last stanza.

> How well the skilful Gardner drew
> Of flow'rs and herbes this Dial new;
> Where from above the milder Sun
> Does through a fragrant Zodiack run;
>
> [65–68]

A sundial of flowers. The world of time is not escaped, but instead is very much present, as present as sexuality itself. The artificial "Zodiack," the sort of thing that dismayed the primi-

[42] Ruth Wallerstein, *Studies in Seventeenth-Century Poetic* (Madison: Univ. of Wisconsin Press, 1950), p. 329.

tivist Damon of the Mower poems, places in a single emblem
the achieved vision the poem has been maneuvering to render. In
this sundial of flowers we recognize the garden for what it is:
a moment of conceptual and verbal stasis artfully poised between
various competing antinomies, capable of accepting either one
because first made capable of accepting both.

Marvell recognizes that no position available in a spectrum
of possible positions that are dialectical functions of one another
is wholly immune from transforming itself into its opposite. Even
the modes of accommodation I have described as inoculation are
at best only just that: accommodations to the unstable nature of
things made all the more unstable to the degree that the human
mind imposes stability within a schema of dichotomous, univocal
categories. Therefore, in "The Garden" and in "Upon Appleton
House," which I will take up now, we find that beautifully balanced mixture of acceptance and denial, of advance and withdrawal whereby Marvell inoculates his vision against attempts
simply to choose one over against the other. Doing such, however,
is like receding through a hall of mirrors: a positive definition of
innocence still reflects its opposite insofar as it only avoids a
malignly negative definition.

Marvell achieves in "Upon Appleton House" a richly qualified
recognition and acceptance of this fact. After surveying the materials that go into this poem, Rosalie Colie finds that "almost
nothing happens twice the same way"; "things are not what
they seem; what they are is unpredictable." And she catches up
exactly its slippery techniques as appropriate vehicles of meaning:

> One condition gives upon another: night and day, dark
> and light, world and estate are all mixed conditions; in
> the poem, experience is always qualified, ambiguous, il-
> lusory, defiant of interpretation, resistant to classification.
> Insofar as possible, the "Discipline severe" must instruct
> that there is no fixed protection either without or within,
> that within may at any moment be turned inside out to
> become without. "In" and "out" depend upon perspective,
> after all, by a perspective of illusion designed to fit our
> experience and to save the phenomena.[43]

[43] Colie, *"My Ecchoing Song,"* pp. 274, 275, 276.

I disagree with her and other recent critics of the poem who say that its main theme concerns the relations between the active and contemplative life.[44] Certainly the poem concerns this traditional conflict as it does also the relations between the house and its occupant, inner worth and outer symbol, nature versus art, and high versus low status; just as *Hamlet* concerns the relation between justice and the guilt that accompanies the enforcement of justice, or Donne's poems concern the logical problem posed by the body-soul relationship. But in all three cases, concerns are not themes. Theme, as I will explain at greater length in the final essay, is the dianoia of the work, its significant whole stated "through" the work (all-pervasive, by the instrumentality of), and therefore is not reducible to any one of its vehicles. The essential theme of "Upon Appleton House" is the accommodations demanded of a mind that begins by formulating the problematics of human life in dichotomous terms.

Several critics have noted the poem's presentation of itself as artifice, as discourse that displays its transformations and metamorphoses as dependent on the perspectives within which the persona sees Nunappleton, its history, and its surrounding grounds.[45] The poem gives us a perspective not only on its subject matter—its various concerns—but also on its own modes of dealing with these concerns. As such, we are invited both to acquiesce in, and to question, the elaborate and sometimes fluid metaphorical transformations the speaker imposes upon the landscape. In being made aware of this extra dimension of the poem-as-poem as well as of the poem-as-vehicle, we are invited simultaneously to ponder, and to discount as much as we feel we must, the speaker's continual joining of opposite motifs, symbols, and valuations. For instance, the opening ten stanzas concern different understandings of the relation between inner worth and greatness, and the outer symbols of this worth, a theme Marvell inherited

[44] Included among those who see "Upon Appleton House" as primarily concerned with the tension between action and contemplation, are Donald M. Friedman, *Marvell's Pastoral Art* (Berkeley and Los Angeles: Univ. of California Press, 1970), pp. 199–200; John M. Wallace, *Destiny His Choice*, pp. 235ff.; M. J. K. O'Loughlin, "This Sober Frame," in Lord, *Andrew Marvell*, pp. 123ff.; and Ruth Wallerstein, *Seventeenth-Century Poetic*, pp. 295ff.

[45] Wallace, *Destiny His Choice*, pp. 235–236; Colie, "My Ecchoing Song," pp. 184, 203–205.

from Ben Jonson. Like Jonson, Marvell realizes how men, because of their inner spiritual poverty, will compensate by creating magnificence of external show. Marvell concludes that a large house only dwarfs the "small" person, while the great one will force the house to "expand."

III

> But He, superfluously spread,
> Demands more room alive than dead.
> And in his hollow Palace goes
> Where Winds as he themselves may lose.
> What needs of all this Marble Crust
> T'impark the wanton Mote of Dust,
> That thinks by Breadth the World t'unite
> Though the first Builders fail'd in Height?

Against this pretentiousness Marvell places Fairfax's true inner worth, which does not need outer panoply. Fairfax can afford to "stoop / To enter at a narrow loop; / As practising, in doors so strait, / To strain [himself] through Heavens Gate" (29–32). This reversal of a snobbish relation between inner worth and outer show leads to a literalizing of metaphor, by which spiritual and material "size" are rendered on the same level:

VII

> Yet thus the laden House does sweat,
> And scarce indures the *Master* great:
> But where he comes the swelling Hall
> Stirs, and the *Square* grows *Spherical;*
> More by his *Magnitude* distrest,
> Then he is by its straitness prest:
> And too officiously it slights
> That in it self which him delights.

Such Clevelandizing recurs throughout the poem, but is not the result of mere conceited cleverness. Rather, such figures in the very act of complimenting make manifest the limits of decorous compliment. The speaker simultaneously indicates the lord's transcendence over outward panoply, while showing, by the figure's very outlandishness, that considerations of external ornament do not really engage the virtuous man at all. The passage calls attention to itself as the panegyrical speech of a speaker who wants to compliment his master for his freedom both from outward ornament, and therefore from the need for compliment.

These opening stanzas define the essential pattern the poem will repeat, in both its content and its poetic technique. The speaker's artifice will invite us to behold conjunctions of image, allusion, and theme in which we are aware of just how, in reality, there are remarkable and surprising points of similarity; while at the same time we see that such conjunctions are, after all, only the creations of a poetic mind bent on both making its myths and discounting them. The stanzas describing the nun's attempt to inveigle Isabella Thwaites, the destined bride of Fairfax's ancestor (XII–XXXV), parody the fusions and separations the poet will work out once he begins his perambulation in earnest. In the nun's rhetoric, innocence and sexuality, piety and pleasure, nature and art, all fuse in a manner that suggests the opposite of Marvell's inoculation. Here, these opposites are rather corrupted by one another, because the nun, unlike Marvell's speakers in "The Garden" and this poem, seems completely unaware of the dangers latent in such fusions. The fusion of action and contemplation gets a suspiciously ambiguous statement in her mouth:

XIII

'Within this holy leisure we
'Live innocently as you see.
'These Walls restrain the World without,
'But hedge our liberty about.
'These Bars inclose that wider Den
'Of those wild Creatures, called Men.
'The Cloyster outward shuts its Gates,
'And, from us, locks on them the Grates.

Coming to the stanza expecting the nun to counterpoise the calm restraint of the cloister against the licentiousness of the outside world, we gradually become aware that she is doing both this and its opposite. The walls of the convent "restrain" the world, while "hedging" their own liberty. This could also mean that their walls protect the nuns' covert licentiousness under the guise of just the opposite. The Bars "inclose" the sexual realm of men, and it requires a double take to notice that the word is indeed not "exclude" or some synonym thereof. The cloister shuts its gates close to bring in rather than shut out. The final line, in such ambiguous context, contains the odd implication that the men are shut inside the convent, away "from us," who would be in that case *outside* the convent. Such ambiguity derives, I think, not from any prurience of the *Maria Monk* type. Rather, Marvell suggests just how liable to mutual interchange the motifs of "inside" and "outside" are, if the person affirming one against the other is unaware of the dialectical dangers.

The nuns continually await the heavenly "Bridegroom" (108), but their tears and prayers have the remarkable effect of making them more sensuously attractive:

XIV

'Our *Orient* Breaths perfumed are
'With insense of incessant Pray'r.
'And Holy-water of our Tears
'Most strangly our Complexion clears.

The ease of this fusion indicates that pleasure and sexuality have not been denied, but rather retained. At one point she says:

XXII

'Nor is our *Order* yet so nice,
'Delight to banish as a Vice.
'Here Pleasure Piety doth meet;
'One perfecting the other Sweet.

Sexuality appears through the coy language that denies it:

XXIV

'Each Night among us to your side
'Appoint a fresh and Virgin Bride:
'Whom if *Our Lord* at midnight find,
'Yet Neither should be left behind.
'Where you may lye as chast in Bed,

'As Pearls together billeted.
'All Night embracing Arm in Arm,
'Like Chrystal pure with Cotton warm.

If the reactions of numerous students can be trusted, these lines evoke a definite, if somewhat uncanny, disgust. Do we not find here exactly that malign mutual corruption of flesh by spirit and of spirit by flesh that Marvell projects in "A Dialogue Between the Soul and Body"?

Fairfax overturns the convent, aware of the nuns' subtle dishonesty. The nun's speech differs from that of the poem's persona on exactly that point where they are most alike: the artifice of their metaphorical conjunctions. But where the persona avoids the dangers of dialectical definition by exhibiting his fusions as artifice, the nun here shows no such awareness. Her artifice is presented as if it were not such, and to that degree she communicates the opposite of the persona's vision: where he envisions fusion under the sign of inoculation, the nun envisions fusion under the sign of mutual corruption.

The next episodes, where the persona artfully metamorphoses the garden, the meadow, the wood, and the river respectively, present us with two movements which are thematic functions of each other. First, each area of Nunappleton's estate is described in images that fuse in metaphor the worlds of action and contemplation, while calling attention to their disparateness. Second, the persona's movement from one area into the next portrays a still further withdrawal from history into a timeless world of pure intuition. The first movement inoculates dialectic by admitting it, the second withdraws from dialectic itself. The second is necessary because Marvell seemed particularly aware in "Upon Appleton House" that dialectic, once brought to consciousness, involves the speaker more subtly in the malign oppositions he seeks to avoid, even as he becomes aware of their true dialectical nature.

The gardens become regiments standing at attention, with flowers turned into flags and musket pans. The mowers in the meadows become likewise an army massacring hay and a bird. The woods are, at various times, Noah's ark (needed to escape the flooded meadows, which are both the innocent world at its creation and the wicked world punished by drowning), a temple, Sibyl's leaves, and an armed fort. The river is likewise a snake and a crystal mirror, both wanton and harmless. The teleology of all this artifice is given in the poem's penultimate stanza:

LXXXXVI

'Tis not, what once it was, the *World;*
But a rude heap together hurl'd;
All negligently overthrown,
Gulfes, Deserts, Precipices, Stone.
Your lesser *World* contains the same.
But in more decent Order tame;
You Heaven's Center, Nature's Lap.
And Paradice's only Map.

Marvell asks and answers in the poem this question: What must be understood and articulated about man's state in a fallen, historical world in order for him to find and possess with some assurance "Paradice's only Map"? His answer is the awareness both of dialectic and of the dangers of this awareness. Marjorie Nicholson points out that the contrast between the "rude heap" in this stanza and the "new and empty Face of things" (442) is a deliberate contrast between postlapsarian and prelapsarian geography.[46] The third couplet of the stanza summarizes how something of the former world may (and must) yet be retained. The "lesser *World*" of Nunappleton manages to contain the same assymetry of the fallen world "in more decent Order tame," precisely because it does contain it, does not refuse it in the name of a nondialectical primitivism, thereby avoiding the malign assault of all those elements of the fallen world which Nunappleton, after all, cannot really escape anyway.

The upshot of these withdrawals is the discovery that no position, no viewpoint or perspective, no metamorphosis is free of its ambiguities. All are recognized as liable to a fall because all have been defined against and therefore in terms of a fall. Two examples, from the beginning and the end of the speaker's peregrinations, will have to suffice.

[46] Marjorie Hope Nicholson, *Mountain Gloom and Mountain Glory* (New York: Norton, 1963), p. 75.

In withdrawing from Fairfax's garden-garrison, the speaker descends in "to the Abbyss . . . / Of that unfathomable Grass, / Where Men like Grashoppers appear, / But Grashoppers are Gyants there" (369–372). As Professor Colie has noted, this inversion results from the fact "that the grasshoppers are sitting, in their usual small shapes, on top of the grass grown taller than men." [47] Once we discover the literal scene we also discover the artifice of the speaker's inversion. But the inversion has foundation in fact; which is, indeed, the "true" perspective?

Through this Alice-like descent we find ourselves in a visionary world where allusions flow together to link with and mutually illuminate each other. Marvell's suspension in this green world leaves him wide-eyed and suggestible:

XLVIII

To see Men through this Meadow Dive,
We wonder how they rise alive.
As, under Water, none does know
Whether he fall through it or go.
But, as the Marriners that sound,
And show upon their Lead the Ground,
They bring up Flow'rs so to be seen,
And prove they've at the Bottom been.

An affirmation of the links between falling and rising, the key to the possibility of the fallen world's salvation, never gets more explicit than this: the poet gives no explanation of the *"felix culpa,"* like Adam's in Book 12 of *Paradise Lost,* but rather dreams the fluidity of these opposites' reciprocity. The men in the meadow are not really swimming in a sea, nor are they even re-enacting the fall of man. We recognize these facts through the poet's ingenious allusions, which on our first beholding them metamorphose men and meadows into types of fall and resurrection. But once we have "unmetaphored" the passage, what then? We become aware of how available are the meadow and its various adjuncts for being converted into such types, of how the rural primitivist world can become the fallen world it is allegedly defined against. The poet affirms nothing except this availability, this potentiality. Later, when the mown hay "seemeth wrought /

[47] Colie, *"My Ecchoing Song,"* p. 205.

A Camp of Battail newly fought" (419–420), and the meadow presents "A new and empty Face of things," both become types of "The World when first created," "a Table rase and pure" (442, 445–446). Nevertheless, the prelapsarian landscape (also an unfallen mind characterized as Aristotle's *"tabula rasa"*) is flooded; which is, after all, only a routine seasonal matter. "But I, retiring from the Flood, / Take Sanctuary in the Wood; / And, while it lasts, my self imbark / In this yet green, yet growing Ark" (481–484). The meadow is initially an area of withdrawal, defined against the garden-garrison, itself likewise defined against the outside world of civil upheaval. But the meadow likewise "falls," or rather, becomes inoculated by the poet's artifice with what it (allegedly) escapes. Not only are evil and fallen nature inoculated, but innocence as well. For, as should be clear by now, both are equally the enemy of the balance Marvell would strike.

The last area of the speaker's experience is the river that winds through the meadow:

LXXX
See in what wanton harmless folds
It ev'ry where the Meadow holds;
And its yet muddy back doth lick,
Till as a *Chrystal Mirrour* slick;
Where all things gaze themselves, and doubt
If they be in it or without.
And for his shade which therein shines,
Narcissus like, the *Sun* too pines.

Like the erotic vegetation of "The Garden," the snake can afford to be wanton because rendered harmless. Its muddiness yields a "Chrystal Mirrour" and its shade shines. The incipient narcissism of the mirror is avoided by being explicitly admitted; but then, this narcissism only mythologizes recognizable physical fact: the sun and the vegetation are reflected in the river.

Here, as throughout, we witness the human mind's transformation of the symbols it finds for externalizing and articulating the categories through which it understands the human condition. The landscape of Nunappleton is neither fallen nor innocent; like the garden, its significance lies not in itself but in the words uttered about it. For it is through words—metaphors, the artifice of human verbal creation—that man makes and utters his accommodations of his fallen nature. Recreating the landscape of Nunappleton into an external correlative to the realizations that govern the speaker's words is the poem's essential triumph. Thus, the speaker demonstrates a high degree of scrupulous discrimination between inside and outside, symbol and reality, and innocence and fallenness. To literalize metaphor as Marvell does in "The Garden" and "Upon Appleton House" is simultaneously to project an outward symbol of inner balance, and to express tacitly the fact that, after all, such balance dwells in no external place, but rather in what the mind makes of that place. Thus are the artifice and theme of "Upon Appleton House" joined.

When Maria Fairfax appears at twilight as, among other things, a new Eve in this new Eden, the poet assures us and her that both of these typological transformations become possible only because of discipline and understanding. Curiously like the Eve of *Paradise Lost*, Maria sums up and orders the landscape around her:

LXXXVII
'Tis *She* that to these Gardens gave
That wondrous Beauty which they have;
She streightness on the Woods bestows:
To *Her* the Meadow sweetness owes;
Nothing could make the River be
So Chrystal-pure but only *She:*
She yet more Pure, Sweet, Streight, and Fair,
Then Gardens, Woods, Meads, Rivers are.

The puns in the penultimate line communicate the essential point here, where "Pure, Sweet, Streight, and Fair" point toward their natural and their human meanings simultaneously. However, puns mark separations of meaning as well as fusions, and in fact Maria contributes nothing to the landscape. She is as different from it as are the two paradigms of meaning the four adjectives single out by their punning. But if the compliment means anything at all, if there is any factual reason for envisoning Maria

Fairfax as a new Eve in a new Eden, it lies in her intellectual and moral achievements, which, like those manifested in the speaker's poetic artifice, have raised her beyond the temptations of snobbish affectation, of "feign'd complying Innocence" (compare the nun's speech), of cosmetic perversion, and of sterile rejection of sexuality (stanzas 89, 90, 92, and 93–94 respectively).

The final stanza of the poem gives a deliberately dialectical emblem of the acceptance the speaker has been striving toward:

LXXXXVII

But now the *Salmon-Fishers* moist
Their *Leathern Boats* begin to hoist;
And, like *Antipodes* in Shoes,
Have shod their *Heads* in their *Canoos.*
How Tortoise like, but not so slow,
These rational *Amphibii* go?
Let's in: for the dark *Hemisphere*
Does now like one of them appear.

Reminding us, as Professor Colie says, "that things are simple nowhere in the world, that all men are sometimes, in some perspectives, upside down," [48] the figures at the opposite end of the earth both reflect and reflect upside down the fishermen at Nunappleton. This triumph of egregious artifice is an unequivocal emblem of what it means to be a rational amphibium.

Night descends, and "the dark *Hemisphere* / Does now like one of them appear." Perhaps Marvell foreshadows the close of Sir Thomas Browne's *The Garden of Cyrus:* "To keep our eyes open longer were but to act our *Antipodes.* The Huntsmen are up in *America,* and they are already past their first sleep in *Persia.*" [49] The movement of time, the quotidian frame of this enactment of human history, has brought round the dark half of the cycle, and Marvell like Browne begins to act his own antipodes. To remain stationary, to refuse the alternating light and dark of human experience is, necessarily, to turn into one's opposite. But since

[48] *Ibid.,* p. 204.

[49] L. C. Martin, ed., *Religio Medici and Other Works of Sir Thomas Browne* (Oxford: Clarendon Press, 1964), pp. 174–175.

the recognition of such has been the condition of his recommitment to time he can say "Let's in" with firm assurance. Discovering the conditions of "these rational *Amphibii*" has yielded full acceptance of the logic of *"Antipodes* in Shoes," and the yearning for retreat from dialectic has so led him to recognizing his complete immersion in it that now he is provisionally free of it.

Transition II

With Marvell we come perhaps to the limits of the lyric's capacity for incorporating dialectic. Spoken by a single persona not subject to counterarguments within the fiction, the metaphysical lyric necessarily limits itself to momentary thrusts of language against the ambiguities of the extralinguistic world. The dynamism of the metaphysical lyric, its peculiar ongoing push from line to line, results from its language's own instability in seeking to encompass these ambiguities. For this reason, such poems continually comment on their own strategies and weaknesses, because each statement progresses beyond the one before it by implicitly or overtly commenting on its inadequacy: a kind of verbal pulling oneself up by one's own bootstraps. Clearly, the metaphysical lyric makes conscious and obvious just those kinds of dialectical eruptions that Bacon's discourse encounters in its commitment to resolving them or keeping them hidden. And in doing so, in accommodating and not shirking the full assymetrical pulls and pressures of both dialectical reality and nondialectical language, the metaphysical poets escape some of the straitening dialectic between the two.

That the accommodation and incorporation of dialectical logic in *Paradise Lost* goes far beyond those achieved by the metaphysical poets is partly due to the wider verbal "spaces" afforded by the epic genre. Beyond this obvious distinction is the further fact that Milton's epic takes as its prime subject a vision of human history unfolding under providential guidance which consciously predicates dialectical processes of that history. There are, of course, some superficial similarities to Hegel in this regard. But Hegel's reification of logical dialectic does not even approach the depths to which Milton explores the ultimately mysterious co-penetration of Providence and human freedom that underpins his vision of history. For the first time in these essays we will be dealing with a discourse that is overtly committed by its fictional narrator to exorcising the malign eruptions of dialectic conse-quent upon attempts to deny it. For this reason, the narrator's own progressive refinement of the language of his song becomes an essential part of the epic's action. *Paradise Lost* is similar to the metaphysical lyric in that both exhibit personae struggling with the recalcitrance of their own language. But Milton manages to encompass the widest context in which dialectic limits and constrains man's confrontation with his world. For Donne and Herbert this confrontation is limited to struggles with matters of intense personal concern. Marvell widens the perspective to exca-vate the poetic and philosophic traditions lying buried beneath the conventions of the seventeenth-century metaphysical and cavalier lyric. For Milton, however, dialectic is nothing less than the warp and woof on which the fabric of universal history is woven. As I shall suggest in more detail in Essay Three, Milton, in explaining the original causes of division and fragmentation in the created world, provides us with the ultimate mythic account of why dia-lectic comes to straiten men in their fallen state.

ESSAY three

Paradise Lost and the Dialectic of Providence

INTRODUCTION

Concluding his *Rhetoric of Religion* with a Shavian dialogue between God and Satan, Kenneth Burke offers an archetype of the cooperation between dialectical opposites in all their multifarious interweavings. The "Impresario, his upper half in formal attire, with ragged pants and worn-out shoes," invites the audience to imagine, if it can,

> every event of universal history, made accessible to contemplation in one momentary panorama that comprises all time and space, in every act, attitude, and relationship (a distillate both perfectly simple and infinitely complex, of what has unfolded, is unfolding and is yet to unfold throughout the endless aeons of universal development).[1]

The reason why the audience cannot imagine such a vision is the main subject of the dialogue itself. Satan says:

> But that odd kind of word they will use . . . with syllables and sentences and whole speeches stretched out through time, like one of their corpses on a mortuary slab . . . that's so different from our single, eternal, Uni-

[1] Kenneth Burke, *The Rhetoric of Religion: Studies in Logology* (Boston: Beacon Press, 1961), p. 273.

tive Word that creatively sums up all, in your exceptional Self [i.e., "The Lord"], combining your Power, your Wisdom and your Love in the perfect simplicity of infinitely complex harmony.[2]

(Because man lives in temporal history he can grasp the unitive divine vision only by fragmenting it into parts, each part struggling to reduce the whole of that vision to itself.) Further, this predicament necessarily flows from the very notion of creation. As Burke points out elsewhere in *The Rhetoric of Religion*, "the possibility of a 'Fall' is implied in the idea of a Covenant insofar as the idea of a Covenant implies the possibility of its being violated." A Fall is likewise "implied in the idea of the Creation, insofar as the Creation was a kind of 'divisiveness,' since it set up different categories of things which could be variously at odds with one another and which accordingly lack the proto-Edenic simplicity of unity."[3]

In his attempt to "justify the ways of God to men" (1:26)[4] Milton had to bridge the gap between the two meanings implied in the phrase itself. These two meanings, as John S. Dieckhoff points out, are either "to justify to men God's ways, or to demonstrate the justice of God's ways toward mankind. . . ."[5] Any justification intelligible to fallen men potentially repeats the idolizing of human knowledge which caused the Fall. If to know Providence adequately, men must achieve (in Burke's or his Satan's words) God's "Unitive Word that creatively sums up all," then Providence must remain always beyond human comprehension. For not only are men creatures, thereby divided from their Creator; and not only are they fallen creatures, thereby darkened in their knowing and weakened in their will to know; but their very means of knowing—discrete concepts and discursive language—present an insuperable barrier to apprehending this "Unitive Word." To climb past this barrier and bring his

[2] *Ibid.*, p. 277.   [3] *Ibid.*, p. 174.

[4] All citations of Milton's works are from John Milton, *Complete Poems and Major Prose*, ed. Merritt Y. Hughes (New York: The Odyssey Press, 1957).

[5] John S. Dieckhoff, *Milton's Paradise Lost: A Commentary on the Argument* (New York: Columbia Univ. Press, 1946), p. 115.

reader with him, Milton took it very much into account, and attempted to turn a barrier into a bridge.[6]

Division, fragmentation, discursiveness: these in Milton's vision characterize human history, man's relations with himself, with his fellow man, with nature, and with God. They also necessarily characterize the epic poem *Paradise Lost,* for it is the narration of a poet who lives in the fallen world, confined by that division and fragmentation his poem purports to explain.[7] To explain, for Milton, is to give causes:

> Say first, for Heav'n hides nothing from thy view
> Nor the deep Tract of Hell, say first what cause
> Mov'd our Grand Parents in that happy State,
> Favor'd of Heav'n so highly, to fall off
> From their Creator. . . .
>
> [1:27–31]

And to give causes he must explain more than the motives of Adam and Eve; he must also, as he said in his student years, raise his mind so that it

> may soar
> Above the wheeling poles, and at Heav'n's door
> Look in, and see each blissful Deity. . . .
> ["At a Vacation Exercise," 33–35]

But as the mature poet saw, "to soar / Above th' *Aonian* Mount," while pursuing "Things unattempted yet in Prose or Rhyme" (PL, 1:14–16) was to risk the danger that he might

---

[6] That the reader's own sinfulness—itself the consequence of the Fall—is intimately taken account of in Milton's rhetoric, and in the poem's whole didactic purpose, has been noted by several recent commentators: Joseph H. Summers, *The Muse's Method* (New York: Norton, 1968), pp. 30–31; Arnold Stein, *Answerable Style* (Minneapolis: Univ. of Minnesota Press, 1953), p. 53; Jon S. Lawry, *The Shadow of Heaven: Matter and Stance in Milton's Poetry* (Ithaca: Cornell Univ. Press, 1968), p. 127; John N. Morris, "Milton and the Imagination of Time," *The South Atlantic Quarterly* 67 (1968):655; and the most intensive study of this matter, Stanley E. Fish, *Surprised by Sin: The Reader in Paradise Lost* (New York: St. Martin's Press, 1967).

[7] For Milton's poetic use of the narrator as fallen witness to that of which he sings, cf. Anne Davidson Ferry, *Milton's Epic Voice* (Cambridge: Harvard Univ. Press, 1963); Michael Lieb, *The Dialectics of Creation: Patterns of Birth and Regeneration in Paradise Lost* (Amherst: Univ. of Massachusetts Press, 1970), p. 55; Summers, *The Muse's Method,* p. 22.

from this flying Steed unrein'd, (as once
Bellerophon, though from a lower Clime)
Dismounted, on th' *Aleian* Field I fall
Erroneous there to wander and forlorn.

[7:17–20]

In short, he must risk the presumption of making himself God,
idolizing his own knowledge, and thereby repeating the sins of
Satan, Adam, and Eve.

Milton escaped this difficulty by first acknowledging how far
short the dialectic of his poem falls in mirroring Divine Providence. *Paradise Lost* reflects the very history that it seeks to
interpret providentially, and exhibits, as its prime medium, discursive movement through time. It embodies a complete action,
which gives at once archetype and cause of the essential pat-
erns of human history to the end of the world.[8] The key to this
history is a providential plan worked out in the sacred history
which the Bible records. But like the Bible, this history is dark
with metaphor and allusion, prefigurative types and consummative
antitypes, which veil this plan at the same time that they disclose
it. As a commentary on the Bible, in the tradition of exegesis
stretching from Philo Judaeus and St. Augustine down to the
Renaissance, *Paradise Lost* assumes an exegetical view of human
language and modes of knowing. Human language can at best
accommodate divine inspiration to human ears and minds, so that
the division between man and God on the cognitive level parallels
and results from that primordial division in the act of creation
itself.[9]

Yet if there is division here, there is also union. The fallen
poet may mediate divine vision through discursive parts that, by
the intricacy of their reciprocal mirroring, repeat in time the
timeless unity of that vision. What "th' Almighty Father from
above, / From the pure Empyrean where he sits / High Thron'd

[8] I am indebted here to both Isabel Gamble MacCaffrey, *Paradise Lost as
"Myth"* (Cambridge: Harvard Univ. Press, 1959), and William G. Madsen, *From
Shadowy Types to Truth: Studies in Milton's Symbolism* (New Haven and
London: Yale Univ. Press, 1968), despite the fact that they differ radically with
each other in their interpretations of the causality of this pattern.

[9] Cf. Madsen, *Shadowy Types to Truth,* p. 82; also Dieckhoff, *Milton's Paradise Lost,* p. 10; and Leland Ryken, *The Apocalyptic Vision in Paradise Lost*
(Ithaca and London: Cornell Univ. Press, 1970), pp. 7–24.

above all highth," saw when he "bent down his eye, / His own works and their works at once to view" (3:56–59), fallen man may also see, once he has acquiesced in the dialectic of part and part concomitant with living a fallen creature in fallen but redeemed time. The dialectic of *Paradise Lost,* consequently, imitates and manifests the dialectic of human history.

[Consequent on creation is the dual potentiality for either harmony-because-of-and-amid-division between creature and God, or disharmony-because-of-and-amid-division. The very fact of division, of separation and partition, contains within itself the consequence that if creation is to mirror God at all, it must be separated from Him. This is a tautology, but not a sterile one. The poem itself incorporates it in a much richer fashion in showing that, no matter how divided among themselves, the parts of creation reciprocate one another because they are first joined to that whole which is God. This relation is primarily mirrorlike, and can reflect in one of two ways: creation, and the moral agents who speak and act for creation, can either see themselves as the mirror of God, or see God as the mirror of themselves.[10] The latter possibility is idolatry, and both idolatry and divine worship are rooted in the same mirroring of God. Idolatry clearly fulfills the possibility of disharmony-because-of-and-amid division, and divine worship fulfills the reverse. This leads to the obvious conclusion that harmony and disharmony are dialectical functions of, as well as mutually exclusive of each other. Their being opposites presupposes the dual consequences latent in the radical possibilities of creation itself.]

The malign possibility of disharmony is realized first by Satan and the fallen angels, and then by Adam and Eve. As a descendant of the latter, the Miltonic narrator inherits likewise their fallen disabilities. Like them after the Fall, he confronts fallen history with a darkened intellect, which tempts every child of Adam to idolize his finite modes of knowing. Since, as Milton insists, self-idolatry is both condition as well as cause of man's

---

[10] Charles Monroe Coffin, "Creation and the Self in *Paradise Lost*," *ELH* 29 (1962):1–18: "As a feature of the created world singular and unique because of his free will and reason, man is, in a sense, furthest from God. In short, he is so much like his Maker as to be nearly independent of Him."

fallen state, and since repentence requires awareness of one's own sinfulness, the poem must purge its language, images, and categories if it is to mediate the transcendent, salvific pattern of divine providence. This purgation the poem achieves by retelling the story of Adam's and Eve's fall, and by locating its cause in their failure to distinguish between the strengths and weaknesses of their prelapsarian intellects. Consequently, the epic's presentation of the dialectic of providence necessarily involves other dialectics consequent upon it and encompassed by it. The following sections deal with three of these.

In the first (The Dialectic of Idolatry) I will examine Milton's treatment of Eve's temptation and fall, emphasizing Eve's failure to recognize the extents and boundaries of her reason. In this manner, Milton presents a negative definition of the self-knowledge needed to grasp the interpenetration of human will and divine command which lies at the heart of providential dialectic. The second section (The Dialectic of Language) explores the ambiguities and pitfalls of fallen language Milton faced and overcame in writing his epic. This dialectic both parallels and results from the dialectic of idolatry. The final section (The Dialectic of Mirroring) concerns the dual possibilities, latent in the providential dialectic, by which both man and poet may choose, through their fallen will, reason, and language, to reestablish harmony with this dialectic.

THE DIALECTIC OF IDOLATRY

Included in the command not to eat the fruit of the Knowledge of Good and Evil was the injunction that the unfallen pair "know to know no more" (4:775). Raphael fills out this exhortation and firmly draws the fine lines separating allowed from forbidden knowledge. If we ask where Eve started to go wrong, we discover that it is when she begins to "reason" about God's command in a manner like the serpent's. The command itself is purely arbitrary and Adam and Eve are required to obey simply because it is a command. Milton expounds this aspect in *De doctrina christiana,* commenting upon a "covenant of works" that God made with Adam:

No works whatever are required of Adam; a particular act only is forbidden. It was necessary that something should be forbidden or commanded as a test of fidelity, and that an act in its own nature indifferent, in order that man's obedience might be thereby manifested. For since it was the disposition of man to do what was right, as being naturally good and holy, it was not necessary that he should be bound by the obligation of a covenant to perform that to which he was of himself inclined; nor would he have given any proof of obedience by the performance of works to which he was led by a natural impulse, independently of the divine command. Not to mention, that no command, whether proceeding from God or from a magistrate, can properly be called a covenant, even where rewards and punishments are attached to it; but rather an exercise of jurisdiction.[11]

If the command itself could have nothing clearly rational about it, then exactly how are Adam's and Eve's reasons brought into play? When Eve early in the temptation says to the serpent that "our Reason is our Law" (9:654), she describes at once the faculty through which she may be seduced, and might have yet stood unfallen.[12]

Reason's part in Eve's temptation and fall is central to Milton's treatment of the dialectic of Providence in *Paradise Lost* for several reasons. First, as this section will develop, much of Satan's temptation depends on Eve's willingness to reason about her own relation to Providence in ways that set her own freedom off against it. Eve is the first human person to be confronted by this dialectic, and she fails to comprehend it to the exact extent she makes her own reason the total arbiter of the logic of this

11 Hughes, *John Milton, Complete Poems and Major Prose*, p. 993.

12 I both agree and disagree with Stanley Fish's argument in *Surprised by Sin* (p. 254) that Eve "is required to perform an act of the will, signifying faith, not understanding, and . . . lapses in logic do not affect her sufficiency. . . ." This statement fails to distinguish between the arbitrariness of the command itself—appealing to this extent only to the will—and the act of reason needed to recognize the consequence of this arbitrariness for its powers. My position is close to that of Merritt Y. Hughes, in "Beyond Disobedience," *Approaches to Paradise Lost*, ed. C. A. Patrides (London: Edward Arnold, 1968), p. 187.

dialectic. In this respect, her temptation functions as one of the many cautionary episodes in the epic, wherein Milton defines negatively the choices the reader must make in order to avoid a similar fall. Second, in falling in precisely this manner, Eve, as well as Adam, bequeath to all generations the same corrupted, rational tendency to define human freedom as an escape from Providence. Third, Milton as a son of Eve and Adam, as well as a divinely inspired poet, must confront the same lesion between physical symbol and spiritual significance that both created when they idolized their own modes of thought, and attempted to make them the measure of God. Consequently, the first pair's failures of reason cause the poet's struggle with the recalcitrance of his fallen language in that both present barriers to understanding and acquiescence in the providential dialectic of man's history.

The warning to "know to know no more," as the temptation and fall informs us, required Eve to reason to reason's limitations. When the serpent proceeds to prove that God's command is unreasonable, the narrator asks the reader to recognize two closely related facts. First, the serpent is quite correct in pointing out this unreasonableness; and second, reason, precisely because erect in the prelapsarian state, contains within itself the seeds of its own hubris. The moment Eve accepts reason as the test of the command ("our Reason is our Law") she is on the way to falling. Her reason would appear to fail, in other words, when she fails to reason to reason's limits, to "know to know no more." But to know to know no more is to call upon an active faculty actively to limit its own activity. The phrase strikes a delicate balance between reason upright and reason so upright as to attempt to go beyond its own capacity. The final act of reasoning, in other words, is recognizing the infinite transcendence of God in His ineffable will. Making reason her law without qualification, Eve falls.

It is important to understand why and how Eve's strength in confronting temptation was likewise her weakness. This important datum of moral self-knowledge, one which after the fact seems to have been necessary to her standing unfallen, was hidden from her in her innocence, to become apprehensible only as a result of the Fall. God prepares Adam and Eve through Raph-

ael's exhortations and narratives, at least as far as they were
capable of being prepared. But the apparently inexorable fact remains, that Adam and Eve can most fully resist evil only after
they have experienced it. The choice confronting the reader might
be put this way: How is it possible to know evil, and still be
good? With the alternative claiming equal consideration: How is
it possible not to know evil, and still be good? Milton puts these
two options perhaps most poignantly in Satan's mouth, who implicitly questions the economy of the poem's whole theme and demands some kind of answer:

> all is not theirs it seems:
> One fatal Tree there stands of Knowledge call'd,
> Forbidden them to taste: Knowledge forbidd'n?
> Suspicious, reasonless. Why should thir Lord
> Envy them that? can it be sin to know,
> Can it be death? and do they only stand
> By Ignorance, is that thir happy state,
> The proof of thir obedience and thir faith?
> [4:513–520]

We will have missed the moral dilemma if we answer Satan's
questions with either the acquiescence of Christian fideism, or the
rejection of the rationalistic secular humanist. Rather, these questions evoke a complex and dialectically defined awareness of the
ways in which it both is and is not death or sin to know, and
Adam and Eve both do and do not stand by "ignorance." Innocence cannot safeguard itself wholly, because the knowledge of
its susceptibility to evil can come only with the loss of innocence
itself.[13]

A substitute for the experiential knowledge of evil is Adam's
and Eve's awareness of a Goodness that transcends their under-

[13] Milton's complex sense of moral ambiguity in *PL* is becoming increasingly
recognized in recent commentary. Cf. Summers, *The Muse's Method*, p. 83; Coffin,
"Creation and the Self in Paradise Lost," *ELH* pp. 1–18; Lieb, *The Dialectics of
Creation*, pp. 16–17, and *passim;* Philip Brockbank, "Within the Visible Diurnal
Sphaere: The Moving World of *Paradise Lost*," in *Approaches to Paradise Lost*,
p. 203; cf., finally, Kenneth Burke's seminal insights into the "logology" of the
good-evil dialectic in *The Rhetoric of Religion*, pp. 174ff., and "Words Anent
Logology," in *Perspectives in Literary Symbolism*, ed. Joseph Strelka (University
Park and London: Pennsylvania State Univ. Press, 1968), pp. 72–82.

standing. In their morning hymn they rejoice in the visible signs
of God:

> These are thy glorious works, Parent of good,
> Almighty, thine this universal Frame,
> Thus wondrous fair; thyself how wondrous then!
> Unspeakable, who sit'st above these Heavens
> To us invisible or dimly seen
> In these thy lowest works, yet these declare
> Thy goodness beyond thought, and Power Divine: . . .
> [5:153–159]

But this awareness is now not enough, for loose in the universe
is another reflection of God, though a perverted one. When God
commands Raphael's visit, he reminds us of the intricate reciprocity of Adam's and Eve's powers and weaknesses:

> Happiness in his power left free to will,
> Left to his own free Will, his Will though free,
> Yet mutable; whence warn him to beware
> He swerve not too secure: tell him withal
> His danger, and from whom, what enemy
> Late fall'n himself from Heaven, is plotting now
> The fall of others from like state of bliss;
> By violence, no, for that shall be withstood,
> But by deceit and lies; this let him know,
> Lest wilfully transgressing he pretend
> Surprisal, unadmonisht, unforewarn'd.
> [5:235–245]

The phrase "though free, / Yet mutable" invites still other con-
nectives: "because free, therefore mutable," "because mutable,
therefore free," "because both mutable and free, able to resist
efforts to make them will away their freedom." And we discover
other things: man might swerve because he is too secure, or because he is "not too secure"; that danger lies within himself,
because physical violence cannot coerce the will; that Raphael's
educational mission, because innocence cannot wholly comprehend
the evil recited to it, can be only provisionally successful.

To impress upon Adam how much he does not know will be

the only realizable goal. The middle four books counterpoint
Adam's natural desire to know, and Raphael's careful distinction
between what he is and is not capable of knowing. Adam himself
tells what things he can understand. He says to Raphael, for
instance,

> nor knew I not
> To be both will and deed created free;
> Yet that we never shall forget to love
> Our maker, and obey him whose command
> Single, is yet so just, my constant thoughts
> Assur'd me and still assure: . . .
>
> [5:548–553]

And yet only a few lines earlier, Adam had asked:

> What meant that caution join'd, *if ye be found*
> *Obedient?* can we want obedience then
> To him, or possibly his love desert
> Who form'd us from the dust, and plac'd us here
> Full to the utmost measure of what bliss
> Human desires can seek or apprehend?
>
> [513–518]

Adam understands that he can apprehend no greater happiness
than he experiences now. But his inability to understand disobedience signals not that Raphael comes in good time, but that no
matter how much Raphael tells Adam of disobedience, Adam will
be limited by the uncomplicated categories of his innocence.

Ultimately, passing the test rests upon Adam's and Eve's explicit willingness to recognize the limits of their own knowledge
in the face of God's transcendence. Raphael makes this point to
Adam several times:

> Yet what thou canst attain, which best may serve
> To glorify the Maker, and infer
> Thee also happier, shall not be withheld
> Thy hearing, such Commission from above
> I have receiv'd, to answer thy desire
> Of knowledge within bounds; beyond abstain
> To ask, nor let thine own inventions hope

> Things not reveal'd, which th' invisible King,
> Only Omniscient, hath supprest in Night,
> To none communicable in Earth or Heaven:
> Anough is left besides to search and know.
> But Knowledge is as food, and needs no less
> Her Temperance over Appetite, to know
> In measure what the mind may well contain,
> Oppresses else with Surfeit, and soon turns
> Wisdom to Folly, as Nourishment to Wind.
>   [7:115-130]

This and a similar passage in the next book (8:159ff.) allow two possible ways of viewing the limitations on man's knowledge: God has deliberately hidden from man that which he is capable of knowing if only God would reveal it; or, God has forbidden knowledge of what man is incapable of knowing. The first presents God as the voluntaristic deity, arbitrarily forbidding a good that is man's by right or at least by nature. This view Satan will persuade Eve to take. The other view derives from the natural law ethic, which says, in Abdiel's words, that "God and Nature bid the same" (6:176). External commands do not enforce but rather remind of the laws built into one's own nature. Insofar as the test commands only voluntarist, nonrational obedience, it invites Adam and Eve to sunder these two views.[14] Eve addresses the tree in her meditation before she eats:

[14] That Eve ought in fact to sunder these two views is argued by Stanley Fish (*Surprised by Sin*). Fish's rejection of the command's putative appeal to reason, thereby making obedience purely a matter of faith (p. 256), is based on the assumption that "if the Fall is explained or 'understood' it is no longer free, but the result of some analysable 'process' which attracts to itself a part of the guilt. Thus freedom of will is denied, the obloquy of the action returns to God (who set the process in motion), and again reason—the reader's reason—has given law to God" (pp. 256-257). The complexity of Fish's philosophical assumptions forbids an extended discussion here. However, two major points can be made briefly: (1) Fish argues throughout his study a voluntaristic viewpoint on the whole poem; and as a consequence, he is committed to viewing freedom of will as impaired to the exact degree that reason presents causes for its choice. The reverse of this position would hold that will is free only to the degree that it acts without "reasons." Fish in this neglects Milton's reason-choice equation (in God's mouth: "Reason also is choice" [3:108]), a formulation which sums up the whole of his attempt to join human reason with the Christian liberty granted by grace throughout his prose tracts. The identification of freedom with "reasonlessness" is both philosophically dubious

Thy praise hee also who forbids thy use,
Conceals not from us, naming thee the Tree
Of Knowledge, knowledge both of good and evil;
Forbids us then to taste, but his forbidding
Commends thee more, while it infers the good
By thee communicated, and our want:
For good unknown, sure is not had, or had
And yet unknown, is as not had at all.
In plain then, what forbids he but to know,
Forbids us good, forbids us to be wise?
Such prohibitions bind not.

[9:750–760]

Here, she interprets the command as arbitrarily forbidding a good she by nature has a right to.

A test that explicitly communicated the information that its purpose was to affirm their own natures would only call upon them consciously to do just that, thereby obviating its very purpose. Because the test elicits their acquiescence in the voluntaristic, transrational side of God's ordaining, it requires foremost an act of the will, not of the reason. But if, as the Father says, "Reason also is choice" (3:108), then rational consciousness must itself

---

in its own right, and also runs totally counter to the whole tenor of Milton's thought from the beginning to the end of his career. It seems to me that a strong case can be made, even regarding the apparent rejection of pagan wisdom in *Paradise Regained,* that Milton was struggling to define dialectically the boundaries (and therefore the contiguous relationships) between faith and reason, rather than rejecting any relation between them at all. (2) Throughout his argument on this matter, Fish identifies reason's operation on the divine command with reason's attempt to ferret out some rational content behind the command itself; i.e., to treat a command of jurisdiction as if it were a command of prudence, and therefore rationally reducible. Clearly, Milton did not view the command in this light, either in *PL,* or in *De doctrina christiana.* On the contrary, as I argue in my essay, the command's main "intelligibility" is that it is not rationally intelligible. But this fact itself, as the dialectical definitions of the limits and strengths of Adam's reason through Books 5 to 8 show, was to be the object of rational acquiescence. The injunction "to know to know no more" assumes the aegis neither of a totally voluntaristic faith, nor of its dialectical opposite, rationalistic hubris. Rather, the injunction calls upon the reason to instruct the will to acquiesce in what is beyond reason. Thus, though I would agree with Fish to the extent it is the will that is being tested insofar as the command is arbitrary, I would have to disagree if this point is taken as excluding the reason's part in recognizing the fact of this arbitrariness and the consequences for itself.

be also tested. Adam explains the parts reason and will play in their continued obedience during his debate with Eve,

> . . . within himself
> The danger lies, yet lies within his power:
> Against his will he can receive no harm.
> But God left free the Will, for what obeys
> Reason, is free, and Reason he made right,
> But bid her well beware, and still erect,
> Lest by some fair appearing good surpris'd
> She dictate false, and misinform the Will
> To do what God expressly hath forbid. . . .
> Firm we subsist, yet possible to swerve,
> Since Reason not impossibly may meet
> Some specious object by the Foe suborn'd,
> And fall into deception unaware,
> Not keeping strictest watch, as she was warn'd.
>
> [9:348–356; 359–363]

As Adam points out here, reason must recognize its own limits. But on the other hand, the will to know more may well push reason beyond its own limits, precisely because the reason by itself cannot do this. Once the reason abides by the will's hubris, a hubris the reason itself partly aids by not knowing "to know no more," it may reach beyond itself to knowledge that it now sees as having been forbidden only by some malign, external, voluntaristic deity. The reason, now seeing this "fair appearing good," informs the will to reach for it.

Once the Fall has occurred, however, both "Soon found their Eyes how op'n'd, and thir minds / How dark'n'd" (9:1053–1054). There is no magical power in the fruit that communicates knowledge, though Eve sees it that way when she eats it. God's command forbade not an object outside of her, but rather, as we see by the result, a purely immanent act. Quite simply, she was not to disobey the command itself, for to disobey the command meant that she would then know evil, and know good only by knowing evil. That is, the test required her to distinguish between obeying the command *per se,* and obeying the command not to eat the fruit. By focusing her attention upon the fruit itself, Satan seduces her into an act of idolatry: imputing to a created object Godlike powers. To pass the test would therefore require her to obey a command that, properly understood, had no intelligibility for her. And doing such would include both "knowing" to know no more and "willing" to know no more.

In the speeches of Satan and the other demons, we see foreshadowed all the characteristics of Eve's and Adam's minds and visions after the Fall. Milton early in Book 1 establishes the satanic vision. No sooner does Satan come to his senses after his fall from Heaven, than he looks about him, and Milton describes how Hell looks when Satan views it "as far as Angels' ken" (1:59). And what "Angels' ken" surveys is an external representation of Satan's own interior landscape:

> A Dungeon horrible, on all sides round
> As one great Furnace flam'd, yet from those flames
> No light, but rather darkness visible
> Serv'd only to discover sights of woe. . . .
>
> [1:61–64]

"Darkness visible" describes not only the contradictory state of Hell itself, but also Satan's mind. Satan retains all the power of thought and language that brought his followers to revolt in Heaven, but now irrevocably twisted and perverted. Whatever illumination his mind brings to bear upon his situation always remains an illumination that is also dark.

If Eve is persuaded to see God as a purely arbitrary, voluntaristic tyrant, we are struck how much she mirrors Satan in this. Unable to see in his fall a wound self-inflicted on his own nature, Satan conceives Hell to be the result only of a supreme magistrate's external imposition. For instance, as we the readers gaze also with "Angels' ken," Hell becomes "Such place Eternal Justice had prepar'd / For those rebellious, here thir Prison ordained / In utter darkness" (1:70–72). For Satan now, God's power was only created by those beneath him who "With suppliant knee" were compelled to "deify his power" (1:112), and he projects God as one "Who now triumphs, and in th' excess of joy / Sole reigning holds the Tyranny of Heav'n" (1:123–124). God is "the angry Victor" (1:169), one "Who now is Sovran" and "can dispose and bid / What shall be right" (1:246–247), and one whom only "Thunder hath made greater" (1:258). This aspect of the satanic vision is most fully developed by Moloch in Book 2, who is determined "rather than be less / . . . not to be at all" (2:47–48). For him, as for Satan, the conflict is merely external, and his revenge is couched in purely military terms:

> no, let us rather choose
> Arm'd with Hell flames and fury all at once
> O'er Heav'n's high Tow'rs to force resistless way,
> Turning our Tortures into horrid Arms
> Against the Torturer; when to meet the noise
> Of his Almighty Engine he shall hear
> Infernal Thunder, and for Lightning see
> Black fire and horror shot with equal rage
> Among his Angels; and his Throne itself
> Mixt with *Tartarean* Sulphur, and strange fire,
> His own invented Torments.
>
> [2:60–70]

Because the fallen angels from the very beginning envision their conflict as an external one only, they cannot understand the self-rending they have performed on their own natures. Likewise, Eve's separation from God after the fall leads her to see him spying on her from some high vantage:

> And I perhaps am secret; Heav'n is high,
> High and remote to see from thence distinct
> Each thing on Earth; and other care perhaps
> May have diverted from continual watch
> Our great Forbidder, safe with all his Spies
> About him.
>
> [9:811–816]

Distinguishing between outer and inner places is consistent with sundering divine command from inner imperative, a further darkening of the reason. Inner spiritual reality and outer physical manifestation can be sundered because of the divisiveness inherent in creation, and for the same reason they always reflect each other. Thus Hell only manifests outwardly Satan's spiritual condition, however much he may temporarily and provisionally fly from it.

On a broader scale, how to understand the spiritual significance behind material symbol is an issue not only for Satan, Adam, and Eve, but for the narrator as well. No physical symbol in the poem has one, univocal ideational referent or moral valence. On the contrary, the radical dual potentiality of the created universe allows for its being grasped by the moral imagination in either a God-directed or Satan-directed manner.[15] Symbol and content can either be reunited in a providential vision of the universe, or be totally sundered, with language, thought, and material creation irrevocably cut off from the truth. And so, by sundering inner and outer meanings the satanic mind condemns itself to being eternally literal minded.[16] Just as Eve idolizes the Tree and bows to it "as to the power / That dwelt within" (9:835–836), so Satan's facile laughter is evoked by the fact that man "by fraud I have seduc'd / From his Creator, and the more to increase / Your wonder, with an Apple" (10:485–487). Because of their fall, Satan, Eve, and Adam cannot understand the relation between symbols and their true meanings, and more broadly, between their own capacity to make "idols" of the mind and the truth of the universe that these idols may or may not reflect. The largest truth they condemn themselves to not understanding is their encompassment by divine providence itself. In attempting to free themselves from their harmony with providence—in choosing to view providence as a purely voluntaristic tyranny external to themselves—they become enslaved to a dialectic that is in fact tyrannical. The divisiveness inherent in the primordial act of creation here realizes the malign possibility of its dual potentiality, and the harmony between God and creature founded in self-knowledge and love turns into a disharmony characterized by idolatry and intellectual blindness. Ultimately, acts and consequences in *Paradise Lost* are always mutually reflexive: to choose

15 On this see Summers, *The Muse's Method,* p. 28; William G. Madsen, "The Idea of Nature in Milton's Poetry," in *Three Studies in the Renaissance: Sidney, Jonson, Milton* (New Haven: Yale Univ. Press, 1958), p. 233; Harold E. Toliver, "Complicity of Voice in *Paradise Lost*," *MLQ* 25 (1964):153–170.

16 Madsen, *From Shadowy Types to Truth,* p. 84.

ignorance of divine providence is to condemn oneself to being enslaved to this ignorance.

THE DIALECTIC OF LANGUAGE

I have already suggested that *Paradise Lost* deals with a kind of knowledge that is ripe for malign potentialities. The three invocations to Books 1, 3, and 7 show that the narrator's consciousness of these potentialities is essential to avoiding a repetition of Eve's presumption. For the language of the poem itself imitates authentically the dual potentialities of the universe, in images, actions, and speeches ripe for multiple moral valences.[17] As both a fallen creature and an aspirant to divine knowledge, the narrator realizes that his instruments for knowing and communicating are tainted by the disease of discursion. The invocation to Book 3 opens in this manner:

> Hail holy Light, offspring of Heav'n first-born,
> Or of th' Eternal Coeternal beam
> May I express thee unblam'd? since God is Light,
> And never but in unapproached Light
> Dwelt from Eternity, dwelt then in thee,
> Bright effluence of bright essence increate.
> Or hear'st thou rather pure Ethereal stream,
> Whose Fountain who shall tell?
>
> [3:1–8]

The alternatives by which God's light may be expressed themselves act out the issue facing the narrator. The problem concerns correct names, correct language to express the "unapproached Light," and he must either identify this Light with the Father, or call it a sequential procession from "Heav'n first-born." The problem is not in God but in human language and thought, which must proceed univocally by identifications and separations.[18]

In aspiring to "the highth of this great Argument," in de-

---

[17] Toliver, "Complicity of Voice in *Paradise Lost*," *MLQ*, p. 154.

[18] Albert R. Cirillo, " 'Hail Holy Light' and Divine Time in *Paradise Lost*," *JEGP* 68 (1969):51.

siring to "soar / Above th' *Aonian* Mount, while [he] pursues / Things unattempted yet in Prose or Rhyme" (1:24, 14–16), the narrator calls for inspiration from the Heavenly Muse. But the narrator can be raised and supported only after he acquiesces in the fact that as fallen creature he is low and dark:

> So much the rather thou Celestial Light
> Shine inward, and the mind through all her powers
> Irradiate, there plant eyes, all mist from thence
> Purge and disperse, that I may see and tell
> Of things invisible to mortal sight.
>
> [3:51–55]

In order to raise his language to where it may safely retell what is beyond his own mortal powers, the narrator must inoculate his language with the disease of fallenness. This inoculation begins, daringly enough, with the beginning of the poem itself. The heroic rhetoric of the first two books, long praised as the height of Milton's epic style, is in fact a parody of the kind of *Paradise Lost* Satan would have written.[19] Off and on we come across lines that could have either the Miltonic or satanic narrator as the speaker. A small example is the narrator's comments after Belial's speech in Book 2:

> Thus *Belial* with words cloth'd in reason's garb
> Counsell'd ignoble ease, and peaceful sloth,
> Not peace: and after him thus *Mammon* spake.
>
> [2:226–228]

We might ask ourselves from whose viewpoint would "ignoble ease" and "peaceful sloth" be reprehensible? From the viewpoint

---

19 Cf. Dennis H. Burden, *The Logical Epic: A Study of the Argument of Paradise Lost* (Cambridge: Harvard Univ. Press, 1967), p. 60; William G. Riggs, *The Christian Poet in "Paradise Lost"* (Berkeley and Los Angeles: Univ. of California Press, 1972), pp. 20–31; also p. 45: ". . . the explicit comparisons of poet and devil in *Paradise Lost* are intended by Milton to demonstrate an undeluded recognition of the satanic potential of his poetic act. . . . By the very act of objectifying such resemblances in infernal analogies to the poet's aspiring flight, Milton is able to keep differences clearly in sight." Mr. Riggs uses this discovery primarily to document the narrator's need for divine guidance in making his own epic flight as unsatanic as possible. He is not concerned with the dialectic between the malign and benign meanings of language in *Paradise Lost* for its own sake.

of the Miltonic narrator, Belial is certainly the archetype of these human vices. But there is another, opposite set of "virtues" from the viewpoint of which Belial could be so judged, an ideal of heroic action in the name of none other than satanic rebellion.

Perhaps the clearest way into satanic parodies of the Miltonic narrator's language is the extraordinary effect of reading through the end Book 2, without pausing, into the invocation that opens Book 3. As Book 2 closes, Satan soars out of chaos toward the light of Heaven, bringing, as we discover later, the Miltonic narrator with him:

> Or in the emptier waste, resembling Air,
> [Satan] weighs his spread wings, at leisure to behold
> Far off th' Empyreal Heav'n, extended wide
> In circuit, undetermin'd square or round,
> With Opal Tow'rs and Battlements adorn'd
> Of living Sapphire, once his native Seat;
> And fast by hanging in a golden Chain
> This pendant world, in bigness as a Star
> Of smallest Magnitude close by the Moon.
> Thither full fraught with mischievous revenge,
> Accurst, and in a cursed hour he hies.
>   Hail holy Light, offspring of Heav'n first-born,
> Or of th' Eternal Coeternal beam
> May I express thee unblam'd? . . .
>
> [2:1045–1055, 3:1–3]

Who speaks these last three lines? The Miltonic narrator, surely, or so at least we may determine as the invocation to Book 3 proceeds. Or is in fact the speaker so surely identifiable? As we read further, disturbing echoes continue to make themselves heard:

> Thee I revisit now with bolder wing,
> Escap't the *Stygian* Pool, though long detain'd
> In that obscure sojourn, while in my flight
> Through utter and through middle darkness borne. . . .

The speaker has been

> Taught by the heav'nly Muse to venture down
> The dark descent, and up to reascend,

> Though hard and rare: thee I revisit safe,
> And feel thy sovran vital Lamp; but thou
> Revisit'st not these eyes, that roll in vain
> To find thy piercing ray, and find no dawn; . . .
> > Thus with the Year
> Seasons return, but not to me returns
> Day, or the sweet approach of Ev'n or Morn,
> Or sight of vernal bloom, or Summer's Rose,
> Or flocks, or herds, or human face divine;
> But cloud instead, and ever-during dark
> Surrounds me. . . .
> > [3:13–16, 19–24, 40–46]

We remember here Milton's own blindness, an autobiographical fact now become poetic symbol for the blindness of the divinely inspired seer who possesses a "Celestial Light" that shines inward (3:51–52). But we may also remember the fallen angels' thirst for the light of Heaven, stated in Beelzebub's speculations that they may someday "in some mild Zone / Dwell not unvisited of Heav'n's fair Light / Secure, and at the bright'ning Orient beam / Purge off this gloom" (2:397–400). And we may, looking forward to the end of Book 3, note that it is "The golden Sun in splendor likest Heaven" that "Allur'd [the] eye" of Satan (3: 572–573). And we may be reminded of Satan's boast before the fallen angels that he would "reascend, / Though hard and rare," when he announces to them that "long is the way / And hard, that out of Hell leads up to light" (2:432–433). And finally, we may also remember the darkness visible of Satan's own interior blindness, yearning for light, but self-condemned to darkness.

In short, the Miltonic narrator's invocation to Heavenly Light at these crucial places echoes disconcertingly the kind of speech Satan himself might have delivered on seeing Heaven again. Both narrators intertwine their discourses, not only here but throughout the first two books. Only after the Miltonic narrator's journey down to Hell and up to Heaven has been inoculated against Satanic perversion of the same journey can this intertwining become loosed, and the Miltonic narrator's discourse enabled to proceed on its own. In the passages just quoted we have the same discourse with two possible and opposite meanings. The satanic praise and yearning signal his ultimate despair, an abortive love of what he has rejected, which will then turn into spiteful hate. But when the Miltonic narrator speaks the same words, they prefigure the renewed grace and vision made possible by the narrator's acquiescence in the fact of his own fallenness and blindness. Here is the clearest case of the Miltonic narrator's inoculating his vision and language. By an achievement of wit overwhelming in the breadth of its reach, Milton demonstrates to the reader that the narrator's vision, and consequently the reader's own, can "see things invisible to mortal sight" only after both incorporate recognitions of how close their vision and language are to those of Satan.

The consequences of this inoculation are radical for the poem's whole meaning. From this point of view, *Paradise Lost* is a poem about itself. More exactly, it is a poem about why such a poem had to be written in the way it was written, inasmuch as the Fall is both the poem's subject, and the event the poem's narrator must take into account in order to write the poem at all. The narrator employs the discursive frailty of human language as a means of purifying this language of its fallenness. The rest of the poem presents a continual critique of its own language, requiring constant, vigilant judgment on the reader's part.[20] When the narrator describes Eden and the unfallen pair, for instance, he carefully inoculates the language against any of the malign possibilities inherent in it. He grants Eden the potentialities for a fall, while carefully defining them with dialectical acuteness as potentalities only.[21] The four main streams of Paradise which, after they "fell / Down" (4:230–231), are sent "wand'ring" (234) "with mazy error" (239), the nakedness of the couple, the "enormous bliss" (5:297) of Eden itself contain, as the overtones of the words themselves contain, the potentiality for malign

[20] Cf. Fish, *Surprised by Sin*, p. 162: "*Paradise Lost* is a primer designed to teach the reader how to interpret it, and especially to interpret it at the point where the characters perform that action which made its writing and reading necessary."

[21] I believe Arnold Stein in *Answerable Style* was the first to take up at large the reader's involvement in the ambiguities of the unfallen Eden through the ambiguities of the narrator's language for describing it; cf., e.g., p. 53.

transformation. In a more extended example Milton lays a trap
for the reader, who will have perhaps forgotten by the time he
reaches this description of Adam and Eve, that his first sight of
them has been through Satan's eyes:

> So spake our general Mother, and with eyes
> Of conjugal attraction unreprov'd,
> And meek surrender, half imbracing lean'd
> On our first Father, half her swelling Breast
> Naked met his under the flowing Gold
> Of her loose tresses hid: hee in delight
> Both of her Beauty and submissive Charms
> Smil'd with superior Love, . . .
>   and press'd her Matron lip
> With kisses pure: . . .

If this passage calls forth a prurient reaction from the reader,
the narrator is ready to credit immediately the mentality wherein
such a reaction finds its proper *locus:*

> . . . aside the Devil turn'd
> For envy, yet with jealous leer malign
> Ey'd them askance. . . .
>   [4:492ff.]

Suddenly interposed between reader and the scene is Satan-as-
voyeur, who then turns toward the reader to present him with the
mirror reflection of his own fallen visage. Not only this passage,
but the whole poem demands likewise the recognition that such a
reaction is due to the reader's own postlapsarian sinfulness. And
if he is to participate in the poem's intended meaning he must
strive to discount the prurience that its language equivocally conveys.[22]

The magnificent descriptions of creation in Book 7 inform the
language of Genesis with a similarly poised, ambiguous moral
valence. In general, the act of creation takes place by a series of
divisions. At the first "Let there be Light," Light "Sprung from
the Deep" (7:243, 245). After this "God saw the Light was

---

[22] I am indebted for the reading of this episode to Fish, *Surprised by Sin,* pp.
104–107.

good; / And light from darkness by the Hemisphere / Divided"
(249–251). A similar division separates the "Waters underneath
from those above" (268). As the mountains ascend, the valleys
sink (285ff.); the moon and sun "divide / The Day from Night"
(340–341), and both are set "opposite" (376) each other, the
moon "With thir bright luminaries that Set and Rose" (385).
The very act of creation itself makes order by first creating division, fragmentation, opposition, rising, and falling.

These and other examples to be discussed in the following
section are part of Milton's statement regarding how physical
objects and human language both may and may not reflect the
providential reality they seek to embody. Raphael says to Adam
and Eve before telling them of the battle in Heaven:

> and what surmounts the reach
> Of human sense, I shall delineate so,
> By lik'ning spiritual to corporal forms,
> As may express them best, though what if Earth
> Be but the shadow of Heav'n, and things therein
> Each to other like, more than on Earth is thought?
>
> [5:571–576]

Raphael justifies using material metaphors for a transmaterial
reality because Earth is itself a reflection, albeit dimly, of Heaven
itself. However, the mirror reflection is not a two-way street:
Earth is like Heaven, but Heaven is not like Earth. Reading
Raphael's statement in this inverse fashion, is to repeat Mam-
mon's attempt to make "Heav'n" resemble "Hell":

> How oft amidst
> Thick clouds and dark doth Heav'n's all-ruling Sire
> Choose to reside, his Glory unobscur'd,
> And with the Majesty of darkness round
> Covers his Throne; from whence deep thunders roar
> Must'ring thir rage, and Heav'n resembles Hell?
> As he our darkness, cannot we his Light,
> Imitate when we please? This Desert soil
> Wants not her hidden lustre, Gems and Gold;
> Nor want we skill or art, from whence to raise

> Magnificence; and what can Heav'n show more?
>
> [2:263–273]

It is also to believe with Satan that his fight with God is only a military conflict, waged with spears, armor, and cannon. It is to repeat Eve's belief that the apple really contains magical powers. And it is, finally, to conceive with Satan his own conquest by the seed of Eve as nothing more than a bruise:

> I am to bruise his heel;
> His Seed,when is not set, shall bruise my head:
> A World who would not purchase with a bruise,
> Or much more grievous pain?
>
> [10:498–501]

an interpretation Michael warns against in Book 12:

> Dream not of thir fight,
> As of a Duel, or the local wounds
> Of head or heel: . . .
>
> [12:386–388]

But Milton's position here is, obviously, not gnostic or manichean. On the contrary, the dialectic of language in the poem balances precisely the ways in which spiritual realities may be reflected in symbols and language against the ways in which they may not. In other cases, symbols and truth symbolized reflect each other exactly. A clear example is the way in which Satan's disguise as a young angel gradually disintegrates along with Satan's inner spiritual life:

> Thus while he spake, each passion dimm'd his face,
> Thrice chang'd with pale, ire, envy and despair,
> Which marr'd his borrow'd visage, and betray'd
> Him counterfeit. . . .
>
> [4:114–117]

Similarly, we may remember God's banishing of Adam and Eve from their physical Eden, once the spiritual uprightness which Eden mirrored has been lost; and how the movements of the earth and the planets are deliberately upset, mirroring a now fallen moral center in the universe. Satan's own physical degradation, far from being imposed by the narrator, as Waldock holds, mirrors his own increasing spiritual degradation, as he moves down the ladder of being from archangel to snake.[23]

We are invited, in either case, to echo the narrator's own blunt announcement in the invocation to Book 7, that it is "The meaning, not the Name I call" (7:5). In general, Milton defines the coalescence of symbol and reality as a function of their distinction, and he demonstrates this distinction by first ironically identifying them. The inoculation of the Miltonic narrator's language requires that it first act out its potential identification with its satanic parody. Such identifications generate the reader's realization of their separation. And this realization in turn allows the resurrection of symbol as a just instrument communicating the transsymbolizable. In short, the language of the poem demonstrates its strengths by first of all demonstrating its weaknesses.

This dialectic of strength and weakness, by which strength is born dialectically out of weakness, parallels in reverse, as I have already suggested, the idolatry that is both the cause and consequence of Eve's fall. Where Eve failed to obey the injunction to "know to know no more," thereby reducing Providence to the categories of her own reason and idolizing her own understanding, the Miltonic narrator reverses the process. He begins the poem by identifying his thought and language not with God, but with Satan, and so demonstrates to the reader the essential recognition in which he too, along with the narrator, must acquiesce if his own understanding is to reach to "things invisible to mortal sight," an understanding of the providential dialectic of history. The acquiescence is made possible, ultimately, because this providential dialectic incorporates not only the harmony of the unfallen couple and angels with God, but also the disharmony of the fallen couple and angels. How these dual potentialities of providential dialectic imply each other is the subject of the next and final section.

THE DIALECTIC OF MIRRORING

Satan's idolatry lies in his recognizing in himself no mirror image but his own. Here, the darkening of his intellect, by which

---

[23] A. J. A. Waldock, *Paradise Lost and its Critics* (Cambridge: University Press, 1961), p. 83.

he cannot respond to anything but the "idols" in his own mind, and the darkening of his outer form coalesce. For his mind can recognize only himself in the images he sees reflected of himself, and this confirms his enslavement to self-idolatry. The reader's self-recognition is initiated in the catalogue of pagan deities. One may with Blake and Shelley see in Satan an archetype of valuable human action, but to do so one must take him out of the context in which Milton places him. As we watch the fallen angels fly off the burning lake the narrator (speaking along with Satan) tells us that they are "Godlike shapes and forms / Excelling human, Princely Dignities, / And Powers that erst in Heaven sat on Thrones" (1:358–360). Who these "Princely Dignities" are depends on the names given them. For "of thir Names in heav'nly Records now / Be no memorial, blotted out and ras'd / By thir Rebellion, from the Books of Life" (1:361–363). The point is that now they have "Got them new Names" (1:365), and these are the names by which "Then were they known to men. . . . / And various Idols through the Heathen World" (1:374–375). Milton here exploits the traditional identification of fallen angels and pagan idols to identify likewise satanic self-idolatry and human fallenness. The Miltonic narrator disengages himself temporarily from his satanic parody to call these devils by their true names. For these devils in later times

> By falsities and lies the greatest part
> Of Mankind . . . corrupted to forsake
> God thir Creator, and th' invisible
> Glory of him that made them, to transform
> Oft to the Image of a Brute, adorn'd
> With gay Religions full of Pomp and Gold,
> And Devils to adore for Deities: . . .
> [1:367–373]

The catalogue of idols thus becomes much more than an imitation of similar catalogues in Homer and Virgil. On the contrary, the Miltonic narrator projects the fallen angels into human history and names them with human language, as must a poem that can name nothing before fallen human history except according to modes commensurate with fallen minds. If the angels fell through self-worship and are truly identified with brutish and monstrous forms, then fallen mankind repeats this idolatry by worshipping them in idols made out of the forms of animals. Like Satan, the idolaters in the narrator's catalogue both see themselves in fact in the "monstrous shapes" (479) they worship, and yet refuse to understand what these mirror images tell about themselves. The reader does (or may) however, and is prepared thereby to understand how to take Satan's own self-projections from here on out. Naming the pagan gods according to their true names becomes an action representing in little the whole poem's essential goal: correct naming of the causes and consequences of the fall of man.

To recognize ourselves as idolaters and narcissists is to recognize, in other words, our being a mirror image not of God, but of Satan. For Satan this recognition comes in the soliloquy at the beginning of Book 4. All the lies, equivocations, half-truths, and self-deceptions in which the fallen angels entangle themselves during the first two books had the one purpose of denying the consequences of their fall. Satan's call to renewed conflict at the end of Book 1, and the debate in Book 2 communicate to the reader that they will always remain fallen to the exact degree that they refuse to admit that fact. If the necessary prolegomenon to repentance and salvation is moral self-recognition, then we are entitled to ask, and Milton required to answer, whether self-recognition, when and if it finally comes to Satan, will in fact issue in repentance. Satan's interior debate in Book 4 proceeds through stages. First he recognizes that his debt to the Almighty was already and always repaid, for "a grateful mind / By owing owes not, but still pays, at once / Indebted and discharg'd"; then, that even a lower place in the heavenly hierarchy would have provoked his ambition; that he was free to accept "Heav'n's free Love dealt equally to all" or to reject it; and that the locus of his guilt and suffering, like the causes of his revolt, lies not in some external agent but within himself (4:42–78). He comes finally to the last question:

> O then at last relent: is there no place
> Left for Repentance, none for Pardon left?

> None left but by submission; and that word
> *Disdain* forbids me, and my dread of shame
> Among the Spirits beneath, whom I seduc'd
> With other promises and other vaunts
> Than to submit, boasting I could subdue
> Th' Omnipotent. . . .
> But say I could repent and could obtain
> By Act of Grace my former state; how soon
> Would highth recall high thoughts, how soon unsay
> What feign'd submission swore: ease would recant
> Vows made in pain, as violent and void.
>   [4:79–86, 93–97]

Caught between fear of derision from those below him, and submission to God above him, Satan is truly the archetypal snob, feeling his worth only when the object of someone else's attention. For him, there are only those beneath, whose high opinion he at once scorns and yet needs, and those above, who are—through his egoistic projection—tyrants and snobs in turn. At the moment Satan clearly recognizes his true state—fallen, self-destroyed, and self-condemned—he turns this recognition back upon himself and reasserts his invincible snobbery. The realization of being low has once again generated the determination to be high. Between enslavement to the opinions of the lesser devils, and his projected enslavement to God, he chooses the former, and in doing so chooses rather to serve in Hell than reign in Heaven.

Milton's insight into the dual potentiality contained in the moment of clearest moral self-recognition for either right or perverse use is one with his total vision of the ambiguous potentiality concealed in the economy of creation itself. And this dual potentiality in all things finite, created, divided from God in the primordial act of creation, makes them at once good, liable to great corruption, and greatly redeemable. Nowhere does the potentiality for either salvation or corruption reach such a crisis stage as at that moment when self-recognition displays itself as capable of generating either renewed love and freedom, or renewed hate and slavery.

We see the second in Satan's soliloquy, and the first in Adam's parallel soliloquy in Book 10. Here Adam has a double task: he must earn the right to forgiveness by himself coming to forgive another. After a longer and even more intense self-examination, Adam finally achieves the same recognition that Satan had earlier:

> Him after all Disputes
> Forc't I absolve: all my evasions vain
> And reasonings, though through Mazes, lead me still
> But to my own conviction: first and last
> On mee, mee only, as the source and spring
> Of all corruption, all the blame lights due;
> So might the wrath. Fond wish! couldst thou support
> That burden heavier than the Earth to bear,
> Than all the World much heavier, though divided
> With that bad Woman? Thus what thou desir'st,
> And what thou fear'st, alike destroys all hope
> Of refuge, and concludes thee miserable
> Beyond all past example and future,
> To *Satan* only like both crime and doom.
>   [10:828–841]

His horrified recognition of his likeness to Satan is at once the moment of Adam's greatest clarity and his greatest freedom. For the choice now is absolute, reduced to forgiveness or damnation; there is no other. The occasion of his choice, as it was before in his fall, is Eve. As long as he insists on castigating her, as he does immediately after this speech, the final acquiescence in his own responsibility will have been denied. He turns her away, but instead of answering his accusations with the same recriminations, she becomes in an instant a type of Christ, conquering the law by refusing to place herself in hardened opposition to it:

> He added not, and from her turn'd, but *Eve*
> Not so repulst, with Tears that ceas'd not flowing,
> And tresses all disorder'd, at his feet
> Fell humble, and imbracing them, besought
> His peace, and thus proceeded in her plaint. . . .
>   . . . both have sinn'd, but thou
> Against God only, I against God and thee,

And to the place of judgment will return,
There with my cries importune Heaven, that all
The sentence from thy head remov'd may light
On me, sole cause to thee of all this woe,
Mee mee only just object of his ire.

[10:909–913, 930–936]

Adam thus has two possible mirror images of himself to conjure
with, that of Satan, and that of Eve (and through Eve, the Son:
"Behold mee then, mee for him, life for life / I offer, on mee let
thine anger fall" [3:236–237]). What Satan cannot stand, what
repels him at the moment of choice, is his recognition of self:
fallen, miserable, hopeless, and above all, contemptible. As with
all snobs, his self-contempt hardens him more in his pride. After
seeing himself in Satan, Adam also repeats Satan's reactions in
turning away Eve. For in Eve he is presented with another image
of his fallen self, the same image he had before, narcissistically
and idolatrously, fallen to worship. To pity her misery will not
simply earn pity for himself: the balance-sheet imperatives of
the Lord's prayer go farther than that. To find her worth forgiv-
ing, to see some redeeming virtue in her repentance, not, in other
words, to fall into a proud self-contempt projected outwards onto
her, to see something, finally, redeemable in himself thereby: this
is the choice presented to him, and he takes it.

At the moment Adam recognizes and acquiesces in his identity
with Satan, he ceases to be like Satan. However, if our rejecting
damnation depended only upon our rejecting our potentiality for
mirroring Satan, the choice would be palpable and easily made.
Milton reminds us through Eve that the choice remains difficult
because the temptation to self-idolatry and narcissism derives
from the fact that man is made in the image of God. Eve's temptation to narcissism delicately poises the ambiguities of the difficulty here. Having become momentarily enamored of her own
image in the pool and been led by God's voice to Adam, Eve hears
from Adam these words:

Return fair *Eve*
Whom fli'st thou? whom thou fli'st, of him thou art,
His flesh, his bone; . . .

> Part of my Soul I seek thee, and thee claim
> My other half:
>
> [4:481–483, 487–488]

Eve may choose to enjoy her own image in herself (as the pool mirrors it), or to enjoy her own image in another, her husband and immediate source of her material being. I think to read her momentary narcissism as foreshadowing the temptation to which she will succumb in Book 9 is incomplete. Both Adam and Eve have been previously described as having "in thir looks Divine / The image of thir glorious Maker" (4:291–292), and Satan himself, when he first sees them, "could love" them, "so lively shines / In them Divine resemblance" (4:363–364). What momentarily attracts her in the pool, and what later attracts her in Adam, are the same image, the reflection of God in human beauty. The important distinction is not merely between sterile narcissism as self-idolatry, and fertile love as loving someone else. The poem distinguishes more thoroughly between loving one's image in the other purely as the image of oneself, and loving one's image in the other insofar as it is in the other. Eve commits no sin in finding herself attractive, because she is, after all, God's image: the temptation to narcissism *is* the image of God. By giving both their due, we become aware of the hair's breadth distinguishing ordered love of one's image in the other, and disordered love of one's image in oneself. Later on the serpent will move subtly in the opposite direction, from an ordered love of oneself as a reflection of the divine, to a disordered love of oneself as a reflection of the divine, when he says to Eve "Fairest resemblance of thy Maker fair, / Thee all things living gaze on, all things thine / By gift, and thy Celestial Beauty adore / With ravishment beheld" (9:538–541). With a smoothness that may even deceive the reader, Satan has moved decisively across the boundary that separates Eve as reflection of the divine from Eve as narcissistically idolizing herself, and it is the fluidity between these two that strikes us rather than their distinction.

Once this line has been crossed, Eve idolizes her own reason, proceeds with the serpent to "reason" about God's command, in turn idolizes the tree as the vehicle of magical powers, and falls.

On Adam's part, a similar transformation of ordered love into disordered love, founded on his beholding in Eve his own image, takes place:

> I feel
> The Link of Nature draw me: Flesh of Flesh,
> Bone of my Bone thou art, and from thy State
> Mine never shall be parted, bliss or woe. . . .
> So forcible within my heart I feel
> The Bond of Nature draw me to my own,
> My own in thee, for what thou art is mine;
> Our State cannot be sever'd, we are one,
> One Flesh; to lose thee were to lose myself.
>
> [9:913–916, 955–959]

In both cases, the dialectic of mirroring appears in its clearest form. Whereas before, Eve was to see her own image in Adam, and both of them in God, at the Fall both reverse this sequence. Adam now idolizes his image in Eve, as Eve had previously idolized her own image in herself under the persuasions of the serpent. As in the dialectic of language, Milton allows no univocal separation between the malign and benign possibilities. On the contrary, the two alternatives are defined consistently as dialectical functions of each other. And as human language may either transcend itself or idolize itself, so likewise man may love the image of God in himself either as the image of God or as that image is in himself.[24]

Finally, the poem itself makes its meaning by complex repeated patterns, in which images, actions, and speeches mirror each other. In this respect, the poem acts out on the structural level of poetic discourse the potential idolatry of which this discourse is itself a vehicle. The poem is potentially idolatrous, in that it reduces transcendent truths and events to fallen language and concepts. The reader is therefore left with two choices. He

---

[24] Gordon Worth O'Brien, *Renaissance Poetics and the Problem of Power* (Chicago: Institute of Elizabethan Studies, 1956), pp. 46ff., presents some suggestive insights into the meaning that "mirroring" had for the Elizabethans, particularly as it applies to Satan's, Adam's, and Eve's "reflexive" mirroring of themselves back to themselves.

may take the images, actions, and speeches occurring on one of the three levels of moral valence—Heaven, Earth, and Hell—as the norm for judging the others. Or he may recognize that the recurrences of the same patterns on all three levels criticize each other, concluding that physical images, actions, and speeches always remain ideationally and referentially neutral, capable indifferently of signifying either the benign motives of Heaven, the malign motives of Hell, or the motives of Earth balanced ambiguously between these two. Obviously, in one sense, the poem directs the reader to choose Heaven, the Father, the Son, and the loyal angels as the norms against which the actions of Earth and Hell are to be measured. But in another sense, the poem directs the reader to discount itself as the discourse of a fallen but redeemed narrator. Even the portrayals of Heaven, the Father, the Son, and the unfallen angels are clearly anthropomorphic, and therefore require discounting as well.

The poem ultimately directs the reader through and beyond itself to the existential life of history and the actual providence controlling that history. *Paradise Lost* is part of history, however much it takes its fable from events happening before history. By explicitly evoking the dimension of the poem as poem, Milton solves the essential problem which such a poem must confront: how may it and its narrator (and its writer as well, John Milton, Englishman), presume to speak the truth about what transcends them. The poem as fable not only measures human history, but it is measured by it as a poem written within it. *Paradise Lost* does not derive its authenticity from itself. On the contrary, its self-discounting leads us to judge it ultimately against those existential norms which we as believing Christians have been redirected to by the poem, and from which we return to judge the poem itself. For this reason, such critics of the poem as William Empson find themselves uncomfortable with it. For *Paradise Lost* claims to give not *a* version of the condition of man in a fallen world, but rather *the* true version. And its truth is ultimately tested not on its internal consistency of fable—image, action, speech—but upon the evoked and poetically formalized human experience of the reader himself. If he does not recognize the truth of the poem, then the poem becomes exactly the reverse of what it presents itself to be. That is, it becomes a verbal "idol," the product of a presumptuous author who has set himself up before his fellow men as somehow gifted beyond them, and who through his God lays down tyrannical, voluntaristic strictures on man's freedom. In short, the poem becomes exactly what its internal self-discountings attempt to avoid: it becomes satanic. And more, its God becomes satanic, and its Satan the liberator of mankind.

Therefore there is a radical dialectical reciprocity between *Paradise Lost* as fable—an explanation and a philosophy of history—and *Paradise Lost* as poem—a discourse written within history and therefore subject to the potentialities for truthfulness or idolatry that it predicates of that history. As fable, the poem establishes a mythic pattern for the actual history of men controlled by Providence. As poem, it discounts itself, directing us through and past itself toward a copenetration between Providence and the existential lives of men that it ultimately cannot fathom, because such fathoming is left only to God. The poem tells the reader what it can. As a didactic, moral meditation on man's condition, it directs the reader to moral self-recognition as a prime condition for repentance and salvation. But the actual existential choice, however much that choice may be defined through multiple versions of itself—whether divinely oriented or satanically oriented—the poem cannot make for the reader. That choice the reader must make for himself within the existential, lived history in which he finds himself embedded. For to read *Paradise Lost* is an act of knowledge, of the intellect, but it is not an act of the will. Certainly no one was more aware of this dimension of *Paradise Lost* than Milton himself, that it should be at best discourse directed to the understanding, and in being directed only to the understanding it is like that warning within a warning, Raphael's address to Adam and Eve:

> Thus measuring things in Heav'n by things on Earth
> At thy request, and that thou mayst beware
> By what is past, to thee I have reveal'd
> What might have else to human Race been hid:

But having done this, both Raphael and Milton can only add:

> But list'n not to his Temptations, warn
> Thy weaker; let it profit thee to have heard
> By terrible Example the reward
> Of disobedience; firm they might have stood,
> Yet fell; remember, and fear to transgress.
> [6:893–896, 908–912]

Transition III

The warnings *Paradise Lost* delivers concern, among other matters, the fact that man's enslavement to dialectic is directly due to his living a fallen creature in a fallen world. Whereas the arguments and language of Donne's and Herbert's poems stand over against the external dialectics they seek to encompass, for Marvell to some extent, and to a much greater degree for Milton, language and history are one. And this means that the dialectical structures that invest both are the same. In *Paradise Lost,* man's immersion in dialectic is credited to an original, disastrous aspiration to a plotless world of unlimited (and spurious) godhood. And this takes us back to Bacon's new science, wherein the same choice was made within categories and myths remarkably like Milton's: the ideal of a primitive Edenic state of complete knowledge of and power over the natural world. Bacon's prose could not overgo the divisiveness inherent in the central antinomical terms of his scientific myth; and Milton's poetry ultimately cannot overgo these either. What distinguishes Milton decisively from Bacon, however, is the way in which he overtly incorporates this divisiveness into his vision of human history, and into the language that mediates that vision. In this respect, *Paradse Lost* warns us that to deny the dialectic which is the manifestation of Divine Providence in history is not only to make dialectic in all its malign aspects inevitable; it is to repeat the original sins of Satan, Eve, and Adam. In choosing to reduce the dialectic between love and justice, command and law, manifestation and hiddenness—which is God—to the univocal categories of their own finite intelligences; in choosing, in other words, to escape dialectic, they fell into a state wherein nothing but dialectic reigns in all of its confusion, fragmentation, and contradiction.

Drama is inherently the most overtly dialectical genre discussed in these essays. In Essays Two and Three, I examined discourses which were made up in whole or in part of their personae's struggles to overcome the partialities imposed by the language and limits of their respective genres. In Shakespeare's plays, a similar struggle takes place, but this time within fictional contests wherein various characters seek to impose the partialities of their own voices and actions on the equal and opposite partialities of other characters. The conflicts between characters embody and parallel the relations between the antinomical terms the characters contest. Though we may note the absence of a single persona in Shakespeare's plays, in contrast to the metaphysical lyric and *Paradise Lost*, we may also discover a kind of compensation for that voice. Those characters, who through their agons reach the most encompassing vision of the dialectical logic governing the actions in which they are immersed, are presented as most triumphant. Within the set of plays I discuss, Prince Hal and Hamlet are these characters. Hal escapes, if only equivocally in *Henry V*, the dialectic of right and power that inexorably controls Richard II, Bolingbroke, the Percies, and Falstaff. And with Hamlet, whose play I discuss last, we come to perhaps the largest, which also means the most ambiguous, tortured, and tragic, vision of dialectic we have yet encountered. In discussing *Hamlet* I will have come full circle, though in Yeatsian fashion on a higher plane, back to my starting point: Francis Bacon. For Bacon attempted in the prose of scientific system what Hamlet attempts in the fictive world of Denmark's corrupt court: total understanding of and control over a world of oppressive ambiguities and assymetries. Like Bacon, Hamlet plots and countermines against forces that divide appearance from reality, and like Bacon, Hamlet dreams of a final complete act that will reduce man's estate to clarity and freedom. Unlike Bacon, Hamlet's highest point of realization, and perhaps Shakespeare's as well, is an understanding that the dialectics of his situation are not encompassed by, but rather encompass the dream and fulfillment of such an act. And yet, despite this obvious and decisive difference in the visions of Bacon and Shakespeare, an overriding similarity comes to the fore: for both, unintentionally for the one, intentionally for the other, dialectic comes to be seen as the only answer to the mysteries that it itself proposes.

ESSAY four

The Dialectic of Right and Power in Eight Plays of Shakespeare, 1595-1604

INTRODUCTION

In this essay I will discuss an issue that concerned Shakespeare from the second tetralogy of history plays (1595–1598), through *Julius Caesar* (1599), *Hamlet* (1601), *Troilus and Cressida* (1602), to *Measure for Measure* (1604). This issue is the complex dialectic between transcendent imperatives of right and the exigencies of power in the world "as it is." He had dramatized this issue in the first historical tetralogy, *Henry VI*, Parts one, two, and three, and *Richard III* (1590–1593), but he did not generate there the sustained and subtle dialectic of the later history plays. At the other end of this period, as *Othello* and *King Lear* illustrate, he was concerned with matters only obliquely connected with this issue. That these plays are chronologically consecutive is convenient for my purposes. In treating *Hamlet* last, however, I break the chronological order of my discussion, because no matter when it was written, it exhibits Shakespeare extending the dialectic of right and power to its profoundest implications.

This dialectic occurs preeminently in the second historical tetralogy. In *Julius Caesar,* the confrontation between ethical norms and the political exigencies that corrupt their exercise stands closest thematically to that in the history plays. *Troilus and Cressida* deals with an issue analogous to the right-might issue: the complex dialectic relating high, idealized motives, and low, cynical actions. *Measure for Measure* concerns the dialectic between repressive legalism, and the license that is both its enemy and its consequence. *Hamlet* includes and synthesizes all of these themes in the dilemma of the man who wants to act for the right reason, only to find this right tainting itself at its fountainhead.

A primary presupposition governing political debate in six-teenth-century England assumed an ideological context dominated by the claims of divinely given authority. What was revolutionary about Machiavelli's thinking in *The Prince* in this regard was not so much his description of political realities divorced from norms of moral right and justice, as rather his implication that claims of right and justice had no place in the discussion at all. J. W. Allen describes this essential distinction between Machiavelli's proce-dure and those of his contemporaries:

> A government, to Machiavelli, princely or popular, had power to do what it could do and no more. Far more im-portant than law was, to him, the power to enforce it. He seems hardly to connect the idea of law with the idea of obligation. He was convinced of the difficulty of effecting changes in law and on this lays stress both in the *Discorsi* and the *Principe*. But whether a ruler can or cannot make law was to him a question of fact simply. The amount of actual power possessed by a government seemed to him to depend little, if at all, on legal theory, to which he never refers. Nor does he make any distinction between power and right; for of "right" he knew nothing. No-where does he ever raise any question as to how far the rights of rulers extend. That question with which, all through the sixteenth century, men were above all to con-cern themselves, did not exist for him.[1]

[1] J. W. Allen, *A History of Political Thought in the Sixteenth Century* (Lon-don: Methuen, 1960), pp. 465–466. Machiavelli puts this point succinctly in Chapter 12 of *The Prince*, when he says: "The principall foundations that all States have, as well new, as old, or mixt, are good lawes, and good armes; and because there cannot bee good lawes, where there are not good armes, and where there are good armes, there must needs be good lawes, I will omit to discourse of the lawes, and speak of armes"; Burton A. Milligan, ed., *Three Renaissance Classics* (New York: Scribner's, 1953), p. 45.

In other words, Machiavelli solved the conflict between power and right by simply throwing out the latter term, thereby implicitly indicting all other political thinkers of employing an irrelevant lexicon. Though Machiavelli was notoriously alone in sixteenth-century political thinking, his example defines more sharply the traditional Renaissance political categories which Shakespeare's plays assumed. As Allen shows at length, sixteenth-century English political thought concerned the implications of an orthodoxy vigorously put forth by the Tudors, for whom obedience was the cardinal virtue and rebellion the most heinous of sins.[2]

My argument here takes off from the conclusions of E. M. W. Tillyard, L. B. Campbell, and Irving Ribner, namely that Shakespeare accepted the basic assumptions about the God-given rights of monarchy, the duties of subjects to this monarchy, and the evils of ambition and rebellion which were the substance of Tudor propaganda, as the limiting terms within which to delineate his own treatments.[3] Nevertheless, Shakespeare dealt with political issues in these plays not in order to justify the political status

---

[2] Allen, *A History of Political Thought*, p. 131: "The 'common-sense' view thus presented in the Homily of 1571 ['If, therefore, all subjects that mislike of their prince should rebel, no realm should ever be without rebellion'] was the view generally taken. The question whether anything ever justifies rebellion and if not, why not, is not being really faced. In England, all through the Tudor period, thinking people are unwilling to admit that there is any real question about it. In this respect England differed strikingly from France, and even from the German countries. Perhaps the most striking peculiarity of England in the sixteenth century was the general refusal to admit that any case can be made for a right of rebellion. Only very late in Elizabeth's reign is the question seriously taken."

[3] Though these three scholars differ among themselves on a number of points, they agree on the essential point that Shakespeare was assuming and expounding what Tillyard calls the "Tudor myth," which controls the older approach to Shakespeare's Histories, and which I am concerned with here. E. M. W. Tillyard, *Shakespeare's History Plays* (New York: Collier Books, 1962); cf., for example, pp. 16–17: "Behind disorder is some sort of order or 'degree' on earth, and that order has its counterpart in heaven. This assertion has nothing to do with the question of Shakespeare's personal piety: it merely means that Shakespeare used the thought-idiom of his age. The only way he could have avoided that idiom in his picture of disorder was by not thinking at all. . . ." Cf. Lily B. Campbell, *Shakespeare's "Histories": Mirrors of Elizabethan Policy* (San Marino: Huntingdon Library, 1947), pp. 110, 125; and Irving Ribner, *The English History Play in the Age of Shakespeare* (Princeton: Princeton Univ. Press, 1957), pp. 26–27, and *passim*.

quo, but rather to test the viability of the theoretical foundations of this status quo. He does this by exhibiting how these foundations contain the seeds of their own destruction. Shakespeare worked out some of the logical possibilities of Tudor orthodoxy in ways that take him far beyond official statements to be found in dozens of tracts and sermons of the time.[4]

First, he assumed a cluster of imperatives, moral categories, and norms, untouchable by the wills and desires of mortal men. These norms appear in the plays I discuss here, except *Julius Caesar* and *Troilus and Cressida,* as divine commands and sanctions. In these two plays classical norms of honor and justice take the place of circumscribing religious norms. All of the major characters in these plays, heroes and villains alike, accept these norms as givens which, by definition, cannot be tampered with: they can be only obeyed or violated. Second, the requirements of rule may very well conflict with what transcendent norms dictate. This antinomy between right and might has, both in Shakespeare's plays and perennially, cognates of a more general sort: antinomies between "is" and "ought," the real and the ideal, what "must be" by transcendent imperative and what "must be" by the ineluctable exigencies of the actual world. Third, these antinomies were absolute. The whole force of Christian ethical thinking had from its beginnings assumed that the absoluteness and eternity of ethical imperatives were coextensive with the ab-

---

[4] More recent studies on Shakespeare's history plays modify the older thesis in various degrees and and in various directions. Cf. for instance, S. C. Sen Gupta, *Shakespeare's Historical Plays* (London: Oxford Univ. Press, 1964), p. 18; Norman Rabkin, *Shakespeare and the Common Understanding* (New York: The Free Press, 1967), pp. 80–81; Wilbur Sanders, *The Dramatist and the Received Idea: Studies in the Plays of Marlowe and Shakespeare* (Cambridge: University Press, 1968), p. 149. A. P. Rossiter, in *Angel with Horns* (New York: Theatre Arts Books, 1961), p. 59, states a position closest to my own: "Throughout the Histories it is the implications of the Comic that shrewd, realistic thinking about men in politics—in office—in war—in plot—is exposed: realistic apprehension outrunning the medieval frame. Because the Tudor myth system of Order, Degree, etc., was too rigid, too black-and-white, too doctrinaire and narrowly moral for Shakespeare's mind: it falsified his fuller experience of men. Consequently, while employing it as FRAME, he had to undermine it, to qualify it with equivocations: to vex its applications with sly or subtle ambiguities: to cast doubts on its ultimate human validity, even in situations where its principles seemed most completely applicable. His intuition told him it was *morally* inadequate" (italics and capitals in orig.).

soluteness and eternity of God Himself.[5] This meant that, compromise however one would, or however subtle one's moral casuistry became, the terms of right and power remained the ultimate circumscribing context within which all discussion and action could take place.

As I will show, the absolute, rigid relations between these terms generate unending flux and flow in debate and conflict. If right and power were always defined in opposition to each other, then interrelations possible between them become reduced to two. One the one hand, the power of right means the power conferred on and held by the ruler according to some transcendent sanction. Within the history plays, this power is untouchable because no man can either confer it or take it away. The "power" in the power of right is nothing less, but also nothing more, than the moral suasion implicit in the ruler's participation in divine sanction. J. W. Allen quotes as a view rather extreme for the sixteenth century in England, Tyndale's written in 1528: "He that judgeth the king judgeth God; and he that resisteth the king resisteth God and damneth God's law and ordinance. . . . The king is, in this world, without law, and may at his lust do right or wrong and shall give accounts but to God only." [6] What happens when a monarch attempts to act only "at his lust" is the subject of *Richard II*. A more accurate reflection of the century's view was Stephen Gardiner's: "Obedience is due, but how far the limits requiring obedience extend, that is the whole question that can be demanded." And Allen goes on to say: "It was, in fact, the question that was being demanded everywhere throughout the cen-

---

[5] This whole doctrine was exemplarily summed up by Richard Hooker in Book 1 of *The Laws of Ecclesiastical Polity;* e.g.: "Law rational therefore, which men commonly use to call the Law of Nature, meaning thereby the Law which human Nature knoweth itself in reason universally bound unto, which also for that cause may be termed most fitly the Law of Reason; this Law, I say, comprehendeth all those things which men by the light of their natural understanding evidently know, or at leastwise may know, to be beseeming or unbeseeming, virtuous or vicious, good or evil for them to do" (London: Everyman's Library, 1963), 1:182. The law of nature which men perceive by their reasons is, of course, part of the all-embracing "second law eternal" to which are conformed all things "which are as they ought to be," p. 155.

[6] Allen, *A History of Political Thought*, p. 128; from *The Obedience of a Christian Man*, 1528.

tury." [7] In other words, just how far the "power of right" extended before it turned into its opposite counterpart, the "right of power," was a moot point in political theory long before Shakespeare wrote his history plays.

But though the issue was not new, Shakespeare's handling of it is. As is obvious, the ruler's power of right had to find its concrete manifestation in physical coercion: he ruled by laws which always had the threat of sanction behind them. But here, in the second tetralogy, is just where the crux of the matter lay. As Shakespeare grasped the paradox in the traditional formulations of the king's power of right, he realized that this right was both beyond coercion, and yet dependent upon it. Shakespeare works out the paradox in this form: right without power cannot stand, and conversely, right that uses power to support itself likewise cannot stand.[8] The sacredness of kingly right and consequently its capacity to command respect depend entirely on a divine conferral, which can never be rescinded by forcible usurpation. But once right submits itself to arbitration by the power of arms, it has already attacked itself, because in so doing it implicitly accedes to and vindicates force's claim to jurisdiction over it. The use of power, as political tract writers never tired of pointing out, must be grounded in right; and yet it cannot be exploited in such a way that it overgoes other rights. Such divinely sanctioned right, because it transcends the rights of ordinary men, contains within itself the temptation to transform an ethical superiority into a superiority of power. The moment this happens the power of right is transformed into its opposite, the right of power. In other words, the orthodox doctrine of the power of right is dialectically convertible into the right of power, not when "power" is overemphasized, but rather when "right" to use that power is overemphasized. The meaning of the phrase "the right of power" should be obvious by now. It means the Hobbesian conception of

---

7 *Ibid.;* from *Concerning True Obedience,* 1553.

8 In the *Pensées,* Pascal's paradoxical mind was drawn to the might-right issue: "Right without might is helpless, might without right is tyrannical. Right without might is challenged, because there are always evil men about. Might without right is denounced. We must therefore combine right and might, and to that end make right into might or might into right," trans. A. J. Krailsheimer (Baltimore: Penguin Books, 1966), p. 56.

right as the power anyone has over some thing or person which he may exercise by physical coercion.[9] In implying the potential for actions based on the right of power, the norms of right in all eight plays are exhibited as at once disjoined from power in their exercise, and as incapable of being disjoined.

THE SECOND HISTORY TETRALOGY

Richard II

In every play of both history tetralogies except *Richard II* the claimants to the throne whose names provide the titles provide also the ground of contention. The fourth, fifth, and sixth Henries, and Richard the Third are so many milestones along a road of never-ending dispute, at which the claims of rightful monarchy momentarily rest, only to be attacked again in the name of those very claims. With both *Richard III* and *Henry V* Shakespeare marks an end: Henry Tudor, as the divinely appointed political savior, concludes the first group, and a Henry Plantagenet, buoyant and pensive by turns, rests in his conquest to conclude the second. But in both cases readers have felt uneasy with these apparent resolutions, because the contest over legitimate monarchal right that began with Richard II is neither totally settled, nor allowed to proceed to settlement. In the first tetralogy and *1* and *2 Henry IV* Shakespeare began with a ready made contention, wherein bickering nobles and rebels all eventually call upon the deposition of Richard II as the ancient act justifying their own actions. The question then arises, that if Richard's deposition and murder are in fact the origin of the quarrels for the throne, what was the totally prior "origin" of this origin? Given Shakespeare's insight into the ways in which power of right invested in the crown can generate dialectically its own destruction, it is appropriate that Richard's downfall results not

[9] In *Leviathan*, ed. Michael Oakeshott (New York: Collier Books, 1962), Bk. I, Ch. 14, p. 103, Hobbes defines the "right of nature" as that "which writers commonly call *jus naturale*, . . . the liberty each man hath, to use his own power, as he will himself, for the preservation of his own nature; that is to say, of his own life; and consequently, of doing anything which in his own judgment, and reason, he shall conceive to be the aptest means thereunto." As he says on the same page, "naturally every man has right to every thing."

simply from an external rebellion, but rather from causes implicit in Richard's own actions.

The cycle of potentially never-ending rebellion thus originates, not in the contention between two antagonists whose claims are divided between legitimacy and pure aggrandisement respectively, but in a single agent paradoxically embodying both. Richard's corruption of his own power of right—the only power of right untainted throughout the history plays—both generates and becomes the model for the dialectic between right and power in the remaining plays of the second tetralogy. Therefore Richard confronts in Bolingbroke's attacks under the "right of power" his own mirror image, a perversion caused by, and consequently matching, Richard's own.

Richard's conception of his political right allows only two alternatives: either he must possess power as illimitable as the divine sanction that created him monarch, or he must be totally abject, without power, status, or even name. The full implications of this attitude appear in act 3 under the pressure of Bolingbroke's landing and Richard's impotence to throw him back. The flight of the nobles crystallizes Richard's predicament by explicitly disjoining the sanctions of right from the necessities of power. Carlisle and Aumerle (3.2.27–36) emphasize that though Richard's right derives from Heaven, nevertheless arms must also be embraced: Richard must arm himself with both divine right and human force. Richard's answer is to rely completely upon the transcendent power of kingly right explicitly divorced from any human foresight or strength:

> For every man that Bolingbroke hath press'd
> To lift shrewd steel against our golden crown,
> God for his Richard hath in heavenly pay
> A glorious angel: then, if angels fight,
> Weak men must fall, for heaven still guards the right.
>   [58–62] [10]

[10] In this essay the following texts are used as sources of quotation: in the Arden edition: *King Richard II*, ed. Peter Ure (Cambridge, Mass.: Harvard Univ. Press, 1956); *The First Part of King Henry IV*, ed. A. R. Humphreys (London: Methuen, 1961); *The Second Part of King Henry IV*, ed. A. R. Humphreys (New York: Vintage Books, 1967); *King Henry V*, ed. J. H. Walter

It is a matter of record that neither in the Chronicles nor in Shakespeare's play does any angel make its appearance to fight for Richard. Richard in effect sunders his monarchal right from any effectual power to defend it, and insists on the power of his mere person invested with divine sanction to turn back rebellion. This call upon the angels yields two complementary points: (1) angels are certainly superior to men; (2) angels, and the transcendent right they protect, because beyond mere force, do not therefore descend to that level to make themselves felt.

Throughout the rest of the scene Richard insists on an extreme either-or view of his situation. Either the rebellion will be overturned by sheer force of his majesty without additional help; or he will despair. The fact that, as the scene progresses, more news comes of actual desertions from his cause does not affect this point. Although Richard must take some position when he finally learns that he simply has no army left, the focus is on the rhetorical gestures with which Richard greets this realization, and the terms in which he incorporates it into a frame of interpretation and acceptance. Richard tends to embrace evil chances the moment that they will not vanish of themselves in the face of his kingly right, and here join together the political and psychological causes that make up Richard's downfall.[11]

In scene 3, Richard and Bolingbroke confront each other. The question of Bolingbroke's landing remains shadowy, from his reappearance in act 2, scene 3, up to this present scene. Though he becomes a rebel in fact the moment he sets foot in England, he justifies his own actions by saying that in seizing his lands and revenues, Richard attacks the monarchal right that gives him (equivocally) that power (2.3.122ff.). There is no question of Bolingbroke's sincerity; or to be more precise, there is no question that Shakespeare gives him overtly any other motive than this. To assume that a downright plot against Richard is under-

---

(London: Methuen, 1967); *Julius Caesar,* ed. T. S. Dorsch (Cambridge, Mass: Harvard Univ. Press, 1955); and *Measure for Measure,* ed. J. W. Lever (London: Methuen, 1965). The texts of *Troilus and Cressida* and *Hamlet* are drawn from *The Complete Plays and Poems of William Shakespeare,* ed. William Allan Neilson and Charles Jarvis Hill (Cambridge, Mass.: Houghton Mifflin, 1942).

[11] Wilbur Sanders, *The Dramatist and the Received Idea,* p. 179, connects Richard's demand for absolute power with his uncompromising despair.

way here is to make crude what Shakespeare takes care to make sophisticated. If Bolingbroke's logic accuses the king, it likewise works against himself. Both are dialectically joined in that each assumes the other a malefactor by a norm of judgment applying equally to both. If Richard's claim on the argument from monarchal right is debased the moment he usurps Bolingbroke's heritage, then he leaves Bolingbroke no choice but to answer in kind, if he is to possess his lands at all. In short, Shakespeare discloses no overt motivation in Bolingbroke for deposing the king before act 3, because up to this point he has none. Shakespeare has Bolingbroke present himself to Richard as a blank page on which Richard must write his own version of his intentions. And Richard's version projects a mixture of personal neurosis and ideological absolutism: Henry has come deliberately to depose him.

It is noteworthy that, in act 3, scene 3, Richard supplies the only reference to deposition, whereas Northumberland's message from Bolingbroke mentions nothing of the sort. Actually, Richard and Northumberland do not agree about what it is they are discussing. In citing Northumberland's refusal to bend his knee, Richard complains:

> If we be not [thy lawful king], show us the hand of God
> That hath dismiss'd us from our stewardship;
> For well we know no hand of blood and bone
> Can gripe the sacred handle of our sceptre,
> Unless he do profane, steal, or usurp.
>
> [3.3.77–81]

The language of appeal to divine sanction is a coin that must be used sparingly, particularly when one is surreptitiously engaged in debasing it oneself. Northumberland's answer simply restates Bolingbroke's intentions: "His coming hither hath no further scope / Than for his lineal royalties, and to beg / Infranchisement immediate on his knees . . ." (112–114). And when Northumberland returns to Richard again, and before he says a word, Richard breaks out with:

> What must the king do now? Must he submit?
> The king shall do it. Must he be depos'd?

The king shall be contented. Must he lose
The name of king? a God's name, let it go. . . .

[143–146]

When the king finally confronts Bolingbroke face-to-face, a director would, it seems to me, be perfectly justified in making Bolingbroke appear somewhat astonished:

> *Bolingbroke:* My gracious lord, I come but for mine own.
> *Richard:* Your own is yours, and I am yours, and all.
> *Bolingbroke:* So far be mine, my most redoubted lord,
> As my true service shall deserve your love.
> *Richard:* . . . What you will have, I'll give, and willing
>   too,
> For do we must what force will have us do.
> Set on towards London, cousin, is it so?
> *Bolingbroke:* Yea, my good lord.
> *Richard:*   Then I must not say no.

[196–199, 206–209]

Richard insists he does what Bolingbroke forces him to do, while clearly manipulating Bolingbroke into the part of the usurper. It is Richard who declares "I am yours, and all," and it is Richard who goes so far as to thrust onto Bolingbroke his cue: "Set on towards London, cousin, is it so?" to which Bolingbroke answers with delicious blankness: "Yea, my good lord." Thus Richard stage-manages his self-destruction.

Both men could be said to cooperate with each other in working out their dialectically related but opposed ends. Both share a notion of the power of right that entails necessarily the right to use power to enforce that right. Both agree, then, in choosing actions which derive from the sanctions of their rightful offices, and which also implicitly attack these sanctions. We have conflict in which both are enemies because both are alike. Appropriately enough, each accuses the other of employing unwarranted power, as distinct from his own pious claim to nothing but his rights in the matter. The consequence is a potentially unresolvable conflict, and the issue is joined for the rest of the second tetralogy. From here on out, enemy will be joined to enemy in a

multivalent repetition of the dialectical pattern first broached in
Richard II.

1 Henry IV

Once become king, Bolingbroke legitimizes his tenuous claim
to the throne through the rites and appearances of order and
respectability. In doing so, he confronts in the rebellious Northumberland, Harry Percy, and Worcester his own mirror image
come back to haunt him. Both Henry and the rebels convert their
base motives upwards, thereby inviting a reconversion downward.
The Percy faction juggles with such motives when Hotspur insists that their rebellion will restore the honor they lost in help-
ing Henry depose Richard. He calls it a "shame" "that men of
your nobility and power" should have cooperated with "this can-
ker Bolingbroke" in putting "down Richard, that sweet lovely
rose." "Yet," he continues, "time serves wherein you may redeem
/ Your banish'd honours, and restore yourselves / Into the good
thoughts of the world again" (1.3.165ff.). This kind of reasoning
appeals to Hotspur, who conceives actions and results almost
entirely as a function of reputation and honor. In the same scene,
however, Worcester more accurately describes their motives. He
knows that "the King will always think him in our debt, / And
think we think ourselves unsatisfy'd, /Till he hath found a time
to pay us home" (280–282). That Worcester predicts (correctly)
how the king will himself predict (also correctly) their justifications for rebellion, shows that they are both of a kind, for they
think exactly alike. Henry's displays of political respectability, as
well as his former allies' rebellion under the banner of restoring
usurped monarchal rights, are thus versions of each other.

Both king and rebels judge themselves and others within mutually exclusive categories of simple right and wrong, high and
low motives, respectable and unrespectable actions. For Hotspur,
the respectable equals insistence on nice points of honor, downright commitment to blows and battle, and exaggerated disdain
of feminine company. The unrespectable for him is anything that
savors of devious policy (the king), or frivolity (the prince). In
the king himself, we find an almost bourgeois anxiety for family
name and honor besmirched in the gutter. In judging by such

simplistic ethical categories, both are unprepared for the ironies of debunking to which they are vulnerable, because these categories conceal their secret sharing in base motives with those whom they execrate and oppose. Thus, Henry's attempts to set himself on the side of order and respectability, and Hotspur and Hal on the side of disorder and tainted action merely invite back upon himself further rebellion. On Hotspur's part, rebellion's pretensions to "honor" mirror Henry's own and also debunk them. Prince Hal's rebellion inoculates moral respectability against the moral decay that it masks in both king and rebels, and becomes therefore both the disease and the cure. Hal's truancy is truly what his father calls it, a "secret doom out of my blood" through which God will "breed revengement and a scourge for me" (3.2.6–7). Hal is of course the appropriate son for Henry, mirroring back to him his own defaults, unmasking his father's "respectability."[12]

In Falstaff, we behold a parody of order and respectability "gross as a mountain, open, palpable" (2.4.221). Falstaff does not present us simply with the embodiment of debauchery and feeding set off against the king's respectability. There is another aspect of Falstaff, not nearly enough commented on, that tempts me to see him as cut quite univocally out of the same cloth. This aspect is Falstaff's hunger for respectability. No one quotes scripture in Shakespeare more than Falstaff, and no one is more a master of the odds and ends of manners and morals, of sermons and proverbs, and of pious exhortation. Falstaff's moral piquancy lies, therefore, not simply in his representing holiday as opposed to Henry's sobriety. On the contrary, his mastery, no less than Henry's, of the rhetoric of moral exhortation and the stances of self-righteous complacency make him an embodiment of moral ambiguity that is formidable to deal with.[13] When Falstaff parodies King Henry's sermon to his son (to come in act 3, scene 2), we perceive that he parodies himself as well. And yet Falstaff

[12] I am profoundly indebted to C. L. Barber's chapter on *1 Henry IV* in *Shakespeare's Festive Comedy* (Cleveland and New York: Meridian Books, 1963), for my discussion of the subplot as inoculating the values of the main plot with needed disorder.

[13] J. Dover Wilson, *The Fortunes of Falstaff* (Cambridge: University Press, 1964), pp. 32–34.

distinguishes himself from Henry in his sometimes complacent, sometimes anguished recognition of the gulf between his high pretenses and the seedy reality. This is the gulf that Henry is committed to denying, that his self-righteousness indeed exists to deny.

Falstaff's mask of moral probity is only one of the masks he puts on and takes off with serene ease and celerity. But if his ability to create for himself various roles and the appropriate rhetoric debunks the actors in the main plot, then Hal debunks the debunker by continually unmasking Falstaff's various personae. When Falstaff says to Hal, "Do not thou when thou art king hang a thief," and Hal answers, "No, thou shalt," Falstaff is immensely taken with the role of hanging judge. When Hal corrects him, and says that Falstaff shall be himself a hangman, Falstaff has little trouble adjusting to this role too (1.2.59ff.). Hal's and Falstaff's understandings of this exchange are carefully distinguished. Hal can relish the moral ironies bound up in the idea of a thief hanging another thief in the name of justice, while Falstaff misses them completely. Hal's facility in wheeling to Falstaff's blind side to score marks him as the one character flexible enough to ecape through the moral ambiguities thrust on all else by their attempts to deny such ambiguities. For Falstaff, as for the king, respectability can only be achieved by "hanging" the thief in himself through hanging other thieves.

When, still later in this scene, Falstaff sighs over the corruptions Hal has led him into, so much so that now he is "little better than one of the wicked," the prince immediately counters with "Where shall we take a purse tomorrow, Jack?" Falstaff easily reverses his field and answers " 'Zounds, where thou wilt, lad, I'll make one." Hal, supreme connoisseur of Falstaff's moral juggling, comments "I see a good amendment of life in thee, from praying to purse-taking" (1.2.88ff.). Falstaff's rhetoric is complex here, for we cannot tell whether he only pretends to the hypocrisy that Hal has corrupted him, or whether he really believes it. Falstaff may at once savor the language of repentance and mock it. These two attitudes, far from being incompatible, are dialectically correlative. For Falstaff, like King Henry and Hotspur, is the first to condemn others whenever he can manufacture some sort of moral edge over them. When anyone in this play affects one side of a moral antinomy in conscious contradistinction to its opposite, he is doomed to enact both opposites, and not know it. Falstaff alternately mocks sober age from the viewpoint of youthful exuberance, and also assumes the persona of that sobriety, castigating youthful debauchery and corruption. Falstaff's counterpart, Hotspur, manages much of the time to convey a deliberately important air of conscious responsibility and non-nonsense dedication to purposeful action, a kind of adolescent pomposity that scoffs at play and women. As such, he is merely the Falstaffian roughneck affecting his antimask. And so there is really a true, and not simply an ironic sense, in which Falstaff is youth and Hotspur age.

Shakespeare presents Hotspur's rebelliousness as a twitchy subjection to certain drives, actions, and reactions, something like a tic. For instance, all of his enemies evolve into the affected popinjay whom Hotspur mimics when Shakespeare first introduces him. He is adept at delineating the affected courtier with all the malevolent relish of Tom Sawyer anatomizing a Sunday-school goody-goody: "He was perfumed like a milliner, / And 'twixt his finger and his thumb he held / A pouncet-box, which ever and anon / He gave his nose, and took't away again / . . . and still he smil'd and talk'd . . ." (1.3.35–40). When he is waxing enflamed against the king he categorizes him in the same way: "Why, what a candy deal of courtesy / This fawning greyhound then did proffer me!" (1.3.247–248). Still later, when reading a letter counseling caution from one of his erstwhile allies, he bursts out with: " 'Zounds, and I were now by this rascal I could brain him with his lady's fan" (2.3.22–23). The ironic parallels between Hotspur and Falstaff on the subject of honorable action go well beyond the two as representatives of excess and deficiency respectively.[14] Though Hotspur and Falstaff are both facile in creating roles for themselves, the essential difference lies between one who is flexible in his role-playing and one who is not. The rigidity of Hotspur's stance allows him to make anarchy in the name of honor and be incapable of distinguishing the two.

[14] Hiram Haydn, *The Counter-Renaissance* (New York: Grove Press, 1960), p. 604.

Unlike Falstaff, he cannot doff his masks when they no longer serve, and his enslavement to these stances he shares with the king.

Falstaff undercuts both of them, in refusing to be bound by any stance, either moral or self-consciously antimoral, and is flexible enough to shift according to the demands of the situation. In this respect, he acts as a kind of lightning rod for Hal, absorbing the malign possibilities of moral equivocation within himself so as to free Hal from these. Therefore, when Hal takes the stool and begins to play his father (2.4.428), he equivocates just as Falstaff does, but with a difference. His mimicking both his father and his boon companion demonstrates his independence of the values of both. When Hal, his own voice speaking through the persona of his father, banishes plump Jack Falstaff, he of necessity banishes his father also, because both old men share the moral ambiguity which their moral self-righteousness attempts to hide and only succeeds in revealing.

But wherein lies Hal's security from this malign dialectic between self-ignorant moralism, and the anarchy of moral relativism? The answer lies in the double valence this relativism gathers to itself progressively through the play. Hotspur, Falstaff, and Henry all become moral relativists in refusing to admit this fact. Hal's moral flexibility on the other hand is positive rather than self-contradictory, because, in not being tied to and consequently controlled by any fixed stance, he can truly achieve independence of its opposite. He knows when to play and when not to play, and this can be said of no one else in the play; in short, what saves Hal is an unerring sense of decorum. Hal knows policy, play, and honor, but in a fashion that does not commit him to a malignly dialectical alternation among them. Nowhere is Hal's sense of decorum more evident than in the scene with Francis the drawer. The complex tone of Hal's tale of drinking with the drawers needs careful consideration:

> *Poins:* Where hast been, Hal?
> *Prince:* With three or four loggerheads, amongst three or fourscore hogsheads. I have sounded the very basestring of humility. Sirrah, I am sworn brother to a leash of

drawers, and can call them all by their christen names, as Tom, Dick, and Francis. They take it already upon their salvation, that though I be but Prince of Wales, yet I am the king of courtesy, and tell me flatly I am no proud Jack like Falstaff, but a Corinthian, a lad of mettle, a good boy (by the Lord, so they call me!), and when I am King of England I shall command all the good lads in East-cheap. They call drinking deep "dyeing scarlet," and when you breathe in your watering they cry "Hem!" and bid you "Play it off!" To conclude, I am so good a proficient in one quarter of an hour that I can drink with any tinker in his own language during my life. . . . [2.4.3ff.]

The meaning of this passage is summarized in the comparison between Hal and that "proud Jack" Falstaff. We see throughout both parts of *Henry IV* Falstaff looking down his nose at the baseness of his companions: such is his "respectable" stance. Whereas Falstaff insists on his moral status precisely because he does not have it and is no more noble in anything than the drawers at the Boar's Head, Hal can afford to drink "with any tinker in his own language during my life" precisely because he is not a tinker born and bred. Like Falstaff, he can take on different personae. But unlike Hotspur, Henry, and Falstaff, who insist they are not like certain depraved types precisely because they are like them, Hal may adapt himself to various persons because he knows that he is not like them. These three each in his own way deny the moral baseness in which they share, thereby dialectically generating the possibility that they will perforce share in it. Hal is committed to denying no aspect of the kingdom and therefore may partake of all parts of it with safety and the certitude that he will never be bound to them despite himself.

The speech about the drawers reveals a divided perspective. The prince is quite frankly flattered by his success, just as flattered, it might be said, as he is ironic at the expense of this feeling in himself. He mocks himself gently as well as them, thereby freeing himself from either snobbishness or its dialectical opposite, unctuous chumminess. And for this reason he can play at various personae with a freedom not granted to the others, who are in Falstaff's words required to give reasons "on compulsion" (2.4.233–234), the compulsion of their self-delusion and self-righteousness. For this reason Hal can eulogize both Hotspur and Falstaff at the battle's end with a freedom that neither of these two could command. Hal, at least as far as the issues raised in *1 Henry IV* are concerned, transcends the malign dialectic that it is the play's main purpose to abrogate.

2 Henry IV

The dialectical structures of the themes in *2 Henry IV* follow upon those Shakespeare explored in the previous play. He introduces here, however, a cluster of motifs concerned with how various characters' moral imaginations fashion expectations, conjectures, and surmises regarding the logic of events stretching itself out beyond the present. As in the previous play, the expectations of all the characters, save Prince Hal, presuppose a univocal, nondialectical, nonconflictual model, with the consequence that expectations and events invariably diverge.[15]

The play opens appropriately with a prologue spoken by "Rumour painted full of tongues," which leads immediately into the main subject of the first scene, an elaborate development of the motif of conjecture. Northumberland hears different tales of the battle from a succession of Messengers. "Rumour is a pipe / Blown by surmises, jealousies, conjectures," announces its allegorical embodiment (Induction, 15–16), and thus prepares for Morton's reminder to the bereaved Northumberland that "it was your presurmise / That in the dole of blows your son might drop" (1.1.168–169). "Yet did you say 'Go forth,' " he continues, "and none of this, / Though strongly apprehended, could restrain / The stiff borne action" (175–177). Morton's comment is well taken. That neither Northumberland nor the rest of the rebels counted on their failure is confirmed by Lord Bardolph immediately after: ". . . we ventur'd for the gain propos'd, / Chok'd the respect of likely peril fear'd" (183–184).

---

[15] L. C. Knights discusses this aspect of the play at length in "Time's Subjects: The Sonnets and *King Henry IV, Part II*," reprinted in *Twentieth Century Interpretations of Henry IV Part II,* ed. David P. Young (Englewood Cliffs, N.J.: Prentice-Hall, 1968), pp. 13–29. A. R. Humphreys also notes this theme in the Arden ed., p. xlix.

In short, one foresees according to one's perception of the logic of events buried in the present. In this play, conjectures about the future run the spectrum from Falstaff's ridiculous delusion that "the young King is sick for me" (5.3.131), to Henry's agonized questioning of "the book of fate" and the "revolution of the times" (3.1.45ff.). Throughout the play runs the irony that though many characters expect one thing and get another, the final event presents itself as that toward which they have been moving covertly all the time. This of course parallels the logic of *1 Henry IV*, wherein denying the undesired implications of one's attitudes and actions brings them back upon one embodied in one's enemies. In *2 Henry IV*, Falstaff, Shallow, King Henry, and the rebels, all in one way or another fall victim to fantasies of expectation (in Shallow's case it is, in reverse, a fantasy of nostalgia), and all suffer actions that truly mirror their just deserts. Falstaff's and Henry's expectations that Henry V will inaugurate a rule of riot and anarchy turn out to be wrong; while the rebels' expectations of honorable treatment are dashed when Prince John presents them the mirror image of their own actions in betraying them.

To begin with Falstaff, the main change in his character here is that he now believes his own pretensions. Far from being the master of his roles, Falstaff becomes the victim of them. He has about him a sometimes unpleasant complacency, redolent of his delusion that he is truly what he says he is: "Jack Falstaff with my familiars, John with my brothers and sisters, and Sir John with all Europe" (2.2.125–127).[16] From being the master of moral prestidigitation, he has shrunk to the king and the rebels in his brittle insistence upon the rights and respect due his role of military hero. As has been noted by others, Shakespeare prepares for Hal's rejection of Falstaff during Falstaff's first meeting with the lord chief justice. Falstaff's ploys we recognize—the alternation between brazen raillery and rather stuffy standing upon status—but here the mixture comes off differently. The first role is heavy with youth's ironic mockery of age: "your lordship, though not clean past your youth, have yet some smack of age in you,

---

[16] J. D. Wilson, *The Fortunes of Falstaff* (p. 95), notes of Falstaff that in "the scenes of Part II he is no longer free, for the simple reason that now he has begun to takes something seriously, namely his own career and ambitions."

some relish of the saltness of time; and I most humbly beseech
your lordship to have a reverend care of your health" (1.2.95–99).
To the chief justice's refusal to play games with him, Falstaff
cannot help bringing to bear the full ideology of youth with fore-
square directness: "You that are old consider not the capacities
of us that are young; you do measure the heat of our livers with
the bitterness of your galls; and we that are in the vaward of our
youth, I must confess, are wags too" (172–176).

The tone of this is interesting. Clearly, Falstaff is not nearly
so insulated from insult as he was in Part One. There he could
play the gay blade in a fashion that made him ultimately immune
to a palpable hit precisely because he refused to be fixed in any
one stance or persona. But in this play he is what he never was
before: testy and stiff, quite without either irony or nimbleness.
In the later encounter with the chief justice, Falstaff's standing
on place descends to the finicky and petulant. When Gower, a
messenger from the prince and King Henry, enters, Falstaff tries
to wind himself into the weighty conversation. When both refuse
to take notice of him, Falstaff is reduced to stuffy point-making:

> *Chief Justice:* What foolish master taught you these man-
> ners, Sir John?
> *Falstaff:* Master Gower, if they become me not, he was a
> fool that taught them me. This is the right fencing grace,
> my lord; tap for tap, and so part fair.
> *Chief Justice:* Now the Lord lighten thee, thou art a great
> fool.
>
> [2.1.184–190]

When Falstaff is called fool here, there is no saving dimension of
wit to his foolery: Falstaff can be called fool with unequivocal
appropriateness, because he is, now, quite clearly convinced that
he is not one.

If we look forward to Hal's rejection of Falstaff, we find the
logic of the action justified when we recognize that Hal judges
Falstaff by exactly that standard of respectability Falstaff has
himself invited.[17] In the Doll Tearsheet scene at the Boar's Head,

---

17 What follows here was suggested to me by a former graduate student,
Miss Hwaja Kim.

Falstaff confronts Prince Hal and Poins, who are dressed as drawers, just after having traduced the prince, not knowing he was present. With an almost instinctive gesture, Falstaff attempts to regain his dignity by insulting Doll and the rest of his companions, thereby bolstering his own sleazy respectability (2.4.291–299). For Falstaff, Doll is "this light flesh and corrupt blood," and Bardolph's face is "Lucifer's privy-kitchen, where he doth nothing but roast malt-worms" (330–331). And when we turn to Hal's rejection—"How ill white hairs becomes a fool and jester! / I have long dreamt of such a kind of man, / So surfeit-swell'd, so old, and so prophane" (5.5.48–50)—we see that Hal rejects Falstaff on the basis of the same standards by which Falstaff rejects his own companions. Whatever we may think of Hal's rejection as a measure of his own "conversion" (an issue I shall take up later), the logic of this rejection is impeccable.

Obviously, Falstaff has not expected this. What he does expect is that his projections into the future will conform to a fantasy of his own making. He believes that he can indefinitely act out his roles of respectable knight, roistering companion, and cynical con-man—all personae rolled into one and coalescing—as if they were not incompatible. When Hal rejects Falstaff, the motifs of both expectation and meretricious conversion of base actions upward come together and illuminate each other. For Falstaff's expectations were precisely a function of his converting low motives upward, of making diseases into commodities. The dialectical countermovement, by which expectations are thwarted and high pretensions debunked, brings back upon Falstaff all those contradictory elements implicit in his delusions. If he truly expects that order and anarchy will meet and marry, then it is appropriate that their incompatibility should be tested on himself. And if his high pretensions have been dialectically caused by his diseases of soul and body, then the full implications of this dialectic will have been made overt finally when his high pretensions are reduced back to their sources, for all to see.

When we come to the rebels, similar aspects of the motif of conjecture and expectation become apparent. In the play's first scene Morton announces that the rebellion will continue, but now made ideologically respectable by the presence of the Archbishop of York: "But now the Bishop / Turns insurrection to religion; / Suppos'd sincere and holy in his thoughts, / He's follow'd both with body and with mind" (1.1.200–203). Such cloaking of rebellion in episcopal robes is of course liable to debunking, a task Westmoreland performs to the archbishop's face: "If that rebellion / Came like itself, in base and abject routs, / Led on by bloody youth, guarded with rags, / . . . You, reverend father, . . . / Had not been here to dress the ugly form / Of base and bloody insurrection / With your fair honours" (4.1.32–41). As in Falstaff's case, the rebels come face-to-face with an event that unmasks their own pretenses to honor in Prince John's deliberate breaking faith in Gaultree Forest. This conclusion is appropriate, because the rebels assumed that their own (meretricious) good faith would be met with an equal good faith on the part of the Prince: *"Mowbray:* Is this proceeding just and honorable? *Westmoreland:* Is your assembly so?"* (4.2.110–111). Shakespeare seems less concerned with the treachery of Prince John and Westmoreland, and more interested in the ways violent political upheavals in the name of idealistic motives invite reactions that, in being equally violent, unmask these idealistic pretensions. Because the rebels implicitly recognize the liability of their motives to debunking they need the archbishop's prestige. But in covering their rebellion with the claims of religion, they likewise hide from themselves the reason for this cover, which is to say, they deceive themselves about their own deceit. When they are faced with the palpable deceit of Prince John, therefore, they are unprepared for it because they refuse to see the same deceit in themselves.

As for King Henry's attitudes toward the prince, just the opposite occurs. He understands nothing of his son, projecting onto him his own subterranean image of himself as lawless rebel (4.4.54–66). It is then only to be expected that, when Hal takes the crown from his sleeping father's pillow, the king should assume that Hal is attempting to depose him. As in the previous play, so likewise here: Hal performs actions that look reprehensible to those who are already secret sharers in them. We find in Henry's harangue at his son a parallel with Falstaff's insulting his companions at the Boar's Head; although his father is not rejected by the prince, however much he may deserve it. We know and Hal knows that the king's vision of England under the young king wherein the "wild dog" of license "shall flesh his tooth on every innocent" (4.5.130–132) is incorrect. This vision is rather the dying king projecting his own misdeeds into the future, blown up into a phantasmagory of chaos. It is the old rebel, regicide, and seeker after order and respectability who speaks here. Once again he has misinterpreted Hal's actions, and once again the king and not the prince is the true offender.

In this play, as in the previous one, Hal becomes the resolution to dialectical conflicts. Though he appears much less in this play, he still demonstrates his freedom from the dialectically generated compulsions of the other characters. He does this primarily through an ironic sense of his own place and status. He first appears in the scene following that in which Falstaff's claims to status reduce themselves to their most petulant. In contrast, Hal self-mockingly puts on a high-toned disgust with himself for remembering such trivial matters as Poins. He agrees that "weariness durst not have attached one of so high blood," yet "it does me, though it discolours the complexion of my greatness to acknowledge it"; and he longs for "the poor creature small beer" (2.2.1ff.). Hal mocks here people's expectations that he should now avoid low companions, be "converted," and put on greatness. But since he never was completely one with his companions, there is nothing to convert.[18] He can mock both rigid respectability and debauchery for the simple reason that he is freed of the dialectical liaison between the two. Further, he gives us a blown-up version of the haughtiness of high place, just as Falstaff does, but with this important qualification: Falstaff believes it and Hal does not.

Hal asks what Poins would think of him if he wept for his sick father. Poins answers that he "would think thee a most princely hypocrite." When asked why he would think so, Poins insists that Hal would be properly judged a hypocrite because of the prince's

[18] C. L. Barber, *Shakespeare's Festive Comedy*, p. 201, makes this point: "Falstaff provides him [Hal] with a continuous exercise in the consciousness that comes from playing at being what one is not, and from seeing through such playing." Cf. also David Berkeley and Donald Eidson, "The Theme of Henry IV, Part I," *SQ*, 19 (1968): 27.

truancy with Falstaff. And when Hal thrusts out Poins's own part in these debaucheries, Poins turns stuffy and defensive: "By this light, I am well spoke on; I can hear it with mine own ears. The worst that they can say of me is that I am a second brother, and that I am a proper fellow of my hands, and those two things I confess I cannot help" (38–65).

The irony of this exchange is complex. First, Hal affects contempt for Poins and his ilk, in keeping with the role of converted prince. Then he avoids the charge of hypocrisy, while at the same time declaring his contempt for those who make it, like Poins himself. Finally, we have Poins affecting respectability, just as Falstaff does. Counterpointed here are two different conceptions of role-playing. Falstaff and Poins, unlike Hal, are unaware how affecting status without some measure of self-mockery will lead only to their affectations being undercut. Hal is not compelled to assert his respectability precisely because, beyond the surmises of any—Falstaff, Poins, his father—he is respectable. If assuming masks of respectability parodies and debases the motives of right and order, then the cure is the ability to assume many roles without being tied to any. When finally Hal assumes the role of king, thrust upon him as it is, he nevertheless grasps it freely along with the necessary judgment that the role entails. And therefore, when Hal rejects Falstaff, he does not reject "all the world," Falstaff's woeful complaint in *1 Henry IV*. What he does reject is the summary embodiment of role-playing, of the coercion that dialectic exerts on one who refuses to accept dialectic—in short, he rejects the malign generation of the appearance of order and respectability out of its base opposite. Quite simply, neither Hal nor Shakespeare any longer needs Falstaff as lightning rod for Hal's role-testing, for Hal is now the master of all his roles.[19]

[19] A. R. Humphreys in the introduction to the Arden ed. of *2 Henry IV* quotes extensively the critical comments of one Mr. Dipak Nandy, a personal correspondent, who, judging by the incisiveness of his remarks, might have contributed much to the interpretation of the play by publishing them himself. Mr. Nandy also sees the rejection of Falstaff as the rejection of the old role-player who is incapable of rejecting his roles himself (p. lx): "He [Nandy] makes three suggestions. First, the rejection dislocates not only Falstaff's self-esteem but our very 'taking' him as a splendid performer in his own role. However reprehensible in real terms, he has appreciatively acted out the great enlargement of comedy,

Henry V

If the general rhetorical stance of *Richard II,* and *1* and *2 Henry IV* has been deliberative, then that of *Henry V* is epideictic. The conclusion of *2 Henry IV* exhibits Prince Hal crowned Henry the Fifth, and allegedly inoculated against the dialectic between right and power. The first three plays ask the audience to weigh this dialectic and the values and rhetorics arising out of it. *Henry V,* on the other hand, concerns not decisions about what must be done, the province of deliberative rhetoric, but rather matters of praise and blame, epideictic rhetoric.

Rhetoric itself, its various favorable and unfavorable uses, makes up much of the play's action. Here, Henry's own rhetoric is hedged against irony by being contrasted with others' rhetorical excesses. These act as lightning rods, carrying off the negative reactions that might possibly accrue to Henry's own speeches. In this manner, one of the play's main actions is refining its own rhetoric of praise and blame.

Henry in this play, as in the previous ones, is the master of his rhetoric, not the slave of it, and wields deftly the particular addresses required in a variety of situations. We see him replying wittily to the dauphin's witty present of tennis balls, speaking sorrowfully yet severely to the traitorous Scroop, heroically to his army before Harfleur and on the day of Agincourt, plainly and simply to his soldiers on the night before, and with disarming self-deprecation in his wooing of Katherine. Clearly the prince who had become "so good a proficient in one quarter of an hour

---

and 'the success of a role depends in large part on the acceptance of the role-player *as a role-player.*' Falstaff not only has been enjoyable, he has shown himself a virtuoso in relishing his part. 'I know thee not, old man' strips him bare of the gorgeous assumptions he has donned for our pleasure, and turns him into an aged cast-off: . . ." Italics in orig. The line of my whole argument about both parts of *Henry IV* commits me to disagreement with Barber's contention (p. 219) that Hal's rejection "goes with a drastic narrowing of awareness." Barber's point depends upon our viewing Falstaff as a legitimate representative, up to the last, of a necessary elements in human life—holiday and the inoculative necessity of temporary misrule. But as I have argued here, it is precisely Falstaff, and not Hal, who by this point in the play represents "a drastic narrowing of awareness," and that Hal demonstrates his freedom from the meretricious visions of riotous anarchy projected by both his father and Falstaff by refusing to be bound in by their equally meretricious visions of their own respectability.

that [he] can drink with any tinker in his own language during [his] life" has not forgotten the uses of rhetorical flexibility after ascending the throne.

In the first act, having listened to the archbishop's lengthy and legalistic justification of his claim to France, he asks with laconic appropriateness, "May I with right and conscience make this claim?" (1.2.96). The wooing scene of *The Famous Victories,* in which Katherine speaks English, is changed so that the bachelor king may court the French princess in English deliberately simple and plain. For if Hotspur only professed plain speech, Henry makes it his own. The contrast between the outnumbered, sick, and ragged English army, and the boasts of the French before Agincourt, provides Henry ample opportunity to present the virtues of "a good heart" behind the appearances of the "plain soldier" (5.2.167, 153). And we may remember Henry's claim that "he today that sheds his blood with me / Shall be my brother" (4.3.61–62), when Montjoy comes after defeat for permission to separate the fallen French nobility from the peasants (4.7.76–80). Henry's common touch—amalgamating his truancy with the responsibilities of kingship—is acted out in the debate with Williams, Bates, and Court, and also in his soliloquy on the burdens of the "idol ceremony" (4.1.242ff.). He suggests nothing of the disingenuous, then, when he says to Katherine: "I am glad thou canst speak no better English; for if thou couldst, thou wouldst find me such a plain king that thou wouldst think I had sold my farm to buy my crown" (5.2.123ff.).

One may question the play's adequacy for dealing with the issues raised in the previous plays. There seems little foundation, however, to the claim that its rhetoric directs the audience to take an unsympathetic view of Henry's policy and soldiership. I suspect that some critics view the play ironically precisely because it lacks the complex vision and ironic crosscurrents of the plays preceding it. Nevertheless, as I have indicated rather briefly, such ironic discounting as the play affords works unequivocally for Henry and against his declared enemies. Viewed apart from the rest of the tetralogy, there seems to me nothing wrong with accepting the play for what it is, on its own terms, and without irony.

But there of course lies the rub: the play is clearly not meant to be taken in such isolation. There seems little doubt, for no critic seems willing to challenge this, that Shakespeare intended *Henry V* to sum up and celebrate a resolution of the serious issues raised in *Richard II* and *1* and *2 Henry IV*.[20] But if *Henry V* is intended to escape the dialectic between low motives and high justifications, does it succeed? My reasons for answering "no" have mainly to do with how Shakespeare sets up the antinomies in the preceding plays.

The dialectic between right and power set forth in the first three plays is irresolvable. That Shakespeare became aware of this fact after *Henry V*, my discussions of the next four plays will attempt to demonstrate. The dialectic in the first three plays demands that any resolution through Hal accommodate the terms on which the dialectic itself has been grounded. "Right" and "power" exist in such a rigidly dialectical relation *vis-à-vis* each other that any stepping beyond this relation in the interests of resolution violates the terms themselves. For this reason, the "logical universe" of the first three plays and that of *Henry V* cannot exist in conjunction with each other. But it is equally clear that Shakespeare makes Prince Hal's "education" the main thread amid the dialectical swirls created by all the other characters. Hal is the one character to reconcile the conflicting ethical stances represented by all the rest—or so he was apparently intended.

Thus two things become clear: first, the ethical dialectic between right and power, and between motive and justification, is made as airtight as possible; and second, Hal is, Houdini-like, to escape from the confines of this dialectic. Shakespeare's attempt to achieve this feat discloses the essential equivocation in his dramatic treatment of Hal throughout the second tetralogy, and explains finally why *Henry V* fails to achieve that resolution which the previous plays both demand and yet frustrate.

I have been proceeding on the assumption that Hal's own

---

[20] Una Ellis-Fermor, "Shakespeare's Political Plays," reprinted in Ronald Berman, ed., *Twentieth Century Interpretations of Henry V* (Englewood Cliffs, N.J.: Prentice-Hall, 1968), p. 54, sums up the position held by several students of the play, when she says "Shakespeare has at last resolved his demands upon such a figure [i.e., a king] into certain clearly defined qualifications and summed them all in Henry V, with his unflawed, hereditary title and his assured possession of all kingly attributes"; cf. also Norman Rabkin, *Shakespeare and the Common Understanding* (New York: The Free Press, 1967), pp. 99–100.

ethical stance remains unchanged from first to last: his famous
soliloquy at the end of act 1, secene 2, of *1 Henry IV* bears this
out. Quite obviously, then, the King Henry of *Henry V* is not a
triumph of progressively learned experience. On the contrary, King
Henry V emerges at the opening of that play as the disclosure of
the ideal king, rather than the achievement of it. If Hal never
becomes a truant, except in the eyes of Hotspur, Henry IV, and
Falstaff—and it is their seeing him as such, rather than his being
such, that is dramatically functional—then there is no conversion
to take place. But if no conversion has taken place, then the triumphant display of Henry in the last play is really a false one,
because it is a triumph that follows upon no real conflict.

The resolution of these antinomies requires that they be dramatically incarnate in the character who is to enact this resolution. Instead, we have a political savior who has never really engaged this dialectic. When we come to *Henry V,* deliberation has
been replaced with praise and celebration, as if the deliberation
had successfully concluded, instead of, as is the case, merely
ceased. C. L. Barber, in discussing how Shakespeare transforms
Saturnalian ritual into a dramatic exorcising of potential anarchy,
makes the essential distinction that *Henry V* blurs. As he points
out, "Shakespeare's plays are full of pageantry and of action pat-
terned in a ritualistic way. . . . The people in the plays try to
organize their lives by pageant and ritual, but the plays are
dramatic precisely because the effort fails." Such characters are
fascinated "with the individualistic use or abuse of ritual—with
magic." They attempt, by making their rituals, to achieve "an
unlimited power to incarnate" the meanings of themselves. But,
he goes on to say, Shakespeare's drama "also expresses an equal
and complementary awareness that magic is delusory, that words
can become things or lead to deed only within a social group, by
virtue of a historical, social situation beyond the mind and discourse of any one man. This awareness of limitations is expressed
by the ironies, whether comic or tragic, which Shakespeare embodies in the dramatic situations of his speakers, the ironies which
bring down the meanings which fly high in winged words." [21] However, *Henry V* employs its ironies primarily to preserve the rhe-

21 C. L. Barber, *Shakespeare's Festive Comedy,* pp. 193–194.

toric of Henry himself from irony. In short, Shakespeare in this play does just what, as Barber sees it, in *1* and *2 Henry IV* he stated caveats against: he tries to make a play out of the "delusory" magic of rhetoric, but without the compensating "awareness of limitations" that irony has contributed to the preceding plays. *Henry V* is not drama in Barber's sense, but ritual, and as such simplifies rather than explores the issues of the whole tetralogy.

This conclusion may appear somewhat lame, considering the generally bad press this play has received. I have tried to show, however, that the play's mixed success derives from pressures from beyond its own boundaries. An irreconcilable conflict occurs in these plays, whereby the logical development of the right-might issue becomes irreconcilable with the dramatic correlatives for this development. In disengaging Hal from this antinomy, Shakespeare insures that he can resolve it with definite, though illusory, certainty and safety. When he finally takes the center of the stage, with no dramatic irony to challenge the thrust of his actions and their motives, we find ourselves disconcertingly back in Eastcheap, with now the king himself at play, but with no Prince Hal to call him to task.

As I shall show in the succeeding sections, Shakespeare dealt with essentially the same issue several more times. But the dramatic correlatives have altered markedly. After *Henry V*, the irresolvability of these antinomies is given its full due, and now their dramatic embodiments must be not comic exorcism and heroic panegyric, but rather bitter comedy and the deepest tragedy.

JULIUS CAESAR AND THE DISROBING OF IMAGES

Like *Henry V*, *Julius Caesar* examines the modes of epideictic rhetoric. In this play, the audience witnesses the ironic debunking to which carefully projected public images of power and high moral principle are vulnerable. In the language of the Tribune Flavius, images are robed in preparation for being disrobed (1.1.64). Brutus, Cassius, Caesar himself, all act out before themselves and one another, the rhetorical gestures of honorable motives, only to find others unmasking these motives and reconverting them downward into their origins in weakness, ignorance, or envy. In this way, *Julius Caesar* continues Shakespeare's critique of the dialectic between transcendent ethical imperatives, and the self-corruption attending these imperatives in the arena of political action.

One might well begin with Caesar, for he is the cynosure of all eyes. He embodies a central cluster of postures and motives, set up before the rest of the play's characters to interpret and mold according to their own predilections. Shakespeare distinguishes carefully between the objective Caesar—the neutral facts of the man himself—and the carefully projected public image of the suprahuman conqueror. He lays out Caesar's deafness, epilepsy, fevers, fears and vacillations, and most particularly his enslavement to others' opinions of his power in order to show that for all the praise and dispraise heaped on him he remains in many respects a quite ordinary human being. All the judgments made about him concern images and fantasies in the minds of the judgers, and are thus distinguished specifically from Caesar the man. And this distinction extends to the other major characters as well. The play's circumscribing irony is that Caesar, Brutus, and Cassius are all destroyed not by knives or mobs or armies, but by images and fantasies which they as well as the rest mutually cooperate in projecting to one another.[22]

Caesar acts before two audiences: the people of Rome, and himself; and his success depends radically upon his projecting successfully the image of a fearless, suprahuman, and immovable force. Caesar is always "on stage"; his habit of talking of himself in the third person suggests a director coaching his star actor. When speaking of "Caesar" he also gives the slightly uncanny impression of an oracle mediating some unseen deity. In interpreting Calphurnia's omen-laden dream, he is wholly concerned

[22] A number of readers of *Julius Caesar* have commented quite fruitfully on the central motif of projection and interpretation of personal images in the play. Among the most incisive are Matthew N. Proser, *The Heroic Image in Five Shakespearean Tragedies* (Princeton: Princeton Univ. Press, 1965); Peter Ure, in his introduction to his collection of essays on the play, *Shakespeare: Julius Caesar* (London: Macmillan, 1969), pp. 14–15; J. I. M. Stewart, "Character and Motive in *Julius Caesar*," *ibid.*, p. 118; Brents Stirling, "Ritual in *Julius Caesar*," *ibid.*, p. 163; Mark Hunter, "Brutus and the Political Context," *ibid.*, p. 204; and John Palmer, "The Character of Caesar," *ibid.*, p. 224. All of the pieces in Ure's volume are reprinted.

with how his refusal to go to the Senate will appear to others. He first tries out the rhetorical gesture of "unquestionable will": "And tell them that I will not come to-day: / Cannot, is false; and that I dare not, falser; / I will not come to-day. Tell them so, Decius" (2.2.62–64). But when Calphurnia suggests the excuse that Caesar is sick, Caesar recognizes that admitting such is also to admit his fears both to himself and to Decius, and consequently his vulnerability. He is left in the rhetorically exposed position of avoiding an action out of fear, while insisting that his refusal is due not to fear but to his power: "Shall Caesar send a lie? / Have I in conquest stretch'd mine arm so far, / To be afeard to tell greybeards the truth? / Decius, go tell them Caesar will not come" (65–68). But Decius knows the soft underbelly of Caesar's "Caesar" pose: " . . . it were a mock / Apt to be render'd, for some one to say, / 'Break up the Senate till another time, / When Caesar's wife shall meet with better dreams.' / If Caesar hide himself, shall they not whisper, / 'Lo, Caesar is afraid'?" (96–101). This is the one challenge Caesar cannot resist.

Clearly Caesar here as elsewhere in the play projects himself as fearless and omnipotent precisely because he is not. Thus he "cooperates" with Cassius's view that he is a mere mortal who has set himself above ordinary men. To this extent, the conspiracy is intended to act out before others the fact that Caesar's public image of suprahuman conqueror is merely a conversion upwards of his mortal infirmities. Like Antony's funeral oration, the assassination of Caesar is a rhetorical gesture of debunking. At the moment Caesar is first struck, Casca's calling upon his hands—holding a dagger—to speak for him rounds out nicely the dialectical logic working in the conspiracy. The rest of the conspirators are acting out their subservience before Caesar, driving him to ever higher rhetorical flights: the moment before he falls he compares himself to Olympus (3.1.68–76). When Casca "speaks" with his hands he rather continues the logic of the diversionary petitions than breaks it. For the subservience of the conspirators is both feigned and real, because they do and also do not believe in Caesar's transcendence.

This ambiguity is most obvious in Cassius. Caesar represents for Cassius the preeminence that Cassius cannot attain, and therefore that which makes him aware of his own littleness. Like Iago,

Cassius "looks / Quite through the deeds of men" (1.2.199–200), and he is an able debunker. Shakespeare wastes no time in presenting, one after the other, all the symptoms of his discontent. We have first his paranoia: "Brutus, I do observe you now of late: / I have not from your eyes that gentleness / And show of love as I was wont to have" (1.2.31–33), followed by the flattering bid for favor: "And it is very much lamented, Brutus, / That you have no such mirrors as will turn / Your hidden worthiness into your eye" (54–56), followed in turn by his denial of all sycophancy (71–77). Still later other characteristics appear, all converging toward a portrait of pride, self-contempt, self-pity, and a perfectly poised love-hate for those he envisions as defining in their "high" nobility his own littleness. Cassius both loves and hates Caesar for the same reason. Caesar is just like himself, an ordinary man, but one who has coerced rhetorically the rest of Rome into accepting his public image as suprahuman colossus. Consequently, Cassius is caught in a further contradiction—he does and does not take Caesar's public image seriously. He finds this image at once the projection of Caesar's transcendence over him, and a mere rhetorical masquerade. Given Cassius's willingness to kill in order to pierce this masquerade, we might say that with no one does Caesar succeed so completely in projecting his public image as he does with Cassius.

However, if Caesar is like Cassius in Cassius's eyes—essentially weak and deserving of no adulation—he is also like Brutus. From Cassius's viewpoint there is a single composite object of Cassius's fantasies, a "Caesar-Brutus," whom Cassius both loves and hates. He achieves a kind of Freudian displacement, and splits the object of one off from the object of the other. And if Cassius's obsession with Caesar discloses a kind of love (in desiring to be like him, a love that is envy), then the hostility that underlies his professed love for Brutus is likewise clear. If one had not already come to suspect as much in Cassius's long temptation of Brutus in act 1, scene 2, his soliloquy after Brutus leaves confirms this mixed attitude:

> Well, Brutus, thou art noble; yet I see
> Thy honourable mettle may be wrought

> From that it is dispos'd: therefore 'tis meet
> That noble minds keep ever with their likes;
> For who so firm that cannot be seduc'd?
> Caesar doth bear me hard; but he loves Brutus.
> If I were Brutus now, and he were Cassius,
> He should not humour me.
>
> [1.2.305–312]

He debunks Brutus's "nobility," for which he had praised him to his face, now declaring it easily seducible by the likes of himself. Including his own self-contempt in this judgment indicates that his need of Brutus to join in debunking Caesar is a need to debase Brutus also. And when Cassius looks at himself through Brutus's eyes, what he sees is contemptible, for he would not humour himself were he in Brutus's place.

The cynicism of Cassius and the other conspirators about their need for Brutus's disinterested motives to cover the assassination is complemented by their respect for exactly that image. And Brutus himself, despite his certainty regarding his own high motives, declares the need for constructing the appearance of high motives. Brutus denies an oath to bind the conspirators, and later, the need to kill Antony. Both actions would remove the assassination out of the realm of pure motives and public ceremony, the guises of which Brutus requires to keep his own actions clean of personal spite. Brutus's doubts on the matter appear obvious in his evasive conversation with Portia, whom, as Brutus's "self, your half" (2.1.274), he must keep ignorant of the plot.

Brutus can be manipulated by the conspirators because of his essential identity with them. It is a truism that Brutus cannot synthesize abstract justice and liberty with the more complex exigencies of concrete political action. Because he murders for the highest of motives, he is eminently susceptible to being debunked by Antony. But unlike either the conspirators or Caesar himself, Brutus is only half-conscious that he engages in rhetorical manipulation. His sincerity is at once admirable and disastrous.

Within the context of dialectically related conversions upward and downward—the essential actions of the play—I do not believe Brutus's idealism, any more than Caesar's "greatness," or Cassius's envy, or Antony's cunning is intended to evoke an isolated sympathetic or unsympathetic reaction from the audience. *Julius Caesar* is not the tragedy of Brutus, any more than it is of Caesar, for the meaning of each of the four main characters cannot be divorced from that of the other three. Brutus's political idealism is simply another variation on the play's main situation, namely the consequences of men's living within a political context wherein power and the evaluations of power are determined by rhetorical projection and destruction of public images.

If in Cassius's eyes Brutus represents the love correlative to his hate of Caesar, Antony represents the Machiavellianism correlative to Brutus's idealism. What Brutus converts upward in his funeral oration, Antony debunks in his. And if the play's essential action involves much rhetorical manipulation, then it is appropriate that its turning point involves the opposite effects on the same audience of two highly rhetorical addresses. The paired speeches of Brutus and Antony enact in little the dramatic logic of the whole play, wherein appeals to transcendent norms and the debunking of these norms in the name of raw appeals to interest and power follow the one upon the other in a matter of minutes. "Honor" through the play's first half has been a key term. Pretensions to it, attempts to convince others of it, and attempts to tear it down again sum up the action. It is therefore appropriately neat that Shakespeare should exhibit the phrase "honorable men" changing before our eyes from praise into ironical blame. Like Brutus, but self-consciously cynical, Antony calls for violence with the language of high motives. And the Roman mob, ironically imitating the conspirators, attacks the conspirators under the noblest of motives: the fact that Caesar has left "To every several man, seventy-five drachmas," to which moral imperative the Second Plebeian responds "Most noble Caesar! We'll revenge his death" (3.2.244–245).

The remainder of the play, apparently so difficult to justify from a structural viewpoint, on the contrary merely extends and concludes the dialectical forces which the first half has set in motion. That the logic of this dialectic requires an appropriate return of the conspirators' actions back upon themselves is obvious. But the agency of this return is not Caesar's spirit inhabiting Antony, but rather that spirit as both Cassius and Brutus embody it for each other. Not generally noticed, I think, is that both Brutus and Cassius accuse each other in acts 4 and 5 of exactly the same failings they had accused Caesar of in acts 1 and 2. When Brutus accuses Cassius of extortion, he overtly assimilates Caesar's crimes to Cassius:

> What, shall one of us,
> That struck the foremost man of all this world
> But for supporting robbers, shall we now
> Contaminate our fingers with base bribes,
> And sell the mighty space of our large honours
> For so much trash as may be grasped thus?
> [4 3 21–26]

In return, Cassius's self-pity, fawning, and love-hate for Caesar are now transferred to Brutus, and as the exchange escalates we see that all the images of honor and power that afflicted Cassius in Caesar he finds again, overtly reproaching him in Brutus. What motivated Cassius's hatred for Caesar likewise inspired his sycophancy before Brutus; and Brutus's conviction of his idealistic righteousness likewise made him vulnerable to this sycophancy. Now both act according to the same motives: Brutus rises up Caesar-like before Cassius as the embodiment of high rebuke of his own ignobility, and Cassius in turn embodies for Brutus the vices for which he stabbed Caesar.

The defeat at Phillipi becomes less a victory for Antony than the final consequence of the self-destruction implicit in Brutus's and Cassius's motives and goals from the beginning. Cassius dies after a final act of foreseeing the worst, the inexorable gloom of a man chafing always against the restrictions and expectations of his own felt inferiority. And Brutus dies to salve his honor. Antony's presence on the battlefield only confirms this final turning of the conspirators' swords against themselves, just as his rise to prominence at the play's center provides the necessary dialectical concomitant to Caesar's, Brutus's, and Cassius's rhetorical manipulations. And that he comes to praise Caesar, as well as to blame the conspirators, results ultimately in neither, but rather in casting doubt on appeals to both transcendent norms and political necessity.

To the extent *Julius Caesar* represents an advance over the second tetralogy, it lies in Shakespeare's having taken a colder look at his attempt to resolve the dialectic of right and power by rhetorical manipulation in *Henry V*. In *Julius Caesar*, as well as in *Troilus and Cressida*, Shakespeare pushes the possibilities frighteningly latent in the first three plays of the second tetralogy to their logical conclusion.

TROILUS AND CRESSIDA AND THE TICKLING OF EXPECTATION

Even more single-mindedly than *Julius Caesar*, *Troilus and Cressida* pursues the dialectic between idealization of ignoble realities, and the debunking such idealization invites. By the end of the play, all characters without exception are caught inescapably in a mechanism whereby meretricious actions and motives both corrupt and are corrupted by the most ethereal of idealisms.

The interrelations between the war and love episodes fulfill this pattern of mutual corruption. Victory, whoever achieves it, is seen as dignifying the prize, namely Helen, while the values of love are envisioned as giving dignity to the war. But if love and war appear as conversions upward of each other, then both are used to debunk each other. On the one hand, Troilus and Paris view Helen as a "theme of honour and renown" (2.2.199), and on the other Diomedes debunks the values that cause her to be so viewed (4.1.54–66). The whole process that guides Helen's fluctuations in the "value market" is rendered ingeniously in Troilus's defense of the war:

> If you'll avouch 'twas wisdom Paris went—
> As you must needs, for you all cried "Go, go,"—
> If you'll confess he brought home noble prize—
> As you must needs, for you all clapp'd your hands,
> And cried "Inestimable!"—why do you now
> The issue of your proper wisdoms rate,
> And do a deed that Fortune never did,
> Beggar the estimation which you priz'd

Richer than sea and land?

[2.2.84–92]

Troilus's argument, meretriciousness itself, illuminates also his own idealized love for Cressida. Troilus says here, in effect, that though Helen was in fact stolen, the Trojan lords, having originally applauded the theft, are now committed to keeping the appearance of honor they put on that theft by continuing to fight "honorably" for her. In short, honorable war is necessary because the cause of the war is dishonorable. As Paris puts it, with less regard for the ethical confusions of the matter: "But I would have the soil of her fair rape / Wip'd off, in honourable keeping her" (148–149).

Here appears in little the logic governing all the idealizations of base actions in the play. The rhetoric of praise is liable to debunking, not because it rightly assumes high values, but because it assumes that a high valuation can transform low motives. To Troilus's insistence, "What is aught, but as 'tis valu'd?" Hector answers "But value dwells not in particular will; / It holds his estimate and dignity / As well wherein 'tis precious of itself / As in the prizer. . . ." (52–56). Yet in the teeth of this canniness, Hector exhibits himself enslaved to worshipping his own idol of chivalry, and votes to continue the war. This chivalry can look for one of the most violent and summary debunkings in the play, when Achilles and the Myrmidons strike him down unarmed after he calls for chivalrous fair play.

Three more or less distinct motif clusters occur in both the love and war episodes: the motifs of expectation, of snobbism, and of idealization. The last I have already explored to some extent, and the rest of this section will show all three of these clusters mirroring each other.

The motif of expectation illuminates the aspirations of Troilus's love for Cressida, though it appears in other connections as well, mainly in Agamemnon's opening speech detailing how "The ample proposition that hope makes / In all designs begun on earth below / Fails in the promis'd largeness (1.3.3–5). The Prologue identifies the main quality of expectation in the play, when in speaking of the war's progress he says "Now expectation, tickling skittish spirits, / On one and other side, Troyan and Greek, / Sets all on hazard; . . ." (20–22). "Tickle" is a favorite word of the corrupted moralist Thersites, who uses it twice for the itch of concupiscence (5.2.56, 177). It appears in the dodderingly lecherous song of Pandarus, where Love "tickles still the sore. / These lovers cry Oh! ho! they die!" (3.1.130–131). And when Troilus delivers his ecstatic speech before his rendezvous with Cressida, we witness his naively lecherous conversion of lust into the purest of mortal experiences:

> I am giddy; expectation whirls me round.
> Th' imaginary relish is so sweet
> That it enchants my sense; what will it be,
> When that the wat'ry palates taste indeed
> Love's thrice repured nectar? Death, I fear me. . . .
>
> $\qquad\qquad$ [3.2.19–23]

Troilus's persistent idealization of Cressida is consistently undermined by Pandarus's senile sexual innuendoes: taken together they form a paradigm of the play's dialectic. The objects of expectation in this play always fail "In the promis'd largeness," and this discrepancy parallels that between idealization of rapacious desire and the reduction of this idealization into nothing but rapacious desire.

In Cressida's pretended coyness, the motif of expectation melts into the motif of snobbism, whereby master and slave jockey for position on a scale of power and subservience. What Cressida says of her own policy in love applies to Achilles in his proud isolation as well:

> Yet hold I off. Women are angels, wooing.
> Things won are done, joy's soul lies in the doing.
> That she belov'd knows nought that knows not this:
> Men prize the thing ungain'd more than it is. . . .
> Achievement is command; ungain'd, beseech.
>
> $\qquad\qquad$ [1.2.312–319]

Cressida's psychology in this play is remarkable and has not often been given its due. The post-Chaucerian tradition of the faithless whore has joined with Cressida's own moral flabbiness to give the appearance that Shakespeare took over the tradition without change; [23] but such is not the case. The subtle relation between her quite sincerely proclaimed (though evanescent) love for Troilus, and her later infidelity to him are in fact one of the play's masterstrokes. Ulysses' disgusted characterization of her as one of the "daughters of the game" (4.5.63) is accurate as far as it goes, but does not envelope the play's total presentation of her dilemma.

Cressida's insistence on playing the aloof "master" of Troilus's infatuated enslavement is motivated by her nervous fear that, having given herself to him, she will not be able to keep him. The advances, withdrawals, and reaffirmations of her love for Troilus in act 3, scene 2 (especially lines 124–133) exhibit her caught up in the bids for power and high valuation no less than Achilles, Ajax, Agamemnon, Paris, or Troilus himself. For her, once she has stepped down from the position of master—tickling the expectation of her lover—there is only the alternate position of abject slave. With these dialectical tensions of her motivation in mind, her enslavement to Diomedes should surprise no one— except perhaps Troilus himself. Diomedes seduces Cressida from her troth to Troilus by the same affectation of masterful aloofness with which she ensnared Troilus (5.2.). The essential paradox of Cressida's motivation is that her need to be desired, by which she swears absolute fidelity to one man, will turn her faithlessly to any other who can offer the same homage.

When Troilus witnesses Cressida's submission to Diomedes, Shakespeare creates a tour-de-force of staging that summarizes the clash of values and judgments in the whole play. Brought by Ulysses to spy on Diomedes's tent, Troilus in his comments is in turn spied upon by Thersites. The counterpoint of all their comments—of Diomedes and Cressida, as well as of Troilus, Ulysses, and Thersites—renders in near simultaneity the dialectical oscillation in the play between conversions upward and downward. Witnessing a replay of his own seduction, Troilus reacts with a

[23] Cf. Robert Kimbrough, *Shakespeare's Troilus and Cressida and its Setting* (Cambridge: Harvard Univ. Press, 1964), for an extended study of the relation of this play to its sources and analogues. Kimbrough himself tends to side with the position that views Cressida as not essentially different from the older versions of her (cf. pp. 107–108).

growing bitterness that is the dialectical reflex of his outraged innocence and simplicity. And Thersites, the embodiment of Troilus's disillusionment, debunks in turn Diomedes, Cressida, and
Troilus. At one point Troilus reels dizzily before the whole spectrum of dialectically related and opposite values the play manifests:

> O madness of discourse,
> That cause sets up with and against thyself,
> Bi-fold authority, where reason can revolt
> Without perdition, and loss assume all reason
> Without revolt: this is, and is not, Cressid.
> Within my soul there doth conduce a fight
> Of this strange nature, that a thing inseparate
> Divides more wider than the sky and earth,
> And yet the spacious breadth of this division
> Admits no orifex for a point as subtle
> As Ariachne's broken woof to enter.
>
> [5.2.142–152]

All of the motifs I have found in the love between Troilus and
Cressida come together in this speech.

They are also repeated in the scenes in the Greek camp. Here,
Ulysses, Agamemnon, and the rest attempt to jolt Achilles out of
his self-centered snobbism. The sleazy comedy of these attempts
arises out of the fact that all the Greeks, except Ulysses, are subject to the same vice as Achilles himself. Agamemnon's clotted
and laboring rhetoric, Nestor's senile wheezings, Ajax's elephan-
tine wit, all betray characters whose dedication to acting out before others the postures of self-satisfied and feisty dignity make
them fit critics of Achilles' own snobbery. Ulysses, in the famous
speech on degree, renders a classic analysis of the snobbery and
emulation operating on all levels of the Greek hierarchy of command:

> The general's disdain'd
> By him one step below, he by the next,
> That next by him beneath; so every step,
> Exampled by the first place that is sick

Of his superior, grows to an envious fever
Of pale and bloodless emulation; . . .

[1.3.129–134]

The ambiguity of the phrase "sick Of his superior" sums up the snobbism that riddles the Greek camp. The scale of snobbery, on which Achilles and Ajax jockey for position at the top, creates that man most powerful whose favors are most sought after. Like Cassius in relation to Caesar, Ajax is at once Achilles' most ardent admirer and most envious of his reputation. Therefore the snobbism of those at the top infects all those below, making them in turn "sick" of all those above.

The battle which ends the play provides the final debunking of all values as well. Troilus's and Diomedes's fight raises from Thersites a caustic remark on the equal depravity of their quarrel: "Hold thy whore, Grecian!—now for thy whore, Troyan!" (5.4.25–26). Then occurs the vicious slaughter of the unarmed Hector, wherein Hector's idealized chivalry confronts its dialectical opposite in Achilles's low opportunism. And finally, we have Troilus's last apostrophe to the Grecian tents ("No space of earth shall sunder our two hates" [5.10.27]), signaling his reversal from the naive adolescent of the first scene. The play ends in a stalemate; no one rises beyond the all-controlling dialectical logic that drives through to final destruction all the values the play has held up for criticism. In the end, Pandarus fumbles out his song and bequeaths his diseases to the audience.

THE DIALECTIC OF LAW AND LICENSE IN
MEASURE FOR MEASURE

In act 5 of *Measure for Measure* the duke returns from his self-imposed exile to test his deputy, Angelo, for violating the laws he was deputed to enforce. Though aware of Angelo's guilt, the duke acts out the surprise that the uninformed, knowing Angelo's reputation for virtuous rigor, might very well experience in the face of Isabella's and Mariana's charges of secret lust:

First, his integrity
Stands without blemish; next it imports no reason

> That with such vehemency he should pursue
> Faults proper to himself. If he had so offended,
> He would have weigh'd thy brother by himself,
> And not have cut him off. Someone hath set you on: . . .
>   [5.1.110–115]

The viewpoint the duke mimics here is nothing less than the simplistic ethic the play tests and criticizes throughout. Within the
sharp dichotomy such an ethic draws between the virtuous and
the depraved, Isabella's charges cannot be accommodated. That
the enforcer of the law might attack his own vices in others, not
only despite but because these vices are also his own, remains in-
conceivable. As the play demonstrates, however, this possibility
derives from the law's own definition against, and consequently
in terms of, the vices it attacks. To the extent that the law is
caused by vice—the existence of vice as requiring correction—the
law must mold its own motives and actions according to the contours of vice, thereby risking the possibility of becoming its mirror
image.

Angelo is not a mere hypocrite. He is not simply a lecher
masked in the robes of authority, as if those robes hid a moral
depravity quite incommensurate with what they themselves sig-
nify. On the contrary, in showing that Angelo's lechery dialectically derives from his devotion to the law, the play tests and
criticizes this devotion. It discovers that if Angelo's license is to
be avoided, then Angelo's version of law and order must have
built into it the realization of how law and order may cause license in the very act of opposing it. In this play the law is inoculated against its own perversions, by having these perversions appear as potentialities within the law itself. The play argues against
neither license nor the law, but against the law-license dialectic.[24]

The ground of this dialectic is the implicit agreement between
law and license, between Angelo, and Lucio, Pompey, and Mistress

[24] My contention here comes closest to that put forward by David Lloyd
Stevenson, *The Achievement of Shakespeare's Measure for Measure* (Ithaca:
Cornell Univ. Press, 1966), when he says that "what disturbs us in this play is
our almost inadmissable perception that below its neat, surface design of evil
committed and evil caught out, *Measure for Measure* suggests evaluations of
Angelo's and of Isabella's behavior which do not conform to the warm, well-lighted
world of institutionalized good and evil we all wish to think we inhabit" (p. 61).

Overdone that the only options sexuality allows are either total restraint or total latitude. Each side generates the other's simplistic recalcitrance by its own, so that the common categories shared by both allow nothing but these two extremes. Thus Angelo's rigor compensates for—and is thus caused by—the duke's self-admitted laxity. Further, the law both creates license and punishes it. Pompey has a valid point when in answer to Escalus's query whether prostitution is a lawful trade he says: "If the law would allow it, sir" (2.1.221–224). Having been created by vice, the law may in turn create vice in allowing it to flourish temporarily without punishment. The duke says that he in effect has "bid them do" the very thing he turns Angelo loose to punish them for (1.3.35ff.).

The other side of this reciprocal dialectic is stated by Claudio as he is being led off to prison:

> *Lucio:* Why, how now, Claudio? Whence comes this restraint?
> *Claudio:* From too much liberty, my Lucio. Liberty,
> As surfeit, is the father of much fast;
> So every scope by the immoderate use
> Turns to restraint. Our natures do pursue,
> Like rats that ravin down their proper bane,
> A thirsty evil; and when we drink, we die.
>
> [1.2.116–122]

The crosscurrents of this passage suggest that the dialectical connection between license and restraint comes about not despite, but because of their sharp opposition. "Proper bane" here means poison, at once derived from one's own nature and matched and fitted to that nature in its destructive potency. Thus the possible check to man's pursuit of his "proper bane" seems also in an odd way to push him on. With the same ambiguity the duke says that "it imports no reason" that Angelo "should pursue / Faults proper to himself" (5.1.111–113). The "reason" so violated is the univocal reason of nondialectical ethical categories, according to which the just man and the sinner stand on opposite sides of a logical and ethical gulf. Nevertheless, the play exhibits the law-license dialectic operating in the little world of Angelo's mind, whereby he pursues both Claudio and Isabella "for" fornication. Further, since the agreement between the motives of law and license require them to absorb all other options into themselves, neither Angelo nor the sinners can budge an inch from one position without running to its extreme opposite. Thus Lucio evokes the language of rigor when commanding Pompey to prison (3.2.64ff.), and attacks the disguised duke as the self-righteous henchman of Angelo. Pompey turns from bawd to hangman in prison and, with the bureaucratic insouciance of a little authority, jokes with Barnardine about his coming execution (4.3.27ff.). And of course when Angelo's sexuality is finally awakened, it will take the form of nothing less than rapacious lust.[25]

Because Angelo refuses to admit his own covert liaison with the vice he attacks—that is, he sizes up his own motives according to a univocal distinction between the two—he generates an action that compels him to admit this liaison. Because she assumes that men will show mercy to those in whom they recognize their own faults, Isabella fairly argues Angelo into propositioning her. Because he has separated himself from the rigor of the law, the duke recognizes his responsibility for Angelo's tyranny.

The debates between Angelo and Isabella sum up the dialectic between law and license in both the little world of Angelo's psychology, and the larger social world. In two scenes (2.2. and 4) the debates proceed through five distinguishable stages, in the first of which (lines 49–80), Isabella and Angelo agree implicitly that the enforcement of the law rests in the will of the enforcer. However, they disagree on the imperative directing that will. Angelo argues that "It is the law, not I, condemn your brother" (2.2.80), while Isabella argues that because Angelo (and all men) are sinful, the deputy has no right to show anything but mercy to her brother. The argument at this stage prepares for the later overt ambiguities latent in their "agreement" that Angelo's will is their central concern ("Look, what I will not, that I cannot do" [2.2.52]).

---

25 Both G. Wilson Knight, *The Wheel of Fire* (London: Methuen, 1968), and D. A. Traversi, "Measure for Measure," *Scrutiny* 11 (1942): 40–58, note this causal connection between Angelo's puritanism and his lust. Knight says (pp. 87–88) "Since sex has been synonymous with foulness in his mind, this new love, reft from the start of moral sanction in a man who 'scarce confesses that his blood flows,' becomes swiftly a devouring and curbless lust."

Stage two lasts from lines 80 to 135, and here Isabella develops Angelo's fallibility almost to the point of calling on him to be cognizant of his sinfulness. Further, in featuring how Angelo can make the enforcement of the law a function of his own will, Isabella inadvertently prepares for just that. She argues against Angelo's insistence that he has aligned his own will with the impersonal will of the law, by reversing the emphasis, and arguing how Angelo does (and may yet) align the law with his own will. Isabella assumes, of course, that she can make the judge's human fallibility yield mercy for the judged. She has yet to grasp how making the law a servant to the judge will make it potentially a slave to his licentiousness as well. When Angelo falls to lust, he doubtless nullifies his previous alignment of his will with the law's. But in so falling, Angelo demonstrates a more important point about the law: the opening and opportunity he seizes for twisting law to his own uses are precisely afforded by the law's self-definition. Angelo's conception of the law goes not a step beyond opposition to lust, and consequently, his whole attention and concern are totally usurped and taken up by lust. When Isabella debunks Angelo's self-righteousness, she inadvertently discloses this self-righteousness as grounded on a total absorption in vice in the act of opposing and denying it.

Stage three begins with line 135 and runs to line 162 and the beginning of Angelo's soliloquy. Here, Isabella brings the liaison between vice and virtue down to a personal comparison between Claudio and Angelo: "ask your heart what it doth know / That's like my brother's fault"; and for the first time Angelo admits in an aside, "She speaks, and 'tis such sense / That my sense breeds with it" (138–139, 142–143). This admission advances the action decisively. When Isabella exclaims, "Hark, how I'll bribe you: good my lord, turn back," and Angelo answers, "How! Bribe me?" (146–147), we sense immediately Angelo's as yet only partially admitted temptation superimposing itself on his customary righteousness. The audience can only infer the varying degrees of Angelo's disappointment and relief when Isabella says that she will bribe him with "prayers from preserved souls, / From fasting maids, whose minds are dedicate / To nothing temporal" (154–156).

Mirroring the audience's puzzlement at his transformation is

Angelo's own. Here we have stage four, the moment when Angelo admits openly that all the values he abides by as the duke's deputy actually draw him on to besmirch themselves:

> What's this? What's this? Is this her fault, or mine?
> The tempter, or the tempted, who sins most, ha?
> Not she; nor doth she tempt; but it is I
> That, lying by the violet in the sun,
> Do as the carrion does, not as the flower,
> Corrupt with virtuous season.
>
> [163–168]

Angelo is amazed to discover the malign possibilities in his commitment to the law. Obviously, Angelo's amazement presupposes the simplistic ethical distinctions that have up to now allowed the malign potentiality of his virtue to remain hidden from him. Angelo develops these ethical distinctions, thereby sharpening his and our sense of the vast discrepancy between them and the dialectic that both affirms and cancels them. "Can it be," he asks, "That modesty may more betray our sense / Than woman's lightness? . . . Dost thou desire her foully for those things / That make her good?" (168ff.). When he discovers that the virgin tempts him where the strumpet does not (180–187), the play passes beyond the point of unmasking simple hypocrisy. Angelo's lust exists not merely hiding behind a mask of pretended virtue; on the contrary, his temptation is real because his virtue is real, if lacking in self-knowledge and humility. The intelligibility in these paradoxes rests in our discovering that the law-license dialectic has become internalized in Angelo's psyche, and his divided motivations war with each other because they have generated each other. Angelo now realizes that he is tempted "To sin in loving virtue" (183).

The outward action of the fifth stage (all of act 2 scene 4) parallels this dialectical transformation within Angelo. Here Angelo and Isabella actually exchange positions. Angelo, taking up Isabella's previous role, argues "Might there not be a charity in sin / To save this brother's life?" (2.4.63–64). In countering this, Isabella emphasizes the greater importance of her chastity, and insists that "lawful mercy / Is nothing kin to foul redemption"

(112–113). She here denies her previous argument that men should be merciful when they recognize others' sins in themselves. In answering "You seem'd of late to make the law a tyrant, / And rather prov'd the sliding of your brother / A merriment than a vice" (114–116), Angelo cynically implies that Isabella had already linked "lawful mercy" with "foul redemption."

As the play shows, mercy can find no place for itself when all moral options are usurped by the dialectic between law and license. The mercy rigorous law shows to its correlative becomes nothing but license itself (*Escalus:* mercy "is not itself, that oft looks so; / Pardon is still the nurse of second woe" [2.1.280–281]). If license is whatever the law does not forcibly control, then mercy is the law's allowance of license. For this reason, Angelo's version of mercy is strict enforcement of the law: "For then," says Angelo, "I pity those I do not know, / Which a dismiss'd offence would after gall, / And do him right that, answering one foul wrong, / Lives not to act another" (2.2.102–105). Within such categories, in short, mercy can be identified only with law or with license, and this split governs Angelo's and Isabella's debate on the matter. "Lawful mercy" for Isabella has no connection with lust. And when Angelo speaks "charity" to Isabella, he really speaks lust, the price of charity.

The essential licentiousness of Angelo's law appears finally in his proposition to Isabella: "Redeem thy brother / By yielding up thy body to my will; / Or else he must not only die the death, / But thy unkindness shall his death draw out / To ling'ring sufferance" (2.4.162–166). Nothing is clearer in this speech than that the power by which Angelo may decree a torturous death for Claudio is the same power by which he is coercing Isabella. It is not a lawful power that does the first and an unlawful power that does the second. Unlawful use of power, perhaps; but Angelo makes perfectly clear to us as well as Isabella that it is precisely the law's conforming itself totally to the arbitrariness of license in order to combat it that allows it to turn into license's mirror image.

However, Shakespeare does not press on Angelo a further rigor in payment for his own. On the contrary, the duke urges just such measure-for-measure justice in exhorting Isabella to accept Angelo's execution. At this point in act 5 (1.401–409), Isabella still believes that Angelo has executed her brother, and in her decision Isabella must now rely on her developed understanding of the drama she has been acting in up to this moment. Mariana begs Isabella to plead for her new husband's life, and the duke reiterates how far Mariana presumes on Isabella's loss of her brother in doing so. When Isabella finally kneels and pleads for Angelo's life, the law-license dialectic is finally transcended, and she shows that she is tied neither to measure-for-measure justice, nor to the license correlative to such justice. As the play demonstrates, mercy becomes possible only after the rigor of the law has convicted both judge and criminal.

In *Measure for Measure* Shakespeare's answer to the problem of right versus power is really only the question restated, but so restated as to advance our knowledge of why it takes its peculiarly problematic form. Nevertheless, none of the seven plays so far discussed isolate the problematics of the question as their overt subject. *Hamlet* does just that, and for this play Shakespeare needed a different kind of hero to exist in a play different from any of the others I have discussed. He needed a hero who was endowed with much of the dialectical insight of the playwright, for this play was to begin where the other seven had ended, with the complexities of dialectic envisioned from the start rather than disclosed only at the end.

HAMLET AND THE TRANSCENDENCE OF DIALECTIC

Hamlet is preeminently a play about the difficulties of doing the right thing for the right reason. In it Shakespeare confronted the widest implications of the right-power dilemma. But though the fact that *Hamlet* deals with this dilemma is hardly a new insight, the play remains problematic largely because of confusions about how it poses this dilemma and seeks to resolve it. Since Hamlet's delay is perhaps the most familiar road into the play's problems and mysteries, I will begin with it.

The question, Why does Hamlet delay? can have two meanings. The first meaning, derived from Bradley and Coleridge and taken for granted by many critics since these, whether they agree with their conclusions or not, assumes that the question elicits some kind of answer about causes. This interpretation invites answers couched in terms of this or that internal or external obstacle, and assumes that to discover this obstacle is to discover what the play (and the playwright) want to say about Hamlet. The other way to interpret this question is to ask, For what purpose does the play exhibit Hamlet delaying? [26] This interpretation assumes a difference between a question a character asks within a fiction, and a question the fiction itself asks of the audience. Thus the question ought to be rephrased as, What is the significance for the play's meaning of Hamlet's delay? This, however, leads to a further question: if Hamlet delays—and as far as he is concerned he does—Why does he not know why he delays? Again, one can interpret this question the same way as the first. That is, one can search for an answer couched in terms of information in Hamlet's unconscious, inadmissable to his conscious mind. This interpretation generates those approaches, Freudian and otherwise, which find it difficult to envision the character Hamlet subordinated functionally to the fiction of which that character is a part. The other way of asking this question is to make it concern the purposes of Hamlet's ignorance within the play's total statement. In this case, the question means: What meaning does the play convey through a character who has, consciously, the will and means to do a certain act, but who does not act, and clearly shows that he does not know why he does not act? In short, What

---

[26] Though I disagree with some of the consequences he draws from it, I am indebted to A. J. A. Waldock's canny remark in *Hamlet: A Study in Critical Method* (1931) that "The delay that exists in a drama is the delay that is displayed. . . . It is not enough to say that Hamlet procrastinates because, as a matter of fact, and regarding the play somewhat as an historical document, we find that he did not act for two months or so. If he procrastinates, it is because he is shown procrastinating. To put it another way, it is not sufficient that delay should be negatively implicit in the play; it is necessary, for its dramatic existence, that it should be positively demonstrated. The delay, in a word, exists just inasmuch as and just to the degree in which it is conveyed"; reprinted in *Shakespeare's Tragedies: An Anthology of Modern Criticism,* ed. Laurence Lerner (Baltimore: Penguin Books, 1964), p. 79. E. T. Schell, in an article published after this essay was finished, "Who Said That—Hamlet or *Hamlet?*" *SQ* 24 (1973): 135–146, deals at length with exactly the same problem, namely, that of distinguishing between transactions between characters, and transactions between the play as a whole and the audience.

is the significance of the "not-knowing"? which is not at all the same as asking *Why* the "not-knowing"? Seen from this perspective, these questions do not invite solutions to some kind of puzzle, as they are too often assumed to do. On the contrary, they invite us to contemplate the furiously innocent and simplistic ethical demands of the hero, as these confront the ethically confused situation within which he must act.

Hamlet's ignorance of his reasons for delaying is itself a positive action in the play. As such, Hamlet's questionings are significant in themselves, not for the answers we may give to them, but for the reactions they elicit from us. We witness a hero struggling with the contradictions entailed by his own ethical imperatives, which contradictions he cannot understand because they are masked from his sight by the innocence of those ethical imperatives. The ghost's command mirrors this innocence in its exhortation "Taint not thy mind" (1.5.85), an imperative implying a simplistic dichotomy between good and evil, the agent of good and the vessel of evil. Hamlet demands an act of revenge totally pure and absolute in its moral valence. Yet to kill Claudius is to share the corruption of Claudius, and consequently to muddy the pristine ethical imperative of revenge in the very act of carrying it out. Therefore the "ought" implicit in the ghost's command elicits from Hamlet an act that is ethically self-contradictory.

This self-contradiction plagues Hamlet throughout the play because he does not understand it. And he does not understand it because his simplistic ethical categories, like Angelo's, cannot take account of an act simultaneously good and evil for the same reason. When speaking of this delay, Hamlet always sees it measured against a norm of simple, pure, and direct action, most directly exemplified by Laertes and Fortinbras. Nothing is clearer than that Hamlet conceives his own mission in exactly the way Laertes views his own revenge for Polonius's death. And yet Laertes acts with a swiftness the messenger compares to "The ocean" which, "overpeering of his list, / Eats not the flats with more impetuous haste" (4.5.99–100), while Hamlet does nothing. Furthermore, Hamlet does not explain his inaction because, as Shakespeare presents him, he does not know either, at least not so as to articulate an explanation.

In fact, Shakespeare could not have remained faithful to the ethical and psychological contours of his hero, had he allowed him to soliloquize on the dialectic he is involved in. Had Hamlet been invested before act 5 with full recognition of the reasons why he delays, he would have been granted this recognition by fiat of the playwright's will, and not as the result of the earned insight the play is dedicated to working out before us. Hamlet could not have intelligibly pursued his revenge while recognizing fully the dialectical contradictions his revenge involved him in, for such recognition would instantly abolish the ethical categories such a pursuit implies and requires. Actually, Hamlet hovers indecisively between these two alternatives: he yearns both to complete his revenge, and to avoid it—both states governed equivocally by the partially hidden, partially disclosed nature of his dilemma.

Shakespeare took the dramatically risky tack of announcing the significance of Hamlet's delay obliquely through the hero's own semi-ignorance of the reasons behind it. In his soliloquies in act 3, scene 1, and act 4, scene 4, Hamlet shows himself more than half aware that he delays because of doubts created by a sensitive conscience—a conscience, we might note, that both drives him on to revenge, and which he would dismiss as a "craven scruple / Of thinking too precisely on th' event." Clearly, the dialectical possibilities of his ethical categories equivocate with each other: either to do the deed or not to do the deed involves his acquiescing in evil.

The matter of Hamlet's doubt about the ghost's honesty puts this point clearly. Hamlet's questioning whether "The spirit that I have seen / May be the devil" (2.2.627–628), like the question of his delay, admits of two interpretations. The first, entailing the apparently irresolvable squabbles regarding whether it is a Catholic or a Protestant ghost, assumes that the audience is to follow Hamlet's own procedure, with the expected answer distinguishing decisively between a soul from purgatory and a devil masking as such. The other interpretation is that the ethical categories underlying Hamlet's query are themselves the point of this action. Hamlet's desire to perform a totally pure act makes him desire also absolute certainty regarding the ghost's own credentials. The function of his test, and consequently of the mousetrap play, is to convey Hamlet's obsessive need to delay revenge until he can reach total assurance about that ethical purity. The fact that he does not kill Claudius after the play—waiting until he can find him ripe for Hell—suggests that the ghost does not really concern Hamlet at all. In meditating on his failure in act 4, scene 4, Hamlet continues to find conscience an obstacle, and he once again announces his puzzlement at a conscience that should drive him on to revenge and likewise holds him back.

As far as reasons for Hamlet's delay are concerned, Shakespeare insures our getting the message by inserting the lengthy and fully developed parallel of Laertes' pursuit of his own revenge. Shakespeare gives us in act 4, in other words, an alternative version of Hamlet's actions in acts 1 through 3. This version moves into parody, with Claudius taking the roles of the ghost and Horatio rolled into one. And in hurling about such terms as "conscience" and "both worlds," and daring damnation in the manner of the Player's Pyrrhus speech, Laertes presents his own version of Hamlet's "To be or not to be" soliloquy. In making the parallel so obtrusive, by far the most developed in the play, Shakespeare both answers the usual query about Hamlet's delay, and moves into the more significant question of the meaning of the delay within the play. To have swept to his revenge, as he vows to the ghost, would have been to end exactly like Laertes, in one way or another controlled by Claudius's corruption in the very act of putatively clearing the world of it. In watching Laertes act so directly, so manfully, and so brainlessly, the audience is intended to recall Hamlet's similar refusal of the craven scruples of conscience—except that Laertes acts and Hamlet does not.

The question the whole play raises through the instrumentality of Hamlet's actions (and even his inaction is extraordinarily vibrant and many faceted) is the same question Shakespeare raised in the second historical tetralogy, *Julius Caesar, Troilus and Cressida,* and a few years later, in *Measure for Measure.* The question is: Is it possible to act on the basis of a pure and dichotomistic ethical imperative against the evil of the world, and at the same time avoid becoming part of that evil? And the play answers, quite simply, No, it is not. When Hamlet announces that "the readiness is all" in act 5, scene 2, he has already become tainted with the evil he would eradicate, not only through his mother's marriage to Claudius, but also when he inadvertently kills Polonius. Here, he realizes that acting and suffering, planning and achievement, good and evil, are categories which, being all that we fallible human beings have to think within, are nevertheless inadequate for grasping the total logic of the "divinity that shapes our ends, / Rough-hew them how we will" (5.2.10–11). Hamlet is finally brought to act out the acceptances thrust upon men by the dialectic of their actions. Only when he becomes the "patient" of Claudius's actions—waiting in the lobby for him to come with Laertes and the rapiers—does he find himself in a position to complete his revenge. But he also knows something else: that he cannot escape the tangles of the logic that binds him to his victim, and his victim to himself. That the venom on the rapier poisons in succession Hamlet, Laertes, and Claudius the same instrument of death turned indifferently on victims and murderers alike—this external business of the play's spectacle carries out the consequence of this logic. For the beholder to have accepted the dialectic by which ethical imperatives and the corruption of ethical imperatives are potentially reciprocal functions of each other is for him to have accepted that which all the plays I have been discussing point toward. Yet none rest so securely in the eye of the storm as *Hamlet,* because only *Hamlet* acts out the tragic acceptance of the questions that dialectic raises as their own answer. The transcendence of dialectic becomes identical with willed immersion in it.

Transition IV

With this discussion of *Hamlet,* I conclude my progress through a purely formalist analysis of these works. The sequence of these essays moved from discourses that most overtly eschew dialectic through discourses that increasingly incorporate it. This progression, as I suggested in the introduction, has been in the form of a shifting proportion. In Bacon's treatises, the greatest resistance to dialectic was balanced by much eruption of unaccommodated contradiction and ambiguity. As I moved through the metaphysical lyric, *Paradise Lost,* and the plays immediately preceding and following *Hamlet,* this proportion gradually shifted. The greater the accommodation of dialectic in the surface of the discourse, the smaller the proportion of dialectic to erupt unintentionally into that surface.

From these discussions arise some constant characteristics of dialectical logic itself. For instance, there is always a dialectic between the surface of a discourse, and the underlying stratum of more or less unaccommodated pressures that this surface both implies and seeks to deny. Correlative to this has been another dialectic: that between the information intended by the author and conveyed through his whole discourse, and the actions and speeches of personae and agents within the discourse, which ironically both fulfill and yet oppose this intention. This discovery leads to still another one. The overriding, all-encompassing "meaning" of the work—what will be called in Essay Five its dianoia— is announced within the work through actions and speeches that, in their nondialectical partiality and univocalness, implicitly oppose this meaning. Finally, the dialectical logic in all these works suggests that enmity and conflict on the one hand, and harmony and resolution on the other are terms that are part of a single continuum of cause and effect. We have seen agents divided against their friends and themselves, and we have seen enemies cooperating with one another in the midst of their conflict. Conflict and resolution, therefore, were seen to imply and even cause each other. In the final essay, I shall extend these remarks in order to explore how the dialectics that each work embodies yield an abstract dialectical logic that all fulfill indifferently. And from this discussion, I shall explore how the dialectical logic that makes all these works at once similar and different allows us to move beyond the dialectic between historicism and formalism in the realm of literary method.

ESSAY five

Dialectical Criticism and Beyond

*"A philosophy for poetry cannot be a rationale of mean-
ing, but, in the end, a myth for the experience of it."* [1]

THE DIALECTIC OF MYTHOS AND DIANOIA

Dialectic occurs, whether within literature or out of it, when
men attempt to put an either-or question to a both-and reality.
The ultimate source of the question is the radical structure of
human thinking insofar as it is governed by the principle of non-

---

[1] R. P. Blackmur, "W. B. Yeats: Between Myth and Philosophy," *Form and
Value in Modern Poetry* (Garden City, N.Y.: Doubleday Anchor Books, n.d.),
p. 61. Essay Five explores methodological territory wherein dwell categories,
terms, and assertions that may appear to some readers barbarous and uncouth.
These are creatures of disciplines lying outside the usual boundaries of literary
studies, *terra incognita* for most literary scholars. My voyages thither have not
been made for captious or eccentric reasons. On the contrary, I have exercised a
prerogative usually honored more in the breach than the observance by literary
critics through the history of criticism from the Greeks down to the present: the
right to borrow, plunder, or steal from extra-literary disciplines whatever capital
is necessary to carry out the critical enterprise. Many believe that the disciplines
making up the study of literature are more autonomous than they really are. On the
contrary, the history of literary criticism from Aristotle and Plato to Wellek and
Warren and Northrop Frye, shows that literary study is peculiarly and consistently
parasitic on other disciplines. Whether from metaphysics and ethics in classical
times, from logic and rhetoric in the middle ages and the Renaissance, from the
sciences and empirical psychology in the eighteenth and nineteenth centuries, or
from political theory, anthropology, psychology, sociology and historiography in
the twentieth century, literary studies have always needed to borrow the lexicons
and grammars of other studies in order to articulate themselves. In this regard, I
invite the reader to explore with me the exigencies and excitement alike bound up
in dealing with familiar literature according to models not usually associated with
it. I have, in short, borrowed heavily from other disciplines the tools I needed to
work with, because I did not find them in my own.

contradiction. Enforced with rigid and tyrannical urgency, this principle continually generates antinomies when it comes face-to-face with a world characterized by diversity and change. When two opponents attempt to resolve an agreed-upon both-and question according to demands for an either-or answer, they absolutize that part of the question that can be resolved according to non-contradiction. Each thereby invites his opponent to attack him under the sign of those elements in the total question which he has excluded. I will attempt in this essay to show, among other things, how the authors I have discussed built into their plots principles and motivations that have as their goal just the kind of absolutizing that causes dialectic. What follows is a kind of abstract schema that applies, with some qualifications, to all of these works.

An agent attempts to bring order out of his world by imposing on it a demand for a total harmony among its competing parts. In doing so he ignores or forcibly denies certain pressures in this world, creating a resolution that is only partial. This partiality in turn generates the opposition of other agents (or principles or realities), which become vessels of those aspects of the total world that the agent had denied or ignored. "World" here means a more-or-less arbitrarily bounded universe of diverse competing parts, and applies indifferently to the limits of concern characterizing a philosophical treatise, a lyric poem, an epic, or a drama.

All of the works discussed in Essays One through Four exhibit such attempts at total harmony and the conflicts resulting from these attempts. Bacon's new science is exemplary, because in one sense its parts are nothing less than the total aggregate of material bodies that make up the universe. The tension between unifying system and diverse natural phenomena parallels that between abstract conceptualization and empirical intuition. Since the new science required the fluid metamorphosis of empirical data into abstract laws, and of intuition into abstraction, Bacon's attempts to eliminate these tensions without violating the terms themselves led to an irreducible dialectic between them. As I suggested in Essay One, separation of antinomical terms, and also the marriage between them, became at once necessary and impossible.

The agent's demand for a (partial) resolution of conflicts usually aims at a static "plotlessness," a state based upon some nonconflictual, nondialectical model. This model implies a dichotomistic set of categories for aligning and distinguishing pros and cons, "good," "desirable," "necessary" actions, attitudes, and values, and "evil," "undesirable," "expendable" actions, attitudes, and values. And according to such dichotomies the agent attempts to set up the first category as the ground of resolution, at the expense of those parts of his world that fall under the second category, but yet are dialectically implied by the first.

Certainly the new science envisions just such a nonconflictual, nondialectical plotlessness. But similar models function, although ironically, in the other works I have discussed. Donne's personae, for instance, envision a verbal discourse wherein the competing parts of various antinomies could be finally harmonized in univocally, logically linked propositions. Like Bacon, these personae strive for a verbal universe totally parallel to and reflecting completely—within the syntax available to verbal language—the extralinguistic world of bodies and souls, stasis and change, faith and reason. But no matter which poles of these antinomic terms a persona begins with, he finds it necessary to confront their opposites, and, more importantly, the contradictions between them. Paradox becomes a standard device, not only for Donne, but for other seventeenth-century poets, because it is the only verbal structure capable of holding in (albeit unstable) solution the demands of noncontradiction in the worlds of human thought and language, and the contradictory demands of extraconceptual antinomies.

The confrontation between an agent who attempts to force his partial resolution, and the competing parts the agent has ignored, is the mythos of a given work. "Mythos," for present purposes, refers to the dynamic, sequential development of conflict, such as I have found in all the works already discussed. The development of a work's mythos is determined by the logical interrelations between the various antagonists, insofar as they are motivated by a reading of the total situation governed by noncontradiction.

The logic of the mythos requires that antagonists agree on some commonly shared issue, which is itself reducible to some unresolvable antinomy between mutually implicative terms. (The antagonists will agree on the pressing importance of the antinomy, the logical interrelations of its terms, the reduction of possibilities to only these two terms, and the insistence that the antinomy must be solved for one term to the exclusion of the other. The meaning or "dianoia" of the mythos is a summary statement of why and how the dialectical logic implicit in the antinomy determines the sequence of events in the mythos. Finally, we can say that the antagonists come into conflict precisely because they refuse to accommodate conflict; that is, they involve themselves in dialectic because they implicitly refuse dialectic.)

Each work considered takes for granted the importance and centrality of its grounding terms. Bacon's assumption that epistemological questions were reducible to the conflict between intuition and abstraction is one example. The metaphysical poets' taking for granted a host of traditional antinomies—body-soul, stasis-change, faith-reason, free will-divine determinism, timeless innocence-historical fallenness, and so on,—is another example. The same can be said of *Paradise Lost*. Perhaps the most fully developed agreement on an antinomical formula can be found in the eight plays of Shakespeare. I showed how the dialectic between right and power, with its satellite offspring, that between high ideals and low actions, informs each one in various ways. As the history of political thought shows, it is not necessary that we reduce human actions to these categories. But if one chooses to do so, as did Shakespeare in one way, and Richard II, Falstaff, Angelo, and Hamlet in another, then agreement upon the antinomical structure of this issue will inevitably lead to dialectical conflict. And if, further, antagonists such as Richard and Bolingbroke, or Hector and Achilles, or Angelo and Isabella insist on a resolution shirking one term in favor of its opposite, this impulse to partial resolution likewise makes dialectic inevitable.

I am indebted for the terms mythos and dianoia to Northrop Frye:

> The word narrative or *mythos* conveys the sense of movement caught by the ear, and the word meaning or *dianoia* conveys, or at least preserves, the sense of simultaneity

caught by the eye. We *listen to* the poem as it moves from beginning to end, but as soon as the whole of it is in our minds at once we "see" what it means. More exactly, this response is not simply to *the* whole *of* it, but to *a* whole *in* it: we have a vision of meaning or *dianoia* whenever any simultaneous apprehension is possible.

The *mythos* is the *dianoia* in movement; the *dianoia* is the *mythos* in stasis. One reason we tend to think of literary symbolism solely in terms of meaning is that we have ordinarily no word for the *moving* body of imagery in a work of literature.[2]

These terms do not correspond to the usual meanings of "plot" and "theme," though they share something with them. "Plot" usually means a sequence of actions governed by an intelligible relation between cause and effect. Here, I use "mythos" for the sum total of the parts of a discourse, its total sequence of words, which would include imagery, diction, gesture, thought, psychological motivation, description, and rhythm.[3] Mythos thus means the essential nature of verbal discourse—a sequence of words—rather than one part of that sequence, the causal connection between the particular external or internal actions of an agent, that is, "plot." The mythos is not what an agent does in a discourse; it is the discourse itself.

Dianoia, following Frye's description, is all the significant cooperating and competing terms of the mythos seen at once according to their mutual implication. A syllogism would embody most obviously this interrelation. The mythos of a syllogism would be the sequence of its terms and propositions, and its dia-

---

2 Northrop Frye, *Anatomy of Criticism* (Princeton: Princeton Univ. Press, 1957), pp. 77–78, 83.

3 I have already discussed in more detail the implications of this distinction in *Mythos and Dianoia: A Dialectical Methodology of Literary Form*, in *Literary Monographs 4*, ed. Eric Rothstein (Madison, Milwaukee, and London: Univ. of Wisconsin Press, 1971), pp. 3–88. This discussion proceeds on more formal, philosophic grounds than does the present one, and is concerned only with the dialectic of mythos and dianoia. Though this present set of essays is essentially an expansion of the earlier one, I deal there with two works I do not discuss here, Jonson's *Volpone* and Shakespeare's *Macbeth*.

noia would be the essential over-arching principles determining
that sequence. However, more must be admitted to make this distinction practically applicable to literary works. The dianoia of a
work is coterminous with its mythos in two different and even
opposite ways. On the one hand, the dianoia sums up the mythos
in stating the logical relations of resolution and opposition that
govern the movement of the mythos. But on the other hand, the
dianoia is opposed to the mythos in the sense that dianoia refers
to the work as an "action-made," and mythos refers to it as an
"action-done."

"Action-made" is the work viewed from the standpoint of the
author's dispositions of his materials, whereas "action-done" is
the work seen as the sequence of actions within it, "authored,"
as it were, by the agent himself. The agent is in implicit opposition to the dialectical logic governing his actions, inasmuch as that
logic affirms a both-and reality in his world, while the agent
chooses to act on an either-or reading of it. Such a distinction
facilitates a further one, namely that between the intentions of the
work as a whole, and the intentions of agents within the work.
Clearly, this distinction implies an ironic distance between what
the author understands about his work and seeks to communicate
to his audience, and what the agent himself understands about his
own actions.

These distinctions are implicit in the previous analyses. The
shifting proportion from Bacon's philosophical prose, on which
dialectic lays the heaviest unaccommodated pressure, to Shakespeare's dramas, where dialectic is most overtly accommodated,
assumes the distinctions between mythos and dianoia, and between the work as action-made and as action-done. There is no
problem in the notion that an author controls and disposes the
sequence of episodes of his own work, and that, consequently, he
has a view of the field of action (which is the work's mythos)
broader than that of any of his characters. This fact is so obvious
that we tend to take it for granted. Clearly, what the action-made
says is what the author says, and is therefore not coterminous
with what one of his characters says in the action-done. In all of
the works I have discussed, it has become apparent that the dialectical logic underpinning their various actions, their mythoi, is

not part of the field of consciousness of any character within those mythoi. The distinction between Donne, Herbert, or Marvell, and their personae, between Milton and Eve, Adam, Satan, as well as between Shakespeare and Richard or Troilus, parallels that between their works' dianoia and their mythos. Dianoia is the total information conveyed by the work as a whole to the beholder, information that elucidates the underlying (dialectical) logic governing and giving intelligibility to the work. The mythos, on the other hand, the action-done by a fictional agent, is a sequence of partial, biased, incomplete actions and speeches that cooperate unconsciously and ironically with the author in announcing that dianoia. As someone once noted, characters in an allegory do not know that they are in an allegory; the same could be said of all fictive agents. For this reason, I have said that a fictive agent's either-or reading of his situation implicitly opposes the author's both-and reading of it. And just exactly how the first becomes a vehicle for announcing the second is the same as asking how a work's mythos becomes a vehicle for announcing its dianoia.

In this last statement I do not want to be understood as making any statement about the writer's intention as it is usually dealt with in discussions of the "intentional fallacy." I mean here only that if a work exhibits a coherent and intelligible dialectical pattern, the author must have as surely "understood" something about dialectic (whether he knew the word or not), as an author who writes in rhyme knows something about similar sounds. In both cases we can infer something about intention after the fact. As my discussion proceeds I emphasize the dianoia of the work as carrying the intended meaning, even in cases like Bacon's where there is every indication that he did not consciously intend such a meaning. Within this perspective, it is the work itself, the mythos, that intends its dialectical dianoia; and one must search farther in the work to determine evidence as to whether the dianoia which the mythos intends is identical to what the author intended.[4]

4 Cf. Quentin Skinner, "Motives, Intentions and the Interpretation of Texts," *NLH* 3 (1972): 393–408. The classic essay on this matter is W. K. Wimsatt, Jr. and Monroe C. Beardsley, "The Intentional Fallacy," in W. K. Wimsatt, Jr., *The Verbal Icon: Studies in the Meaning of Poetry* (New York: The Noonday Press, 1960), pp. 3–18.

A consequence of these distinctions is therefore that the dianoia of the work will state "ironically" the dialectical logic that comes to control a mythos precisely because the agent within it has chosen implicitly to deny it. We might say that the purpose of the action-made, that is, the meaning of the work as intended by the dianoia (and perhaps) by the author, is to exhibit through the conflicts in the action-done exactly how and why these conflicts come about. That is, the dianoia states the full dialectical logic in the both-and relations among the competing parts of the mythos, which parts compete with one another because the agent of the mythos has insisted on acting within an either-or reading of these relations.

Before going on, however, I would like to obviate one possible misunderstanding about my use of the term *sequence* in discussing the dialectical dynamism of a plot. The ordinary way of proceeding in reading a lyric or a narrative or watching a play is to begin at the beginning and end at the end, moving between these two points in simple sequential order in time and syntax. But in reading a poem or beholding a play according to the ordinary sequence, the reader finds that not only does what comes first illuminate what comes after, but also vice versa, what comes last illuminates everything that came before. I would argue that there is no one natural way of reading a poem or a narrative: there is only the fact that, by reason of the sequential one way street nature of verbal discourse, we must first proceed through one sequence before we proceed through any other. But that "first" is prior only in an instrumental, pragmatic sense, and not in any evaluative or logical sense. Certainly, the first sequence does itself carry some of the meaning of the work: the fact that in this sequence *this* causes *that* to happen later is obviously important for the meaning; but it is only one of the parts of the total mythos of the work, and not that mythos itself. Therefore I do not intend the notion of dialectical generation of part out of part to be taken to refer only to a before-after sequence. Part generates part, not simply *vis-à-vis* each other, but rather as all parts confront in their partiality the whole; and they stand in relation to one another only after they stand in this primary one.[5]

[5] Cf. Wolfgang Iser, "The Reading Process: A Phenomenological Approach," *NLH* 3 (1972): 279–299 on the interrelation between the process of reading and

All of this discussion has been leading up to a summary statement of the principles of dialectical logic itself, a kind of schema for all conflicts in a mythos. The three-part schema that follows establishes essential relations that are almost never, save in some fully articulated philosophies, found concretely in their purity. The movement from the first to the second proposition, and from both to the third is not that of formal syllogistic implication. They could be stated in any order, because they are all three distinguishable "moments" of the same dynamic process:

> 1. A resolution of antinomies is always partial, thereby containing implicitly the potentiality for conflict.
> 2. A conflict of antinomies presupposes a ground common to both, and thereby contains the potentiality for resolution.
> 3. Both resolution and conflict, since they contain the elements of both in potentially reciprocal relationship (propositions 1 and 2 taken together), are themselves related as mutual cause and effect.

These three statements are not "moments" in the sense that they can always be found at three separate points in the sequence of a mythos, although that is sometimes the case. Rather, each statement, taken one at a time, is inadequate without the other two for rendering the total dialectic in a mythos, because the pressures of all three moments occur at all points in the mythos. They are moments, as it were, in the reader's process of assimilating the total action of a mythos to its dianoia. Ideally, the centripetal relations of all a dianoia's terms would be grasped in a single intuitive glance of the mind. The three propositions as I have stated them here are really attempts to look at the same logic from three viewpoints that distinguish, step-by-step, the logical interrelations between conflict and resolution implicit in any part of a mythos: the inception of conflict, its progress, as well as its resolution.

The schema employs the most all-inclusive elements of a dialectical action. The agent's drive toward partial resolution re-

---

the discursive sequence of the work itself. Also, Stanley Fish, "Literature in the Reader: Affective Stylistics," *NLH* 2 (1970): 123–162.

sults in conflict to the extent that he attempts to split a both-and situation into antinomical options under the pressure of non-contradiction. This conflict likewise generates (partial) resolution, insofar as opponents agree on the antinomy itself as the common ground of their quarrel, as well as agreeing further that resolution (that is, victory) is the goal both are fighting toward. The resolution is always only partial, because of the obvious fact that in victory only one side can win. In short, (the terms of the antinomy which control the logic of the conflict likewise provide the terms of the final resolution.)

The first moment names situations in which harmony reigns, but at the expense of only partially encompassing the total claims of the situation putatively resolved. Thus all peace potentially contains war. By the same token, all war potentially contains peace, because the opponents are already "at-oned" in their agreement on the mutually exclusive (because antinomic) options available for resolution: the second moment. (Pseudo conflicts occur when the opponents assume different grounds of contention, and if they fight at all it can be only over which grounds will be accepted by both.) The third moment sums up the reciprocal causality between resolution and conflict named in the first two moments. This moment is the paradigm for the dianoia of any plot, because it states the abstract model for relating terms of resolution and conflict that the mythos exhibits in competition with each other.

This three-moment schema can be found imbedded in all the works considered. I have not introduced it until this late stage for the reason stated in the introduction: I wanted to let the works speak their specific dialectical structures with a minimum of dialectical terminology, in order to let the necessity of this schema announce itself fluidly out of the discussion.

The first moment occurs at those points in Bacon's treatises where he attempts to define the "marriages" most central to the new science: between intuition and abstraction, and between empirical data and abstract laws. The potential for conflict is built into Bacon's own working definitions of these four terms, definitions which overtly deny, and therefore require, a *rapprochement* among them. The second moment appears in Bacon's struggles to achieve this *rapprochement,* wherein appears nothing so much as their incompatability. This incompatibility, however, announces the common ground that the various opposing terms share. The intuition-abstraction antinomy represents, for Bacon at least, two extremes of a single continuum, namely, the whole human person, made up of both senses and intellect. For him, both sensible intuition and immaterial abstraction are *données,* the essential instruments wholly conditioning man's knowing anything at all. And the ground common to the data-system antinomy is founded on this one. In searching for the fewest and most general laws that control the vast body of discrete entities that make up the natural world, Bacon was likewise committed to making compatible the two realms of being in which these two existed: the time-space continuum, and the "spaceless," "timeless" realm of thought. Having assumed that these two antinomies circumscribed the logical and physical "spaces" wherein the new science was to dwell, Bacon attempted to conceive these two spaces as one and the same, continuous and unbroken, a single "space," at any rate, where intuition and abstraction, and data and system could, or ought to, join together. Consequently, his treatises continually exhort this marriage. The third moment occurs at those points, discussed in Essay One, where we discover that fusion and separation of these antinomical terms are reciprocal functions of each other. Bacon's statements on the marriage of empirical and rational faculties, the doctrine of forms, the doctrine of the idols, and on the Eden myth are the most important. Here, the dialectical causality mutually implicating these terms in rigid polarization becomes most obvious to the reader. One might say that Bacon never manifests so openly the enslavement of his key terms to dialectical logic as at those places where he spends the greatest energy and eloquence in trying to extricate these terms from this enslavement.

In metaphysical poetry, the three-moment schema occurs similarly. In this case, however, the poets seem to have "intended" dialectical logic in ways that Bacon did not. The first moment occurs in the attempts of various personae, as they embark on their lyric discourses, to resolve the respective antinomies with which they are concerned. For brevity's sake, I shall cite only

Marvell. The personae in "The Garden" and "Upon Appleton House" begin their poems by attempting a withdrawal from one side of various antinomies into the realms implied by the opposite side. History, the flesh, fallenness, and human endeavor are rejected in favor of a timeless spiritual purity, primitive and contemplative. As this withdrawal proceeds, however, the personae find it necessary to take account of what they have putatively left behind: attempted partial resolution generates renewed acknowledgement of conflict and opposition. This is the second moment of dialectical logic. The third moment appears at those points where, in the personae's metaphorical and allusive conjurings, these opposites flow together; and both personae and reader realize that the impulses to resolution of the first moment, and the divisive ones of the second imply each other. Taken together, and only in this way, Marvell manages to achieve adequate naming of the mixed nature of human existence. [The grounds of this dialectic are, in general, the same for Marvell as for Bacon, as well as for Donne and Herbert: the fact that man indisputably lives simultaneously in two worlds. Man's fusing flesh and spirit, and consequently his potentiality for both sin and salvation, as well as his inability to create modes of contemplation that escape action in fallen history—these givens of the human condition create the reciprocity of conflict and resolution.]

[Something of this last statement applies to *Paradise Lost* as well. As I showed in Essay Three, Milton finds human history guided by a Providential Dialectician, whose eternal plan contains as part of its "determinism" a clause insuring human freedom. The dialectical interaction of external law and inner nature, obedience and rule, falling and rising, plus all the satellite antinomies attendant on these, manifest the third moment of dialectical logic in *Paradise Lost*. This third moment is likewise announced in the poem's language. Here, the potentialities for both "fallen" and "resurrected" meanings announce in truly epic puns of universal reference the reciprocity that binds together man's fall and man's salvation. The first two moments occur at those points in the poem where Satan, Adam, and Eve attempt to break down this reciprocity, and to reorient their own natures, their relations among

themselves, God, and the universe according to a limited, nondialectical harmony centering on themselves. They would affirm
their own natures against God's law, rule divorced from obedience, and rise to spurious godhood without the fall attending it,
thereby bringing back on themselves the second moment of dialectical logic. And yet this second moment, the point where they
are most at enmity with God and themselves, contains likewise
the grounds of future harmony. As I showed in Essay Three, the
various ways in which these creatures mirror God become the
grounds both of their possible divorce from Him, and of their
possible reconciliation. If the essence of dialectical logic is, from
one viewpoint, constraint, rigid continuity between cause and effect, it is from another the ground of individual freedom. That
Satan, Adam, and Eve are creatures of God and consequently
mirror Him offers them the possibility of making that mirroring
either benign or malign. For this reason, the third moment of
dialectical logic, by which likeness and difference, enmity and harmony are reciprocal, comes in two forms in *Paradise Lost:* the
malign reciprocity with God chosen by Satan, and the benign
reciprocity chosen by Eve and Adam.

In Shakespeare's plays, the first moment lies in the attempts
to resolve right into power and, conversely, to cover base actions
with high rhetoric. This brings about conflicts within and among
the antagonists, wherein right and power entangle themselves in
mutual opposition and mutual corruption. The second moment announces further that such opposition and corruption only become
possible because both the playwright and his characters assume
that the imperatives of right and the necessities of power must
somehow dwell together in the arena of human action. Even though
right and power may pull in opposite directions (and even because of this), the major characters in these eight plays move
actions that aim at some coalescence and harmony between them.
As I showed in Essay Four, the second moment apparently became increasingly problematical for Shakespeare, something one
sees particularly in moving from the second historical tetralogy to
Julius Caesar and the plays following. What grounds are there,
ultimately, for allaying the strife between the motives of right
and the evil actions these may cause? As *Hamlet* shows, Shake-

speare seems to have concluded that the potentialities for conflict and resolution so reciprocally embrace each other in human endeavors that the third moment, interpreted as a tragic, dynamic, and irresolvable riddle, announces that neither Hamlet, nor Shakespeare, nor we his audience can do more than affirm that third moment itself as ultimate: "The rest is silence."

It would seem, therefore, that the third moment of dialectic is the schema for a work's dianoia. The dianoia is the total information delivered to reader or audience which, when reduced to propositional, thematic form, states the dialectical logic that causes, controls, and carries out the actions of the work's mythos. We behold in the mythos the agents' attempts to impose some sort of resolution, some sort of nonconflictual model on the world around them: the first moment. We behold the conflicts and reachievements of partial resolutions that this attempt generates: the second moment. But when we grasp the interrelation between attempted denial of conflict and resultant conflict, between the ideal of a nondialectical world and the dialectic that attends the attempt to enforce that ideal, we grasp the work's total meaning, its dianoia. And this dianoia states the intelligible, mutual causality governing both conflict and harmony, the third moment of dialectic.

THE OBJECTIVE, EXPRESSIVE, AND DOCUMENTARY DIMENSIONS OF THE LITERARY WORK

The difficulties raised by the split between historicist and formalist criticism which I discussed briefly in the introduction derived from the dual status of past literary works as at once past and present to the modern reader. A schema has been lacking for rationalizing the relations between these two dimensions, as well as a critical approach that can take both dimensions into account and see them as functions of each other. Without such a unifying schema, the work will necessarily remain an unresolved duality, approachable in some ways as a product of its culture and interpretable only in its terms; and approachable in other ways as an autonomously structured producer of its culture, interpretable only in terms of its internal, formal structure.

This difficulty can be illustrated briefly even in such usual, practical matters as source study. One of the reasons for discovering a work's sources in previously constructed plots, conventions of genre and character, philosophical ideas, and so on, is to distinguish an author's indebtedness for such material from his originality in what he does with it. Usually, the author's additions and changes are cited as evidence of his originality, and the matter can only be allowed to rest at that, whereas it is exactly at this point that the difficulty arises. Are these additions and changes themselves wholly cut off from external, culturally conditioned categories? From such an analysis this would have to be the conclusion. The hunt for sources presupposes that the literary work is a sunderable combination of traditional elements and original genius. It assumes that once the former is discovered, the latter will stand out as the surd left over, so to speak. Consequently, historicism and formalism agree that by dividing the work this way they can arrive, together, at an explanation of the total work. But in fact an "explanation of the total work" in this fashion is exactly what is impossible, because there would be no "total work" left to explain. On the contrary, source study reproduces the split between historicist and formalist analysis in the work itself. What is left, on the one hand, is only so much of the work as can be abstracted and assimilated back into still other works. The remainder is then credited to the "original genius" of the author, who then by definition becomes ahistorical, without contact with or dwelling in the context of tradition he has putatively assimilated and made new. In reflecting this gulf between historicist and formalistic approaches, the literary work can be explained neither in its indebtedness to tradition (the work as product of its culture), nor in its uniqueness (as a producer of its culture), because the work is fragmented and in a sense disappears from view. Without the capability of showing how tradition and originality are dialectical functions of each other, both approaches end up illuminating nothing at all. In short, the work as a copenetration of tradition and originality makes itself available to understanding only to the degree that a liaison between historicist and formalist approaches becomes possible.

Dialectic makes such a schema available because it specifically interrelates the basic terms of these splits—resolution and conflict, whole and part—so as to exhibit the terms of these antinomies as functions of each other. I shall show in this section that three different but coterminous dimensions of the literary work itself must be distinguished, each constituted as a dialectical antinomy. These three dimensions derive from an essay by Karl Mannheim entitled "On the Interpretation of *Weltanschauung*" (1921–1922), where he asks the same question: How is it possible to move from a document's overtly intended meaning considered in itself, to its relation to cultural context? Mannheim distinguishes three dimensions of meaning the document may have for the cultural historian: the objective, the expressive, and the documentary. The objective is its intelligible meaning considered according to its own short-term purposes, the meaning the reader may grasp who possesses already a knowledge of its language and enough information to interpret what it says.[6] Within literary studies, formalist criticism is primarily concerned with this meaning, as are glosses on diction and topical references, and to some extent analytical bibliography. The expressive meaning corresponds to intention or motive. Mannheim treats this dimension as the "emotional element," and seems to mean by it something roughly analogous to "significance." Thus a legal document may say such-and-such, its objective meaning, but its significance is its actually intended effect within a limited context of specific laws, legal controversy, and so on.[7] I modify Mannheim's own definition, keeping nevertheless the notion of the literary work as expressing something about itself that goes beyond communication of content. The third meaning is the documentary, which Mannheim explains in part this way:

> The incorporation and projection of both "objective" and "expressive" meaning is a matter of conscious effort for the artist. By contrast, the third dimension of meaning— documentary meaning—is not an intentional object for him. It can become an intentional object only for the

[6] Karl Mannheim, "On the Interpretation of *Weltanschauung*," in *Essays on the Sociology of Knowledge,* ed. Paul Kecskemeti (London: Routledge & Kegan Paul, 1952), p. 45.
[7] *Ibid.,* pp. 46, 49.

recipient, the spectator. From the point of view of the artist's activity, it is a wholly unintentional, unconscious by-product.[8]

About the documentary dimension, Mannheim says further that "the totality we call the 'genius' or 'spirit' (of an epoch) is given to us in this mode of 'documentary' meaning; this is the perspective in which we grasp the elements that go to make up the global outlook of a creative individual or of an epoch." [9]

The notion of "unconscious" meaning needs to be specified. Clearly, Mannheim is not referring to psychoanalytic categories for distinguishing subliminal forces and information buried in the individual psyche, though this might be part of "unconscious intention" in a specific instance. Rather, the term refers to the necessary "partiality" of any presupposition which the culture itself assumes to be "absolute." One of Mannheim's followers, Werner Stark, makes this point clearer:

> . . . What concrete men see of the world and in the world, and how they see what they do see, depends . . . on a socio-historical principle of specification, of crystal- lization, of ordered selection and co-ordinating construc- tion, and that principle is inherent in the axiological or value-structure prevailing at the time. The world of the absolute cannot be grasped by us humans. How can the finite mind hope to lay hold on the infinite? By our whole constitution we are forced to live in a universe of re- stricted awareness. Our world-view will always be relative, however "natural" we who live within it may feel it to be.[10]

The "unconsciousness" that characterizes the documentary di- mension of a verbal artifact lies in the fact that it, as well as the culture of which it is a part, takes its own schemas for "con- structing" the world for granted, as if they were natural or eternal or absolute. Similarly, each verbal artifact exists "in a universe of restricted awareness," the universe of its own con-

[8] *Ibid.*, p. 55.   [9] *Ibid.*, p. 48.

[10] Werner Stark, *The Sociology of Knowledge: An Essay in Aid of a Deeper Understanding of the History of Ideas* (London: Routledge & Kegan Paul, 1958), pp. 118–119.

cerns and discourse. To this extent, no single work can take account of and exhaust deliberately and consciously the total categories, conflicts, and values that make up the whole culture of
which it is a part. This is what Mannheim means when he says
that the work's documentary dimension is "wholly unintentional,"
an "unconscious by-product": namely, that no work or its writer
can be wholly aware of how his work participates in the total
"socio-historical principle of specification" that grounds his whole
culture. This participation can be grasped only by a spectator
who stands outside that culture.

In one sense these three dimensions are abstractions from individual texts, but in another they are not. Taken collectively,
these dimensions uncover the radical dialectic that regulates and
informs every stage of a work's phenomenal, discursive progress.
They make clear and formalize perceptions of the basic conditions that make possible not simply a discourse's communicating
this or that specific content, but rather the discourse's communicating anything at all. This means that the moment one begins to
understand a discourse that assumes some kind of antinomical
categories, one has already implicitly contacted that discourse's
objective, expressive, and documentary dimensions.

The Objective Dimension

We encounter first the phenomena of the discourse itself. At
this point we are concerned only with intelligibility and understanding in their ordinary senses. We may proceed through *The
Advancement of Learning,* or *Paradise Lost,* or *Richard II,* asking such usual questions as: Why and how does a particular statement relate to what went before and will come after? What is the
cause of Satan's fall? How am I to understand Richard's peculiar
tendency to dethrone himself? Here we move along with the syntactical, logical, or dramatic sequence of the discourse, fitting the
pieces together as we go. We intentionally and provisionally identify with the agents of the discourse, or its personae or terms, and
to that degree we do not (yet) take any ironic perspective on
these. Once having perceived what Frye calls the whole *in* the
discourse, we likewise become aware that this whole is made up
of "cooperations" among its "competing" parts. We understand

that the enmity between Henry IV and the Percies, Hamlet and Claudius, between body and soul in Donne's poetry, or intuition and abstraction in Bacon's treatises is not random. The terms of these contests were chosen together, because each one of these mutually implies its opposite. Further, we discover that these contests come about because the fictive agents carried them out in implicit opposition to the dialectical logic that controls them. We see that antagonists (whether agents or concepts) within the action-done of their discourses "cooperate" despite themselves both with each other and "with" the author in announcing the author's intended statement, the dianoia of the action-made. At this point one has discovered the work's objective dimension, that is, the fact that the work's mythos is dialectically related to its dianoia. The accompanying diagrams use Donne's "Loves Infinitenesse" and the dialectic between love-as-unchanging and love-as-changing that informs that poem, as an example:

```
┌─────────────────────────────────────────┐
│                                         │
│         Objective Dimension:            │
│         Mythos-Dianoia dialectic        │
│                                         │
│    ┌────────────────────────────┐       │
│    │                            │       │
│    │   The phenomena of the     │       │
│    │   literary work, e.g.,     │       │
│    │   "Loves Infinitenesse"    │       │
│    │   Love-unchanging or       │       │
│    │       Love-changing        │       │
│    │                            │       │
│    └────────────────────────────┘       │
│                                         │
│   (A)  Love-unchanging or Love-changing/│
│   (B)  Love-unchanging and Love-changing│
│                                         │
└─────────────────────────────────────────┘
```

The objective dimension is composed of the dialectic between mythos and dianoia, between the work as action-done under the impulse to escape dialectic, and the work as action-made, which "intends" to communicate the logic controlling the dialectical action that this impulse creates. This dimension has been the main subject of Essays One to Four. In "Loves Infinitenesse" the speaker attempts to resolve the antinomy between love as a dynamic, growing attachment, and love as a constant, totally given and received. The speaker's attempt assumes the contradictory, mutually exclusive status of these two aspects of love, whereas the dianoia of the poem—what the speaker announces "unconsciously" about his attempt—illuminates the fact that both aspects of love are yet somehow one.

The Expressive Dimension

In discovering so much, we are prepared for discovering something about this mythos-dianoia dialectic itself. This is the fact—now isolated in its own right—that the dianoia appears through, by means of, the mythos in opposition to the phenomenal discourse that makes up this mythos. This is another way of putting a point made earlier: the agent's attempt to read his situation in an either-or manner implicitly opposes the both-and reading affirmed in the whole discourse by the author. The personae of the metaphysical lyric, Adam, Eve, and Satan in *Paralise Lost,* and such characters in Shakespeare as Richard, Bolingbroke, Falstaff, Angelo, and Troilus, all attempt to avoid the dialectical implications of the terms on which they choose to ground their speeches and actions, thereby generating in their actions-done dialectical comeuppances. The dianoia of the work announces itself through, and in opposition to, the phenomena of the mythos: this is the work's expressive dimension.

The dialectic in this dimension is between what is "phenomenal" in a literary text, and what is "announced" about that text through the phenomena, a distinction made by Martin Heidegger in *Being and Time.*

" *'Phenomenon'* signifies *that which shows itself in itself,* the manifest." [11] Heidegger distinguishes phenomenon from appearance while showing at the same time their intimate connection. The example he uses is the symptoms of a disease:

> The emergence of such occurrences [symptoms], their
> showing-themselves, goes together with the Being-present-
> at-hand of disturbances which do not show themselves.
> Thus appearance, as the appearance 'of something,' does

[11] Martin Heidegger, *Being and Time,* trans. John Macquarrie and Edward Robinson (New York and Evanston: Harper and Row, 1962), p. 51.

not mean showing-itself; it means rather the announcing-itself by [von] something which does not show itself, but which announces itself through something which does show itself. Appearing is a *not-showing-itself.* . . . In spite of the fact that 'appearing' is never a showing-itself in the sense of "phenomenon," appearing is possible only *by reason of a showing-itself* of something. But this show-ing-itself, which helps to make possible the appearing, is not the appearing itself. Appearing is an *announcing*-itself through something that shows itself.[12]

Heidegger's distinction states the essential way in which dia-lectical logic occurs within a mythos. This logic can only an-nounce its presence through the phenomena of the mythos, and can never appear "in itself." A conflict's full dialectical structure will not show itself overtly in the expressed statements of the agents, because the conflict's very existence presupposes that each partisan is partial. Each partisan is controlled by and his posi-tion contained within and made possible by the dialectical logic implicit in his conflict with his antagonist. This simply means that both sides ignore the partiality of their positions in order to ab-solutize them; that is, they remain unaware of the dialectic bind-ing them in opposition to each other. For this reason the reader cannot expect overt statements of the dialectical logic to appear phenomenally in the work itself. The only exception would be agents who have already worked their way through the dialectics of their mythoi so as finally to transcend them, and to be able to comment on them. Hamlet might fall within this category; with reservations, this would apply to the Miltonic narrator of *Para-dise Lost,* and the persona of "Upon Appleton House," and per-haps some of the lyrics of Herbert and Donne.

Therefore dialectical logic will always be announced through the whole mythos of a given discourse, and consequently can never appear as one of its parts. Further, this logic and its three moments can have no existence apart from the concrete linguistic and aesthetic structures that make up the discourse. The phenom-ena of any discourse does not hide dialectic beneath its surface;

12 *Ibid.,* pp. 52–53.

rather the phenomena depend radically on the presence of dialectic. And this presence can be disclosed only by following and allowing the intelligible structure of the discourse—what one sees and understands—to unfold itself untrammeled.

In the expressive dimension the work "expresses" something about its phenomena over and above, but also through, what the agents or personae in the discourse say themselves. This dimension does not comment directly on the work itself, but on the mythos-dianoia dialectic discoverable in the work's phenomenal surface. It takes over the whole objective dimension—the mythos-dianoia dialectic—and discovers what essential logic of dialectic is announced through this dimension:

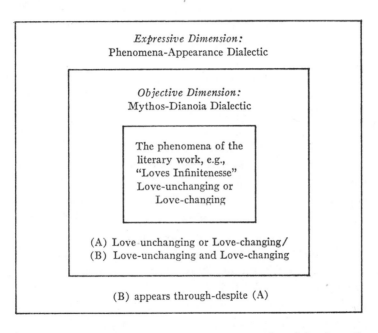

Expressive Dimension:
Phenomena-Appearance Dialectic

Objective Dimension:
Mythos-Dianoia Dialectic

The phenomena of the literary work, e.g., "Loves Infinitenesse" Love-unchanging or Love-changing

(A) Love unchanging or Love-changing/
(B) Love-unchanging and Love-changing

(B) appears through-despite (A)

The expressive dimension comments on the objective dimension in two ways. First, it uncovers the fact that a work's dianoia can only appear, be announced, "through" the phenomena of its mythos—that is, through the opposition of the mythos to the dianoia. Second, the expressive level takes over the total objective dimension—now become phenomenal to the critic's perception—and seeks to discover what in the objective dimension announces itself for analysis on the documentary level. As regards "Loves Infinitenesse," the expressive dimension of that work comments now, not on the concrete dialectic of love as at once changing and unchanging, but on the dialectical logic that governs the ways in which the "and" of the dianoia makes its appearance through the "or" of the persona's overt formulation of the antinomy. The expressive dimension also takes note, for instance, that the mysterious divine economy of salvation can only announce itself through the mythoi of Herbert's persona, which are overtly dedicated to resolving the paradoxes of this economy into clear verbal distinctions. It formalizes the fact that the total meaning of Shakespeare's second tetralogy—the dialectical entanglements of right and power—announces itself only through the phenomenal actions of characters who attempt to reduce this tangle in various partial, simplistic, and corrupting ways. It raises to the reader's consciousness the "mythic" fusions of antinomies implicit in Bacon's treatises, which only make their appearance through phenomenal discourse that attempts to keep the terms of these antinomies in separate compartments.

The Documentary Dimension

Finally, the documentary dimension uncovers information implicit in the expressive dimension, that is, in the dialectic between phenomena and appearance. This dimension has been implicit in the three-moment schema of dialectical logic discussed in the previous section, whereby resolution and conflict cause each other. These relations, considered "platonically," in abstraction from the dynamism of the mythoi they generate, are fixed and rigid. Though resolution and conflict may lead each other around in a potentially never-ending sequence, the cause of this sequence is the unchanging dialectical relation between resolution and conflict, which is itself "eternally" constant. Thus, in all the works discussed, I have pointed out how the specific antinomies informing each work are themselves fixed and absolute, to the extent all of these works treated their antinomies as by definition irresolvable. Abstraction and intuition, body and soul, human and divine will, creation-as-unity and creation-as-separation, and right and power: all of these antinomies spark their specific embodiments in a mythos of science, the metaphysical lyric, Milton's epic, and

Shakespeare's dramas precisely because all of these works are grounded on the assumption that, by definition, each term excludes and yet implies the other. Looked at from this viewpoint, these works are constituted dialectically as a result of being regulated dialectically. But this causal relation is also reversible: these works come to be regulated dialectically *because* they are constituted dialectically. That is, dialectic comes to regulate each work precisely because, as action-done, each work rejects such regulation.

The two different ways one can read this dialectic parallels the two different ways of viewing the work as both action-done and action-made. If we look at the action-done from the viewpoint of action-made, we can say that the work is constituted dialectically because the author intended it as such. In this respect, the author, overtly or implicitly, exploits the rigid causality relating the three moments of dialectical logic so as to construct discourses the coherence of which depends on these moments leading each other around with strictness and precision. However, if we look at the action-made from the viewpoint of the action-done, the constitution-regulation dialectic reverses along with the reversed perspective. Now it is apparent that the action-done becomes dialectical both because of and despite the agents' attempts to force an either-or resolution on the both-and conflicts of their world. In short, in attempting to escape dialectic, the agents become enslaved to dialectic. Consequently, the work comes to be regulated dialectically—that is, it announces its regulation by the dialectic of its dianoia—precisely by trying, as it were, not to be dialectical.

This then is the content of the expressive dimension which the documentary dimension takes over and formalizes: the dialectic between phenomena and appearance is likewise a dialectic between the phenomena as constituted dialectically and the phenomena as regulated dialectically. What "appears" through these phenomena is that dialectical constitution and regulation are themselves dialectically related.

The documentary dimension, in a sense, reunites what had been theoretically split in the objective and expressive dimension. The ineluctable fact is that the work as action-done and constituted dialectically, and the work as action-made and regulated dialectically are nevertheless the same work. The documentary

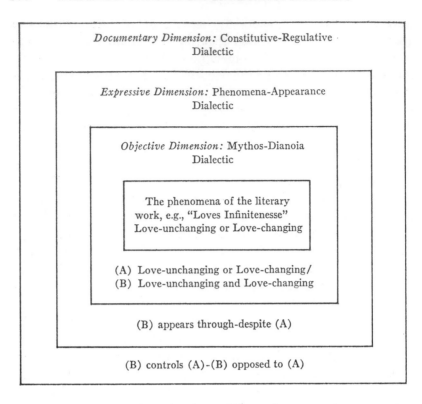

dimension sponsors this identity, while at the same time asserting the paradox of how the work makes its meaning. The work signals, or intends, a meaning that is the sum total of its parts. And yet these parts manage to speak this meaning through short-term, local actions and verbal behavior that are overtly directed to denying it. Like the characters in *Paradise Lost,* where agents in the discourse which is human history fulfill the providential plan even through actions that are overtly intended to thwart it, so in all the discourses I have considered: what the discourse says as a whole action-made—namely, how and why it is regulated dialectically—is by means of actions within the action-done that become constituted dialectically in the process of attempting to escape such regulation.

As I stated above, these three dimensions concern the conditions that allow discourses to communicate not just this or that content or issue to the reader, but anything at all. Another way of saying this is to point out that these three dimensions are implicit in the reader's understanding of and response even to the surface phenomena of Bacon's treatises, or the metaphysical lyric, or *Paradise Lost,* or Shakespeare's plays. And for this reason, I have said that these dimensions are not really abstractions from the works I have discussed. Rather, they are three stages the reader may go through in attempting to discover the radical categories and logic in terms of which these works are organized and intelligible.

One need not bring each dimension to consciousness; and for the most part, when we read anything involving antinomical categories for short-term purposes, we do not do this. The information delivered by these dimensions, once they are isolated specifically as dimensions *of* these works, is such, however, that were that information not latent in our understanding, understanding itself would be absent.

These dimensions essentially say the following:

"Once one begins to understand the conflicts in, say, *Hamlet,* or 'The Garden,' or the *Novum Organum,* one also begins to assemble a rudimentary understanding of dialectical logic in general. When one discovers that the personae in these works, as in the rest, are circumscribed by antinomies that they cannot resolve, one likewise discovers that these works as a whole 'say' something about these antinomies that goes beyond what these specific personae 'say' about them. At that point one already implicitly acquiesces in the mythos-dianoia dialectic, and the various ironic discrepancies between action-done and action-made. In so doing, one also (again implicitly) acquiesces in the appearance-phenomena dialectic, because this dialectic—the work's expressive dimension—is implicit in perceiving its objective dimension, the mythos-dianoia dialectic. And still further, by the same process, one acquiesces (whether conscious of it or not) in the work's documentary dimension. This dimension lays bare the dialectic between dialectical constitution and dialectical regulation that has already informed one's perception of the first two dimensions. That is, one assumes this dimension the moment one assumes the appearance-phenomena dialectic, which, in turn, one assumed when perceiving the work's mythos-dianoia dialectic. And finally: one assumed *this* dialectic the moment one began to grasp the logical necessity governing indifferently the struggles in Bacon's prose, in the metaphysical lyric, *Paradise Lost,* or Shakespeare's plays."

The ground of this assertion is simple: author, text, and reader in one way or another share a single condition—all take for granted the law of noncontradiction. As I have shown, the mind's demand that antinomical assymetries make sense to it according to identities and distinctions dictated by noncontradiction is the main cause of dialectic. The demand for noncontradiction means that antinomies must be resolved, and be resolved into either identities or distinctions, not into a third thing. But the mind's confrontation with antinomical realities seems to demand exactly that: that the mind acquiesce in their being structured in a both-and fashion. And since the mind can conceive anything and understand anything only in an either-or fashion, the confrontation between both-and realities and either-or categories generates dialectic. Consequently, once even the most superficial understanding of the logical underpinnings of any of the antinomies in these works is achieved, the three dialectical dimensions become implicit in that understanding.

To understand these works' objective meanings one need not take cognizance of the expressive and documentary dimensions implicit in them. However, these latter dimensions do allow one to discover the liaison that bridges the gulf between the objective meaning of each work and its cultural context. In the next section I shall explore a single principle that will illuminate at once both the unity among these works in Renaissance culture, and the avenues along which they diverge from and even stand in opposition to one another. The dialectic between dialectical regulation and constitution—disclosed in the documentary dimension of each work—will be developed as this principle. The documentary dimension of each work discloses both the radical dialectical logic that constitutes it, and the dialectical regulation it shares with every other work discussed here. It is this regulation that makes possible many diverse dialectical structures, while dictating the rigid logic that governs them. Insofar as these works share a common set of antinomical structures that Renaissance culture at large took for granted, each of them will be seen to realize various specific dialectics that, taken together in their uniqueness and diversity, cooperate in producing this culture. We shall see, in short, that the unity of the Renaissance lies in the shared categories within which Renaissance men disagreed.

THE DIALECTIC OF RENAISSANCE LITERATURE:
HISTORICISM AND FORMALISM REVISITED

A view of the works considered here, which takes account of their uniqueness as well as their linkages with one another and therefore with Renaissance culture at large, must first get past the dialectic between historicism and formalism that I broached in the introduction. As I pointed out there, these two approaches agree in sundering the literary work and literary study along various axes: external influence versus formal coherence as ways of explaining meaning; the literary work as irrevocably past versus the work as eternally present; the literary critic as totally conditioned by his culture versus the critic as dwelling in an ahistorical present. As I suggested there and will develop further, in agreeing to this division of labor, these two approaches can offer no way of explaining either a work's ties to its culture or its uniqueness and originality. The reason for this is that neither approach engages at all the specific phenomena that the other specializes in; consequently, a work's originality as well as its debt to tradition—which logically and historically are functions of each other—disintegrate into diverse atomistic parts with no connection. Obviously, the ancillary relation of criticism to literature has been reversed, and methodological splits now determine the fissures along which the work itself may allegedly be analyzed. Historicism cannot explain a work's structure of meaning, because it dissolves the work back into still other works of its context. In reverse, formalism cannot explain it, because in presupposing every work's total isolation from its context, and therefore its total uniqueness, formalism is left either with developing a wholly new critical construct for each work, or (usually the case) interpreting every work as if it were written in the twentieth century.

In my introduction I began not with the Renaissance but with the methodological difficulties accompanying a study of Renaissance literature which scholars and critics must face in the present. In this respect I grounded these essays within their historical perspective, which is not the seventeenth century, but the twentieth century. I submit that it is impossible to divorce the consideration of Renaissance literature from the problems raised by the historical perspective one must take on it. And since this historical perspective in the 1970s is complicated by the methodological problem of the historicism-formalism dialectic—a dialectic specifically concerned with historical perspective—the place of Renaissance works in Renaissance culture, and one's twentieth-century perspectives on this question are problems that must be solved together.

To begin where I left off in the introduction, I will take as my text a recent statement of the problem by Wesley Morris in *Toward a New Historicism:*

> The dilemma that a new historicist faces consists in explaining the *aesthetic* relationships between the work and its cultural-historical environment, a relationship that is structural as well as thematic. To do this he must confront the damning circularity of the historicist tautology, the approach to literature that explains the meaning of history in terms of the particular works which comprise it and conversely interprets those same works in terms of that historical meaning. The new historicist must argue that the individual work stands free of its historical context while it simultaneously draws its audience toward that context. Logic, of course, ultimately runs afoul of such a paradox, and we may never be able to develop a completely satisfactory explanation of an historicist aesthetics.[13]

Others, such as Robert Weimann, Roy Harvey Pearce, Murray Krieger, and E. D. Hirsch have formulated the problem in similarly paradoxical terms.[14] As I showed in the introduction, the

[13] Wesley Morris, *Toward a New Historicism* (Princeton, N.J.: Princeton Univ. Press, 1972), p. 13.

[14] Robert Weimann, "Past Significance and Present Meaning in Literary History," *NLH* 1 (1969): 91–109; Roy Harvey Pearce, *Historicism Once More:*

problem becomes paradoxical because both historicists and formalists have tacitly agreed to set up in antinomical form the two dimensions of a literary work's historical status: the historicists see it as a product of its culture, and seek the causes of its meaning in other verbal artifacts of that culture; while the formalists divorce the work from its culture, seeking the causes of its meaning in the internal, organic structure of its parts. As a consequence, both factions have ended in an irresolvable, dialectical stand-off, because the work's dual status cannot, in this manner, be resolved, nor will the critical problem go away merely by being ignored.

Consequently, historicists and formalists have come to act as do several of the characters in the works I have discussed here. That is, like Richard II, Henry IV, Falstaff, Percy Hotspur, Troilus, and Angelo, they have surreptitiously taken over the very position they were attacking. Thus the historicist commits himself to internal analyses of background texts (if he is not, that is, to commit himself to infinite regress in the search for sources), and the formalist implicitly assumes the universality of his own norms of literary structure. Further, the past-present dialectic created by splitting off the recreation of the past from present meaning, has merely meant that both factions equivocate, each attempting, like Falstaff, to be old and young simultaneously. That is, they both attempt uncritically to reap the benefits of taking at once past and present perspectives.

One begins to realize that at issue here are not just methodological quarrels, but quite practical matters of critical division of labor. The question is not whether historicist or formalist criticism ought to be employed to the exclusion of the other, but rather how, once they are employed together, they can agree on boundaries between them that will not set them in malignly dialectical opposition. The historicist will demand, for instance, as regards the objective dimension of a literary work, how one can begin to analyze that dimension without taking into account a

---

Problems and Occasions for the American Scholar (Princeton: Princeton Univ. Press, 1969); Murray Krieger, *A Window to Criticism: Shakespeare's Sonnets and Modern Poetics* (Princeton: Princeton Univ. Press, 1964); E. D. Hirsch, Jr., "Three Dimensions of Hermeneutics," *NLH* 3 (1972): 245–261.

whole range of contextual items, from vocabulary, topical references, and biographical data to larger questions of audience, conventions, and genres. From this viewpoint, the procedure outlined in the previous section might seem to founder at the outset, since it presupposes rather a large fund of information about the cultural context of these works. The formalist, on the other hand, might be amenable to the objective and expressive dimensions of a literary work, while balking at its documentary, and would wonder whether that dimension was not just another, concealed attempt to make the work purely a function of its historical context.

My procedures in these essays for the most part take for granted much information already in print and well known, to Renaissance specialists at any rate, in the areas of literary history and cultural backgrounds. My reason for not citing such information at length derives from my working conception of these works as at once products and producers of their age. I have set aside here, in other words, a small though important body of literature from the late English Renaissance, in order to enact in this arbitrarily delineated microcosm methods of analysis that might be applied to a still larger group from the same era. In this respect, I have implicitly in the first four essays and overtly in this essay treated each work as part of the context of all the others. And in so doing, I have pursued a notion of cultural context that to some extent, at least, cancels the division between the work and its context, and replaces it with the dialectic between the culture as regulative-of-itself and culture as constitutive-of-itself. To put this point in more traditional terms, I have attempted to transform the gulf between cultural context or background sources, and the individual literary work into a dialectical relation, wherein each literary work (and for that matter, every verbal human artifact) of a culture is at once text and context.

Those who know the work of Ernst Cassirer, particularly *The Philosophy of Symbolic Forms,* will recognize my indebtedness for the concept of culture that has been operative here. This concept assumes the following points: (1) Culture equals the total shared agreements binding a group of people at a particular time and place, regarding the nature of the universe and the powers that cause and control it, man's relation to it and to his fellow men; plus all the rituals and artifacts through which the members of that culture mediate and reaffirm these agreements among themselves. (2) All artifacts that a culture produces are symbolic forms, embodying parts of these shared agreements. (3) To the eye of the historian, all that he possesses of documentation is nothing more nor less than such of these artifacts as have survived. (4) The historian, insofar as he assumes that a culture is a relatively homogeneous creation of these shared agreements, can seek to understand that culture only through discovering the interrelatedness among these artifacts. (5) The terms and grammar of this interrelatedness are not automatically phenomenal on the surface of these artifacts. On the contrary, the most basic categories of agreement and understanding within a culture, because they are so much taken for granted by that culture, will not so rise to consciousness as to appear phenomenally in the surviving artifacts themselves. The historian must therefore strive to interpret the phenomena of these artifacts so as to discover the underlying presuppositions of form and value that announce themselves through the phenomena. My guiding rule in this respect has been Cassirer's own statement, that

> the critique of reason becomes the critique of culture. It seeks to understand and to show how every content of culture, in so far as it is more than a mere isolated content, in so far as it is grounded in a universal principle of form, presupposes an original act of the human spirit. . . . Thus, with all their inner diversity, the various products of culture—language, scientific knowledge, myth, art, religion—become parts of a single great problem-complex: they become multiple efforts, all directed toward the one goal of transforming the passive world of mere *impressions,* in which the spirit seems at first imprisoned, into a world that is pure *expression* of human spirit.[15]

From this viewpoint, when the literary historicist divides culture into background and foreground he merely hypostatizes a

[15] Ernst Cassirer, *The Philosophy of Symbolic Forms,* trans. Ralph Manheim, 3 vols. (New Haven: Yale Univ. Press, 1953), 1: 80–81.

division that his own method requires, and treats it as if it really existed. One might even note here a secret alliance with the formalist, insofar as the historicist automatically assumes that he might study *A Mirror for Magistrates* in order to illuminate Shakespeare's history plays, but not the reverse; and this despite the demonstrated immense popularity of the former in Shakespeare's time. Thus do our own present perspectives subtly "corrupt" us in our very attempts to shake free of them. Like the formalist, the historicist chooses out for scrutiny those artifacts that continue to have significance in his own time.

On the contrary, we have no choice but to view every treatise of Bacon, every poem of Donne, Herbert, Marvell, and Milton, and every play of Shakespeare as part of the context of one another. For this reason I have eschewed the usual preliminary background annotations, because each individual analysis was an exercise at once in historicist and formalist criticism. And also, for this reason, I have made little defense so far of my use of dialectic as a tool for investigating works which were written at a time when the term meant only a division of logic.[16]

We should get straight, however, just what constitutes the relevance of terms derived from the history of thought of post-Renaissance times. D. W. Robertson states quite clearly the historicist's objection to such usage:

> Freudian psychology [Robertson's example of a misused modern grammar of terms] is a part of a "universe of discourse" with a nexus of relationships to other elements in that "universe." To insert it into an earlier universe of discourse where no such nexus exists is to create absurdities. That is, Freudian "complexes" have about as much place in discussions of Shakespeare as have carburetors or semiconductors. It cannot be emphasized too urgently that any age in the past can be understood only when we analyze it in so far as is possible in its own terms. If we can begin to understand those terms in their own context, we can begin to understand the age, but if we impose our

16 Walter J. Ong, S. J., *Ramus, Method and the Decay of Dialogue* (Cambridge: Harvard Univ. Press, 1958), pp. 59–63, and *passim*.

own terms on it, we might as well be studying ourselves rather than the past.[17]

This is a strong statement and argues quite articulately a viewpoint held staunchly by many modern professional literary students.

Several assumptions made here, nevertheless, require modification. Robertson's "universe of discourse" corresponds to his later statement (p. 31), that "the past is, in effect, a series of foreign countries inhabited by strangers." In arguing for the complete gulf between present and past cultures, as well as that between present and past lexicons, Robertson falls into just the historicist equivocation I have examined both in the introduction and in the present essay. As Mannheim and Stark have pointed out, to analyze the past "in so far as possible in its own terms," if we mean by that only the actual lexicons and grammars extant in the past's surviving artifacts, is to commit oneself exactly to not understanding the past. One must, of course, distinguish. Matters of glossing topical reference and vocabulary, in general the area of studies taken up by "literary annals," are clearly necessary for the simple, beginning understanding of a text on its objective level. But one must distinguish "glosses" and "interpretation," as well as noting their mutual implication. Too often the historical critic will assume that a gloss on a passage, that is, noting what lexicon or event outside the work is employed in the passage, constitutes an interpretation of the passage. Such glossing is of course indispensable. But referring to other works as background of a particular passage implies a possible infinite regress. For one must know the appropriate lexicons and grammars to interpret these works as well, and so on. Actually, the only lexicon and grammar available for interpreting a passage is that provided by the work itself. For the relevance of an outside gloss must be determined by querying its significance in the work, which becomes then not merely "identical with" an outside reference, but rather actively dictates which, of several possible glosses, is relevant. And so, a gloss is not only important for

---

[17] D. W. Robertson, "Some Observations on Method in Literary Studies," *NLH* 1 (1969): 28–29.

interpretation, but interpretation in turn "interprets" glosses. Consequently, the lexicons of contemporary "universes of discourse" do not automatically make themselves available for interpretation, but rather must be sought out with a notion of their possible relevance already rather firmly in mind; which notion, of course, presupposes a certain amount of interpretation. And this interpretation, however tentative, is something the historical critic can only perform by starting within his present perspective.

The question of twentieth-century grammars of terms, however, has yet to be confronted. Robertson's sundering of past from present universes of discourse suggests the notion that we must strive to do away with the second in order to use the first. But is such ever done, or even possible? I would suggest that even attempts to purify one's own lexicon of terms and employ only terms derived from a past universe of discourse at once transform that universe from a past into a present one. If one examines such a monument to the historicist method in Renaissance studies as E. M. W. Tillyard's *Elizabethan World Picture,* one discovers the imposition of post-Renaissance categories concealed under the very attempt to get behind these. The very concept of a "world picture" is a post-romantic tool of historical synthesis, owing much more to Herder, Kant, and Hegel than to anything that Renaissance thinkers produced. To assume that indeed a wide variety of statements about the cosmos, man, society, religion, politics, and so on in a given culture is liable to synthesis into an organic whole, is to assume something that Renaissance thinkers were only beginning to discover. This is not to argue that Tillyard gives us a fiction in the guise of truth. It is rather to point out how much of the truth in that study is indebted to the author's availing himself of the very perspectives and categories allowed him precisely by his not living in the Renaissance but in the twentieth century. That Renaissance thinkers thought in terms of correspondences among various planes of existence is something that Tillyard discovers and documents. But what allows Tillyard to synthesize the evidence that discloses this kind of thinking is a grammar of categories that is definitely post-Renaissance. In short, thinking in correspondences involves a Renaissance grammar; the discovery that such thinking constituted in fact a "world picture" is indebted to a nineteenth- and twentieth-century grammar.

One ought also to be alert against taking statements made within a culture that appear to synthesize large, synoptic visions of that culture's own world view as being such in fact. Modern studies of Renaissance thought, such as Tillyard's, seem to do just that. Implicitly such documents as Hooker's *Laws of Ecclesiastical Polity* and Spenser's *Fowre Hymnes,* precisely because they make such general, synthetic statements, give the appearance of conveying some of the documentary information underlying Renaissance thought structures. What appears through these documents, however, is something different, something which they take wholly for granted: namely, the notion that the cosmos as the Renaissance saw it is available to being rationalized within categories of coherence and hierarchy, which categories Spenser, Hooker, as well as many others, never questioned. That others such as Bruno and Machiavelli did question them illustrates only the fact that the Renaissance produced, in some isolated individuals, the seeds of a later perspective that was to transcend its own. Therefore, *The Laws of Ecclesiastical Polity* and the *Fowre Hymnes* have also to be examined to discover what more basic, presupposed categories of value and structure appear through their objective dimensions; and such works have no more privileged place for the cultural historian than works whose objective dimensions are concerned with non-abstract, concrete matters of everyday life.

I am not attempting to justify my own viewpoint by pointing out an aberration in an otherwise exemplary product of historicist scholarship. I rather want to indicate that the distinction between present and past universes of discourse is a useless distinction, if it means only their being mutually exclusive. Beyond the level of necessary glossing performed by literary annals and to some extent by literary history, the recovery of the essential structures and values that characterize the Renaissance or any other period can mean nothing else than the translation of them into a present set of structures and values, because it is only in the present that we can stand in order to perceive them as such.

Such grammars exist only within specific verbal artifacts, and can be treated specifically and consciously as grammars only by abstracting from these artifacts and synthesizing them. Such abstracting and synthesizing, however, becomes possible to the extent one stands outside of them, so as to achieve perspective on the radical paradigms of coherence and value that underlie them and make them possible. In this respect, then, such paradigms announce themselves through the phenomena of the verbal artifacts that incorporate them and take them for granted. And just because these paradigms are taken for granted, they cannot appear phenomenally—become available, that is, to the historicist who consciously limits himself to the perspective of "the typical Elizabethan"—but only announce themselves to one who refuses such limitation. To the extent that the literary historian avails himself of grammars contemporary with the work he wants to illuminate, he does so not because he recreates himself also as a contemporary of that work, but rather because he recreates such grammars in the present. And, as I argue here, such recreation is possible only because he exists in the present.

Robertson's notion of the past as a "foreign country" is a metaphorical hyperbole at best, and an absurdity at the worst. If in fact we take this notion strictly, then the past is totally closed to us, and the consequence is historical scepticism. Under this condition there is, by definition, nowhere we can start to recreate the past, no lead into that past. But the very fact that historians, as well as historical critics, do manage to recreate the past in rather immense detail, indicates that there are some ways in which the past is a "foreign country" and some ways in which it is not.

My own justification for using a "dialectical" grammar lies in the fact that the works I have discussed exhibit on their surfaces structures set forth in antinomical terms. And as I have shown, dialectic necessarily follows upon antinomical structures, wherever they are found. The problematics of antinomies themselves never become phenomenal in Renaissance literature (save on the documentary level), for the simple reason that, as far as one can tell, Renaissance writers took for granted that antinomies were built into the structure of reality, thereby cutting themselves off from any possibility, later made available to Kant and Hegel for instance, of achieving perspective on their essential logical structures. I would suggest, finally, that recognizing the difference between past grammars and past grammars recreated in the present exercises a check on the modern critic, whereby he may distinguish between what he finds in the culture and what he brings to it.

If, then, all grammars that a critic can use, whether drawn from the past or the present, must become actively present to him, then the solution to the dialectic between historicism and formalism is to be learned from the very works I have studied here: the solution is the acceptance of the dialectic itself. Only if present standpoints are accepted as the necessary base from which we can recreate past standpoints, will the equivocations of both historicism and formalism be avoided. In tending to identify being and knowing, both positions assume that the mind of the critic cannot be in two places at once. The historicist presupposes that thinking like an Elizabethan means that he must somehow become an Elizabethan; while the formalist places the literary work and himself in a timeless present wherein both putatively partake of identical categories of existence and meaning. My argument accepts the dialectic between past and present necessarily thrust on the literary student. I would go even farther, and say that he can "be" in either past or present only by being "in" both simultaneously. As E. D. Hirsch has pointed out, this "doubling" of perspective is something we do all the time in literary studies, as particularly illustrated in our grasp of ironic significance.[18] In place of the covert equivocations between the two dimensions of literary works entangling historicism and formalism, I would substitute a conscious development of the methodological consequences flowing from the dialectic between them.

Even the modern critic examining twentieth-century literature is subject to this dialectic. There is a curious bias on this kind of interpretive situation that is the reflex and converse of the historicist's bias. Whereas the twentieth-century critic must supposedly make a conscious effort to put aside his own cultural presuppositions to recreate a culture foreign to him, the modern critic interpreting literature contemporary with him is already allegedly endowed with the necessary cultural data because he is

[18] Hirsch, "Three Dimensions of Hermeneutics," *NLH* 3: 251.

contemporary with it. Whether he knows it or not, the twentieth-century critic who interprets a twentieth-century poem not only brings to this poem his own built-in repertoire of culturally conditioned categories, he learns something about his status in the twentieth century as well. Insofar as he interprets the poem self-consciously as specifically a "twentieth-century" poem, he is acting as an historical critic, with all the deliberate detachment and objectivity of a critic reading Ben Jonson—or as little.

Since there is literally no distinction between verbal artifacts and their cultural background, the recreation of a past culture is indistinguishable from a study of the individual verbal artifacts that make it up. To this extent, then, historicist and formalist analyses are identical. The historicist must always interpret his documents, whether in the foreground or the background, and the formalist can only analyze any literary work to the extent, as Heidegger insists, that he partakes of the same stream of history as that work itself. Therefore, to analyze a literary work is at once to exact an interpretation of it and to interpret a manifestation of culture.

The bugaboo of subjectivity versus objectivity, that relic of Descartes's transhistorical ghost in an historical machine, needs to be viewed in historical perspective as itself a product of the Renaissance's instinct for absolutizing. Of the advantages granted by perceiving man's consciousness as the consequence of historical causes, not the least is the distinction he can now draw between those areas of his world which are historically conditioned and those which are not. E. D. Hirsch, consistent with his distinction between past meaning and present significance, indicates that a similar distinction must be drawn between those parts of a critic's spiritual world derived from cultural sources, and those wholly indigenous to his own unique experience. "If an interpretation is grounded in the interpreter's entire *Welt*, it will no doubt be different from any past meaning, since undoubtedly a person's entire spiritual world will be different from any that existed in the past." Nevertheless, "the very introduction of 'historicity' as a chief characteristic of *Welt* means that a boundary has been drawn, since historicity is not the chief component of a person's spiritual world." On the contrary, "the domain of shared cultural experience" may well be the lesser component, although Hirsch is uncertain where the line should be drawn. His conclusion on this score, however, turns the subjectivity-objectivity antinomy inside out. The selectivity that governs any person's spiritual world determines as well those culturally shared experiences that enter into it, and "since the spiritual universe that actively governs an interpretation is limited and selective, no inherent necessity requires this delimited world to be different from any that existed in the past." [19] In short, awareness of one's place in the stream of history allows one then to bracket this place provisionally, set it aside, and gives rise to the possibility of what R. G. Collingwood calls the "renenactment" of past history in the present:

> The processes of nature can therefore be properly described as sequences of mere events, but those of history cannot. They are not processes of mere events but processes of actions, which have an inner side, consisting of processes of thought; and what the historian is looking for is these processes of thought. All history is the history of thought.

> Thought can never be mere object. To know someone else's activity of thinking is possible only on the assumption that this same activity can be re-enacted in one's own mind. In that sense, to know "what someone is thinking" (or "has thought") involves thinking it for oneself.[20]

As W. H. Walsh clarifies Collingwood's point here, we reenact the thought of a past person not in the sense that we

---

[19] *Ibid.*, pp. 253–254. Hirsch's disagreement with Heidegger for his purposes does not prejudice my use of both for my own. Hirsch opposes these distinctions to Heidegger's insistence that man's consciousness is totally and completely conditioned by history (p. 251). From my own viewpoint, however, immersion in history provides the very possibility for distinguishing, as Hirsch does, between that part of private consciousness that shares in historical context, and that which does not. The sense in which I emphasize the interpreter's partaking in the same stream of history as does the work itself, means that the private *Welt* of both (earlier) work and (later) interpreter comes to be, and even to be "private," within the same historical continuum.

[20] R. G. Collingwood, *The Idea of History* (New York: Oxford Univ. Press, 1956), pp. 215, 288.

achieve the identical act of thought, but rather we rethink the same content of that act.[21] In this way, then, following Hirsch, we can grasp how a critic in the present recreates the intelligible structures of meaning of past literary works. The identity of the critic with the past audience implied by the work does not, therefore, derive from emptying ourselves of our subjective, culturally conditioned categories, but rather from plunging back into our subjectivity, and realizing that that subjectivity can reenact the intelligibility of a past precisely because the subjectivities of author, contemporary audience, and modern critic alike only exist bound within the stream of history, though not identical with it. The work presents itself to be rethought by the critic, no matter when it was produced, only because both work and critic exist immersed in history, and it is this immersion that guarantees the critic's capability of contacting it.

The literary critic must confront these literary works' dual status as both past and present by taking account of another duality, that ranged along the axis between the cultural content and the uniqueness of the individual text. So far, this section has concerned transforming the gulf between historicism and formalism into a reciprocal relationship. Such methodological rearrangements, however, are inseparable from further revisions of our perception of the context-text duality that created the critical quarrel in the first place. In the rest of this section I shall explore how the documentary dimension outlined in the previous section allows us to take account of the indebtedness of these works to their cultural context and of their uniqueness, without sacrificing one to the other. This dimension is Janus-faced, for it articulates and defines the literary work as a part of the context of still other works, yet autonomous. It will finally appear that context and text, the work as a product and as a producer of its culture, really name different, partial perspectives on the same integral whole: the individual work as both constituted and regulated dialectically.

The term "Renaissance," as I have been using it here, means

21 W. H. Walsh, *Philosophy of History* (New York and Evanston: Harper and Row, 1960), p. 92.

something different from the established fact that all these works were written in England in the first seventy years of the seventeenth century. Calling these works "Renaissance" for this reason is actually an empty tautology. That they were all written at the same time and in England is usually used to justify interpreting one work by reference to other contemporary works. In turn, the common label "Renaissance" is affixed to them all when it is discovered that, indeed, all share certain ideas, images, structures, and so on. In short, the work is "Renaissance" because the work is "Renaissance." This is another and more superficial example of a tautology mentioned earlier, whereby a work is turned into a gloss on itself by being reflected in other works that can be found to mirror it: A is like B because B is like A. The question, What does the term "Renaissance" refer to? means something else here. It concerns whatever categories for asking and answering questions of the world can be found in many works written at roughly the same time, taken one by one. It seeks further the common ground on which these works agree to disagree as the fundamental condition of their being divergent manifestations of the same, homogeneous culture. If commonly shared categories are what make up a culture, then when they occur contemporaneously they are part of the same culture. And if that culture is more or less by convention called "Renaissance," then these commonly shared categories make individual works equally and indifferently "Renaissance." *

---

* What Brian Stock says about modern, academic demarcations of the "Middle Ages" necessarily applies to our conception of the "Renaissance" also ("The Middle Ages as Subject and Object: Romantic Attitudes and Academic Medievalism, *NLH* 5 [1974], pp. 527–547). That is, since as he notes "the Renaissance invented the Middle Ages in order to define itself," and since the modern conception of the "Middle Ages" is inherited from the historiographical self-preoccupations of the Enlightenment and the Romantics, our concept of the "Renaissance" is likewise open to the same revisions he calls for regarding the Middle Ages. One of the characteristics of the period we call "the Renaissance" was that it called itself a Renaissance, at least insofar as it delimited itself from an earlier period of "darkness." The name and its various meanings are part of the cultural phenomena to be studied. Methodologically, we equivocate on the label itself, insofar as it applies indifferently both to the period as an object of study and to our own, present methods of studying it as a subject. We should rather refer to "a certain period in Western Culture that thought of itself as a 'Renaissance.'" Such revision would facilitate avoidance of such tautologies as claiming a work to be Renaissance be-

My deliberate refusal to start with any assumed notion of what makes up "Renaissance culture," such as would have necessitated preliminary background studies regarding "the thought of the age," "what Shakespeare was taught in grammar school," "the Elizabethan World Picture," and so on, has been based on my conviction that such real or fictional entities external to the works I examine in these essays have no privileged status or authority. If these works themselves will not yield a notion of Renaissance culture, what will? Clearly, homilies, sermons, commonplace books, astronomical treatises, sixteenth-century translations of Ovid are no more (and no less) "Renaissance" than *The Advancement of Learning* and *Hamlet*. In this respect, as in others, I have joined historicist and formalist approaches in these essays, because I examine here Renaissance artifacts in the attempt to find out, among other things, what makes them specifically "Renaissance."

My point resembles that made by several other critics who have concerned themselves with the same problem. For instance, Roy Harvey Pearce asserts that "the literary work has as its end the objectification of such historical data as may be formed into ideally possible wholes." This means that "the greatness of a literary work is an index and an assessment of the possibilities for greatness of the culture out of which it has come. . . . All cultures, thus, through their great writers, manifest the *possibility* of greatness. What art teaches us is the degree to which that possibility has been realized." [22] In a similar vein, Murray Krieger directly confronts the individual literary work's place in its culture from the viewpoint argued in these essays:

> In moving from the literary context to history, the critic can learn from the work what it was in the culture that he as historian should be looking for, even if without the work's illuminations he could not see it. From the front end of history, our vantage point, the poet's activity may

cause it was written in the "Renaissance." We would, in other words, free ourselves from enslavement to the cultural categories we would study, in order to distinguish the Renaissance's definition of itself from our own definition of it. Such distinction, as I have already argued, traditional historicism closes itself off from.

[22] Roy Harvey Pearce, *Historicism Once More*, pp. 27, 36.

indeed look like the imitation of what has already been formulated elsewhere in culture; but to the extent that he has imitated truly existential and pre-conceptual forces, one cannot know what was being imitated until after the poet has made it perceptible—which is to say, after he has created it to show what it was he imitated.[23]

The literary work is not merely "imitative" of its culture; on the contrary the culture is created by—is in fact nothing else but—the work and others contemporary with it. I would push Pearce's statement even further than he intended it, and say that not only the "great" literary work, but all expressions of men within a culture or period of a culture, manifest the "possibilities" of that culture. "It is the essence of a civilization that whatever its intellect conceives becomes a part of it." [24] That is, from my own viewpoint, these works realize the possible structures and values allowed by their culture's own unified and unifying categories for asking and answering questions about the world at large.

To elucidate my point from another angle, I must return to Mannheim whose essay on *Weltanschauung* contains such a wealth of insight into its problems. He distinguishes between two ways in which a work may be related to its culture, the "causal" and the "interpretive." He insists that "there is no causal relation between one document and another; we cannot explain one as the causal product of the other but merely trace both back to the same global unity of *Weltanschauung* of which they are parts." What "interpretation" does "is to take some meaningful object already understood in the frame of reference of objective meaning and place it within a different frame of reference—that of *Weltanschauung*. By being considered as 'document' of the latter, the object will be illuminated from a new side." [25] This notion frees the historicist critic from the limitations of a narrowly causal mode of interrelation, whereby cul-

---

[23] Murray Krieger, *A Window to Criticism,* pp. 64–65.

[24] Johan Huizinga, "A Definition of the Concept of History," in *Philosophy and History,* ed. Raymond Klibansky and H. J. Paton (New York, Evanston, London: Harper & Row, 1963), p. 8.

[25] *Essays on the Sociology of Knowledge,* p. 81.

tural wholes can be established only in terms of direct sources, influences, and so on. While allowing for such kinds of connections, an interpretation of a work's place in its culture allows also not only for the likeness between source and text, but for the difference as well. And in allowing for such difference, the "unity" of source and text, as well as of text with "causally" unrelated texts, makes way for a notion of "Weltanschauung" that conceives of it as located nowhere else save in those texts themselves.

As I showed in Essays One through Four, an identical paradox occurs in a variety of literary texts, which in turn suggests that this paradox is a thought structure shared by Renaissance culture as a whole. That is, the Renaissance would seem to embody generally shared agreements to ask and answer questions of its world in antinomical form. At the same time, as these works indicate at least, the other face of this agreement is a common demand for the resolution and destruction of antinomies. In short, the Renaissance was committed to seeking either-or solutions to both-and problems, solutions at once sought as necessary and discovered to be impossible. If, as this limited sampling suggests, the culture of the Renaissance consists (at least in part) of such an agreement, then the Renaissance may be considered as a whole made up of parts, by analogy to the internal structures of each of its verbal artifacts. This time, however, these parts are the individual artifacts themselves. Each of these works would therefore compete and cooperate with the others in manifesting, each in its limited, partial way, some sort of similar dialectical concern. From this viewpoint, Renaissance culture becomes an overarching, circumscribing mythos, collectively constituted out of all the human artifacts that embody and reflect that culture, each in its own, incomplete, partial manner. The dianoia of this cultural mythos would be, then, the dialectical logic that creates and regulates widely divergent, yet dialectically related, manifestations of itself in all the human artifacts that equal that culture.

This argument, the reader may note, moves increasingly toward a tautology that may appear perilously close to the kind of tautology I have just condemned. I would appear to be saying that a culture is made up of those human artifacts, agreements, rituals, institutions, and so on that unite in producing it. In one sense, this is exactly what I am saying. The movement of this argument is actually toward a way of defining context and text as two names for the same thing, or perhaps the same thing looked at in two different ways. If culture equals the total collection of human artifacts, then the equation is obviously reversible. The intention here is to allow this reversibility, while at the same time giving full due to the ways in which this equation also creates divergence. So, in this respect, the context-text equation is just as tautological, and just as little tautological, as the first two moments of dialectical logic: they are logically interrelated, and they refer to the same process. Therefore, they are (equivalently) versions of each other, but they also state dialectically opposite situations.

In fact, as I shall show now, it is precisely the three-moment schema of dialectical logic, outlined in the first section, which defines the context-text equation as at once tautological and not tautological. This schema controls the cultural, contextual arena in exactly the same manner as it controls the dialectical structures of the individual literary products of that culture. In doing so, it makes intelligible how a culture such as the Renaissance can be united by the very culturally shared categories that allow and even dictate much diversity and disagreement. The objective, expressive, and documentary dimensions each disclose dialectical ligatures among these works, and the three-moment schema operates in a similar fashion in each dimension.

"A resolution of antinomies is always partial, thereby containing implicitly the potentiality for conflict"—this is the first moment. It is enacted, first, in the objective dimension of these works. This dimension concerns the mythos-dianoia dialectic as it is embodied in various specific subject matters. These would include the abstraction-intuition antinomy in Bacon; language and thought versus reality in the metaphysical lyric; providence and human freedom for Milton; and right and power for Shakespeare. The "resolution" here means that all these works agree in developing the dialectics allowed by these various antinomies. The conflict implicit in this moment lies in their separately attempting to reduce their culture's general antinomic way of thinking to one specific antinomy or set of antinomies. Each work would thus

more or less explicitly claim to be a central, representative sum-
mation of the human condition as the Renaissance saw it. Both
Bacon and Milton made such a claim overtly. Bacon envisioned
the boundaries of the new science encompassing nothing less than
the whole realm of human knowledge and existence. Sciences and
philosophies tend to involve themselves in such massive aggrandisement, to the degree that they take total inclusion of the cosmos as a radical criterion of truth. Fictional works, when they
make such claims, do so in more covert, senecdochal fashions.
Paradise Lost resembles the new science, since it extends its
metaphorical reach to include the whole of human history. For
Shakespeare, the ethical dialectic of good and evil, wherein both
appear as dual potentialities of a single continuum of human energy, sums up the central human concern. Marvell's "Upon
Appleton House," though more fragmentary than *Paradise Lost,*
makes a similar claim for its own "summary" character. The
compass of concern is narrowest in Donne's and Herbert's
poetry, though Donne's obsession with epistemology, and Herbert's with the economy of salvation, clearly sum up two concerns which the Renaissance agonized over at large.

There is another, more specific antinomy that several of these
works join in competing over. In its broadest form it would
align the achievement of a plotless, transhistorical, spiritual state
of pure existence and intuitive knowledge against a discursive,
historical, fallen state of mixed ethical and epistemological conditions. Bacon's new science would fall down on the first side
(though his ethics and politics in the *Essays* would not). This
would be likewise true for the personae of Donne's and Herbert's
lyrics, and with some changes, for Satan, Adam, Eve, Richard II,
Angelo, and Hamlet, insofar as all of these demand realization of
some transcendence beyond the here and now. Probably Milton's
epic narrator, and the personae in Marvell's "Garden" and "Upon
Appleton House" would illustrate most completely the other op-
tion; as would no doubt the Hamlet of act 5. This broadly defined antinomy controls overtly the specific choices realized by
these various writers and fictional personae. In this respect, then,
Milton and Bacon, for instance, exhibit their indebtedness to a
shared cultural category, inasmuch as they differ quite sharply

within options allowed by the same antinomy. Bacon's belief that man can reach Eden again through knowledge, and Milton's equal and opposite belief that the desire for (at least inordinate) knowledge caused the Fall would likewise link them in precisely dialectical opposition.

At this point, the second moment of dialectical logic appears in the objective dimension—"a conflict of antinomies presupposes a ground common to both, and thereby contains the potentiality for resolution." That is, the various competitions and disagreements noted above disclose the underlying agreement they all share. All of these works, and their writers, are "at-oned" with each other, in sharing a common antinomical mode of asking and answering specific questions about the human condition. This in turn leads to the conclusion that it is precisely this agreement that conditions and allows their diversity.

Such a conclusion is summed up in the third moment: "Both resolution and conflict, since they contain the elements of both in potentially reciprocal relationship, are themselves related as mutual cause and effect." This kind of causality is not that which Mannheim distinguishes from "interpretation." It does not refer to direct "indebtedness," a standard category of explanation for traditional historicism. It rather refers to the fact that these works' agreement upon antinomical categories in general likewise creates, or causes, the possibility for each to embody this agreement in distinct, autonomous, unique verbal realizations. Thus Bacon's and Marvell's agreement and opposition are reciprocally "causal" of each other, only to the extent that agreement on the man as angel-man as historical antinomy, for example, will "cause" them to disagree if, as they did, each chooses one side at the expense of the other. Of course, this is not quite true of Marvell, and the fact that it is not suggests that the dialectical causality joining them is not as pristinely symmetrical as one might want for the purposes of simple example.

The objective dimension concerns only agreements about choosing different subject matters or treating the same subject in divergent ways. It does not disclose these works' differing manners of accommodating the dialectical logic shared by them all. This matter is disclosed in the expressive dimension, the dialectic between the verbal surface, the work's "phenomena," and the dialectical logic that appears through this surface.

The phenomena-appearance dialectic determined the sequence of works discussed in the first four essays. There, I moved from Bacon, whose work involves the greatest unaccommodated eruption of dialectic, to Shakespeare's plays, where dialectic is most overtly accommodated, through metaphysical poetry and *Paradise Lost,* where the phenomena-appearance proportion shifts progressively. Here, one might just as well begin with the third moment, which sums up the first two moments in any case. As I showed in the analytical essays, each of these writers essentially asked the same question: How can the antinomical structure of things (that is, thought, the natural world, God, history, and so on) be accommodated? Each of the actions-done in these works takes place under the insistence that antinomies must be resolved; and the dianoias of each answer with equal insistence that the resolution of dialectical antinomies is impossible. Consequently, each work, whatever its specific subject matter, confronts the same paradox implicit in an antinomical view of reality, the notion that resolution of antinomies is at once necessary and impossible: this is what they share. How each work confronts this paradox, that is, how each work adjusts the dialectic between its phenomenal surface (always involving some rejection of dialectic) and the appearance of dialectic through this surface, determines how they differ.

I am not suggesting here a limited number of possible accommodations and adjustments dictated by the overarching dialectical regulation imposed by the culture at large. Rather, as the sequence of my analytical discussions has attempted to illustrate, there would seem to be a limited spectrum, enclosing an indefinite number of possibilities, along which these works could be ranged. Bacon's new science and *Hamlet* would seem to be, as far as the selection of works here is concerned, the two extreme, limiting cases. In Bacon, there is the greatest gulf between nondialectical surface and unplanned appearance, or eruption, of dialectic. In *Hamlet,* the phenomenal concerns of the hero—his overt statements and actions—incorporate most completely an awareness of the dialectical logic controlling the world of the play. Here, dialectic between phenomena and appearance is at a minimum. In the metaphysical poets, this dialectic is very much present, appearing through the lyric personae's attempts to reject it. *Paradise Lost* stands yet closer to Shakespeare's plays in that the epic narrator is overtly concerned with the dialectics in his fable and his own language.

In the expressive dimension of these works, then, we find divergences that yet remain functions of an over-all community: a community of agreement on the necessity of accommodating dialectic within discourses that are variously structured to that end. The mutual reciprocity between likeness and difference stated in the third moment illuminates these works as alike in enacting various accommodations of an identical logic. And this logic in turn can be seen as dictating the limited spectrum of (indefinite) possibilities for accommodating itself, on which all these works can be placed. At this point, the third dialectic that includes and controls all the rest becomes apparent: that between dialectical regulation and dialectical constitution. This dialectic is disclosed in the documentary dimensions of these works, and is the single principle that defines the copenetration among them, allowing them to be seen at once as products of and producers of their culture.

The previous section explained how each work becomes constituted dialectically through and despite its agent's attempts to avoid regulation by the dialectical logic implicit in his actions. In expanding this dimension to take in the whole mythos of Renaissance culture, the same dialectic repeats itself. "Repeats" is not wholly accurate; "reduplicates itself" is perhaps more to the point. This is because the Renaissance culture which dictated that these works formulate the human condition in antinomic categories is nothing else but these works themselves, plus all the many other expressions of Renaissance man not considered here. This overarching dialectical regulation is at once imposed on these writers, and is freely chosen by them, since they all cooperate among themselves in asserting it. At once, the other side of this regulation comes to the fore: the agreement to ask and answer such questions likewise imposed the imperative to resolve these antinomies. Consequently, each of these works, with

varying degrees of deliberateness, enacts attempts to escape from
dialectic into some nondialectical resolution. In the broadest
cultural perspective, each work announces its common regulation
by the identical culturally imposed dialectical logic. And, in
turn, each becomes constituted dialectically, according to the indefinite number of variations that dialectical logic can allow.

All of these works enact, in the microcosms of their own
verbal universes, the overarching dialectical logic governing the
culture which they unite in being at once products of and producers of. In the documentary dimension, the difference between
text and context becomes actually dependent upon which viewpoint one takes, since the regulation-constitution dialectic is
identical for each work and for the culture at large. The assertion that each work becomes constituted dialectically through
attempts to escape dialectical regulation, and the assertion that
Renaissance culture becomes constituted dialectically through
attempts to escape dialectical regulation state the same content,
but seen from two opposite viewpoints. One can begin, as I have
done in this study, with individual works, and gradually build
toward a reconstruction of their cultural context. But having
done so, I have reversed the process in this essay, and discussed
the ways in which their cultural context dictated the various antinomic categories within which they might agree to disagree. But
though the sequence of discussion requires that these perspectives
be laid out and taken up one by one, the cultural and literary
reality remains integral and whole. Like the writers I have discussed in these essays, I too have had to violate the integrity of
my chosen subject matter, to break it down into mutually competing and cooperating parts, in order to disclose the all-encompassing dialectical logic that both binds them together and sets
them at odds.

The cultural determinism of the historicist and the artistic
freedom of the formalist need not be seen as enemies of each
other, and mutually exclusive. On the contrary, the creative freedom that these writers exercised, perhaps preeminently over all
other contemporaries, was itself grounded in their acceptance of
the dialectical regulation their culture proffered them. For as all
of these writers, perhaps even Bacon, testify, the other face of

dialectical determinism is the tragic freedom which that determinism enforces. These writers witnessed to the fact that, as Milton's God insists, man is determined to be free.

In this way, then, I have attempted to sum up the main positions argued through this whole study. It is possible to reach a perspective on the works discussed here that allows both their uniqueness and their indebtedness to their culture to be taken account of, without sacrificing one to the other, or splitting one off from the other. Here, likeness and difference, agreement and disagreement, context and text, work as product and as producer of its culture, are all seen to be dialectical functions of each other, and therefore as reciprocally causal of each other. Each literary work exhibits its originality and uniqueness *vis-à-vis* the originality and uniqueness of other contemporary literary works, in a way that allows the historicist to treat it as at once unique and culturally indebted. Further, present significance and past meaning can now also be seen as dialectical functions of each other, and thereby implying each other, because the literary work's continued survival from its own "present" into a later one is through an uninterrupted historical continuum in which both it and the critic are imbedded. And because this continuum is a temporal one, it both links the critic to the work and separates him from it. In surviving from past into future, these Renaissance literary works bring their culture with them, while establishing that culture as irremediably past. To recreate the meaning of these works in the present the critic must likewise (and necessarily) *re*create them: the work as both past and present, as both culturally determined and unique: all the terms of these antinomies are implicit in the same critical act.

One final point must be made in this section, and that an important one, about an assumption that underlies everything I have been saying in this fifth essay. This concerns what, if anything, my dialectical analysis of these works as specifically "Renaissance" separates them, and the Renaissance in general, from other cultures and periods of culture? On the one hand, my analysis of dialectic in its appearance within the three dimensions of a literary work has implicitly claimed a kind of universal validity. On the other, I have continually insisted that the Renaissance was a period which specifically featured such dialectic. What then distinguishes such dialectics as they appear in the Renaissance from such, if any, that appear, for example, in the middle ages and the eighteenth-century enlightenment?

In order to answer these questions, one must distinguish between the logic of dialectic as a kind of "platonic" structure, existing "eternally" implicit in all antinomical thought structures of any time and place, and the ways various cultures and periods have shown themselves accommodating these antinomies. What seems to be universal in dialectic are the following items: (1) The law of noncontradiction. This seems to be, throughout all the cultures I am acquainted with, an assumed regulator of thought. One may find in certain Eastern philosophies attempts to assert certain "coincidences of opposites," for example, Lao Tzu, but such occurrences do not deny that noncontradiction is operative, they rather affirm it. (2) Insofar as dialectic results from the confrontation between noncontradiction and a world of diversity and change, then dialectic will occur wherever this confrontation is pushed far enough for men's minds to perceive this conflict between noncontradiction and such existential "contradictions." (3) Wherever men take up issues and agree upon their antinomical structure, dialectic will occur; and the dialectic between mythos and dianoia will occur in those works wherein antinomies provide the substructure.

The Renaissance showed itself overtly, in the human artifacts that produced it, as dominantly concerned with questions that could be put in antinomical form. Its artifacts exhibit a high amount of irritation with antinomies, as witnessed by the many attempts to solve them. Further, dialectic arose in the Renaissance in the areas of philosophy, theology, and science, because all parties to the quarrels in these areas agreed that whatever final system of answers might be arrived at, must conform to an all-embracing, "absolute" viewpoint—that they must conform to such criteria as completeness, coherence, all-embracingness, and finality. Thus the wars and struggles during the Reformation resulted because all sides were agreed that the Christian religion should conform totally to one set of doctrines and disciplines. And since many factions disagreed on what this set should be, dialectic was inevitable.

In a culture, however, where people agree to disagree in a wholly different fashion, that is, where there is a certain amount of agreed-upon pluralism, differences remain unmediated, and therefore unfought over; and consequently, dialectic will not be a dominant form in that culture. The eighteenth-century enlightenment is a period where dialectic is not a dominant form. This situation is due to science, whereby it was generally assumed that many riddles in the natural and human worlds could be brought harmoniously to resolution within a single, univocal system. Such realities as did not fit within science were simply relegated outside the pale, as in the case of some poetic theories and some theologies. Dialectic between science and poetry, or science and religion would arise, therefore, only in those cases where one side or the other insisted on extending its own realm to enclose the other. But as long as it was agreed that science and poetry simply existed in unrelated universes of discourse, there could be no dialectic between them.

In general, then, it might be concluded that a culture becomes dialectical to the exact degree that it assumes that differences of viewpoint must be resolved within a single, coherent, all-embracing system which will be final or eternal. In reverse, dialectic will take a subordinate position within a culture where competing and differing viewpoints can be compartmentalized in relative isolation from each other. The middle ages in some areas, mainly theology and philosophy, were highly dialectical. But in many other areas of social and economic concern the period was not, mainly because the hierarchies of medieval culture were relatively agreed-upon and their various strata set off from one another. Only when, for example, the papacy and the empire reached for each other's dominant realm of concern do we find a real dialectic on a number of antinomies: time-eternity, body-soul, political-spiritual, and so on, which split the archetypal Christian man in half, without either fusing these halves, or totally sundering them.

On this question I have reached the boundaries which the selectivity of this study will not legitimately allow me to cross. If anything, I can on the matter of comparing cultures or periods only suggest. The Renaissance opens itself up to us as an era tormented by oscillations between demands for absolute viewpoints and the discovery of the relativity of viewpoints. That it never resolved this dialectic was a main reason why dialectic throve. And within the limits of this study, only on matters such as these are answers of any assurance possible about Renaissance culture.

And yet this culture in its diversity and unity becomes manifest only to strangers—we ourselves, living outside of the Renaissance, but enabled to grasp it in its entirety precisely because of our alienation from it. Within the action-done which is the Renaissance we find no studies of "the dialectic of Renaissance thought structures," for in being circumscribed by dialectic, the men of the Renaissance could only wholly partake hotly in that dialectic. One must wonder continually at the highest visions of their own world that the Renaissance's greatest writers have bequeathed us, which show us how far the Renaissance could reach toward a total, conscious enactment of its own moment in history. These works live neither in the past of the Renaissance nor in the present of the twentieth century, but rather in both cultures because both cultures are imbedded in the same stream of history; and we can become "Renaissance men" again precisely because both they and we are historical. Only by accepting and accommodating the dialectic of past and present, by refusing to attempt a transcendent, plotless, timeless state outside of history can the past become present, and a culture's dual status as at once past and present be, momentarily in the mind of the reader, reenacted.

BEYOND DIALECTICAL CRITICISM

The dialectical criticism I have examined here parallels many formulations in intellectual disciplines outside modern criticism as well as within it. The indebtedness I noted in the preface indicates only the texts I am aware of as influencing my own thoughts on the subject, but this does not explain fully my being drawn in the first place to dialectical criticism as a useful tool in literary studies. The main thought structures of the nineteenth and twentieth century are themselves concerned with various dialectics. Hegel, Marx, Jung, Einstein, Bohr, to name a few, have established the realities of the twentieth century primarily in terms of antinomical polarities and the dialectical relations between them. Literature as well as literary criticism from Coleridge to the present treat dialectical structures with ever-increasing self-consciousness. Dostoevsky, Flaubert, Proust, Faulkner, Eliot, Stevens—again, to name a few—exhibit this self-consciousness in formulating their worlds in terms of various malign and benign dialectics. To explain my own predilection for dialectical analysis, therefore, would be for me to attempt a viewpoint transcending my own, a viewpoint available only to those in the future who have themselves gone beyond dialectic.

And yet, to the extent dialectic becomes increasingly phenomenal in the verbal artifacts of our modern culture, as it was not in the Renaissance, dialectic has already been transcended in principle. My own analysis of dialectic into a three-moment schema, whereby the paradoxes, contradictions, and logical riddles of dialectic are resolved into clear, univocal concepts reciprocally related, is itself a kind of "meta-dialectic." And already art forms from mid-century to the seventies exhibit a movement beyond dialectic. Various "chance" art forms—aleatoric music, theater of the absurd, fragmented movie narration, confessional poetry— move away from the highly structured, centripetal frameworks of polarized thought structures which dialectic requires for its existence. These forms attempt to escape the rigid causality of dialectic into events and happenings where each moment exists in total independence from those that come before and after.

To the extent that literary criticism moves beyond the historicist-formalist dialectic into realms where time-honored antinomies such as subjective-objective, past-present, and internal-external no longer hold sway, it too will require new categories to formulate and mediate new and newly discovered realities. Yet to so do, literary criticism cannot escape its past. It can only revolt against this past within the categories that that past provides. Its attempt to transcend dialectic, already implicit in its increasing awareness that dialectical antinomies are not ultimate, that they can be rationalized without sacrificing either term to the other, can mean only that dialectic will control this transcendence by providing the springboard from which transcendence must take off.

I shall attempt to speculate here in a very limited and tentative way (what speculations are not limited and tentative?) regarding the directions literary studies may turn in the immediate future. As Robert Weimann points out, once the twentieth-century critic becomes aware that he can no longer treat the past as dead, that the very survival of past literatures into the present presupposes that the critic himself is immersed in the same history he studies, the projection of this survival into the future cannot be ignored. This means, among other things, that present standpoints are themselves dynamic and changing, and that literary history will not be able to cope with this dynamism, as once it did through its historicist and formalist incarnations, by attempting an ahistorical, timeless viewpoint governed by the outworn myths of scientific objectivity and the eternal presentness of literary structure. The dialectic between the present and the past need no longer generate ideals of transcending dialectic into a plotless world outside historical time. On the contrary, the awareness that one's moment in present history allows the separation and distinction, as well as the fusion, of present significance with past meaning will have, hopefully, exorcised these specters once and for all.

But if dialectic is accepted as a necessary condition of our twentieth-century way of seeing things, then what, if anything, announces itself through this acceptance? Once dialectic becomes phenomenal, not only on the expressive and documentary levels of modern literature and criticism, but (as it already has) on the objective level as well, what more basic thought structures lie implicit in this phenomena, making it possible? Such speculation risks the ironies of future historians, who may investigate twentieth-century attempts at self-analysis with the same categories of partiality and unconsciousness that twentieth-century historians and critics have used for investigating past periods. Nevertheless, our own moment in history is one in which we have not only transcended past perspectives in general, but past perspectives on the historical process itself. Our own viewpoint therefore gives us this much advantage: that we may confidently confront our own future fully aware that it too will be historically conditioned, and that it too can observe us only insofar as it is likewise immersed in the same stream of history as are we ourselves.

As I have shown in these essays, dialectic provides a means of understanding likeness and differences, stasis and change, cooperation and conflict—the very stuff of history—as reciprocal functions of each other. Dialectic-as-regulative controls dialectic-as-constitutive of specific human actions and creations, primarily through men's attempts to thwart the dialectical process itself. Having said as much, one may then wonder how far dialectical regulation may be escaped to the degree that one (and one's culture) overtly and deliberately incorporates dialectical consciousness into one's dealing with present-day antinomical realities. Game theory gives us one such attempt, except that it merely takes for granted dialectical interchange and reciprocity between opponents, and only attempts to work out a sophisticated calculus which rationalizes and predicts dialectical sequences. In a certain sense, these essays themselves have been a kind of exercise in game theory, though without benefit of mathematical calculi. In both cases, dialectic is not transcended, but only used. But if it is so used, then as I suggested before it is also already transcended in principle; that is, a view of dialectic that can formulate its inner logic has already "gone beyond it."

Does the full consciousness of how dialectical logic structures and controls conflicts mean that now conflict can itself be so rationalized as to be rationalized away? Is a scenario feasible wherein men, with full knowledge of how their conflicts inflict upon themselves a rigid dialectical liaison with their enemies, might attempt to resolve conflicts by developing negotiation techniques in which "meta-dialectical" arguments play a decisive role? As I have argued, the very existence of dialectical situations presupposes that men attempt to force upon all concerned some sort of absolute resolution wherein there is always a surd of unincorporated reality left out, thereby creating the possibility of renewed conflict in the future. Dialectical analysis thus criticizes the absolutizing instinct indigenous to Western thought and culture, in favor of recognizing the inescapable partiality of all resolutions and the "at-oneness" of all opponents. Therefore, such projected eschatological escapes from dialectic into a final resolution of all antinomies, as were envisioned by Hegel and Marx, seem to be dead ends, if only because they surreptitiously reimport this absolutizing instinct as a governing principle, however much this principle is placed at the end of the dialectical process. On the contrary, dialectical analysis would seem to teach us—as Donne, Herbert, Marvell, Milton, and Shakespeare saw—its own inescapability.

This line of thought seems to lead us to—*mirabile dictu!*—a still further dialectic: dialectic must be transcended, and dialectic cannot be transcended. The absolutizing instinct that creates dialectic absolutizes dialectic at its own peril. And yet these essays seem to point to the conclusion that dialectic is, willy-nilly, absolute, that the ultimate structure of human thinking, insofar as it becomes possible only through the law of noncontradiction, cannot help but allow it to be such.

All of which brings me back to my original, and more limited, question. What future does literary criticism have once the inner laws of its own dialectic become phenomenal? If dialectic is absolute, how can it be transcended? But if we recognize that dialectic is absolute, have we not already transcended it? This dialectic between the necessity and the impossibility of transcending dialectic creates, I think, its own modes of accommodation. Whatever "transcendence" means here, it does not mean escape. We do not become free of our place in history by projecting an ahistorical perspective on that history. By the same token, the dialectical structure of literature, and the dialectic between historicism and formalism that that structure enforces cannot be escaped because now known, understood, and rationalized. The reason for this is that precisely *what* is known, understood, and rationalized is our own involvement in the phenomena we would contemplate, our own dialectical attachment to it in the very act of placing it out there to be investigated as objectively as we think possible. Our immersion in dialectic in the very process of transcending it is, I think, what announces itself through all of my present discussion.

The future of literary criticism, insofar as glimmers shoot out from that darkness to us, points toward increased self-consciousness of its dynamic reciprocity with the literature it studies as a prime condition of its flourishing at all. Sharp divisions between objectivity and subjectivity, extrinsic and intrinsic analysis, past meaning and present significance will increasingly cease to control the questions literary students ask of literary texts. In their place will appear dialectical categories that allow the reciprocity of these traditional antinomies, plus a host of others, their fullest range. All competing claims will be given their due and fully allowed, not at the expense of each other, but rather as functions of each other. Professional competitions will doubtless continue, but, hopefully, no longer intent on dismembering the literary work and dragging off pieces to be devoured separately in libraries and studies. On the contrary, the full dialectical status of the literary work, the prime reality that literary students serve with wonder, earnestness, and fierce reason, will reassert itself to teach us how to grasp its inviolable integrity as an integrity at once of and beyond its parts.

Index

Allen, J. W., 160–161, 163–164
Anderson, F. H., 15, 32
Aquinas, Thomas, 27–28; analogy, xvi
Aristotle, xvi, 3, 20, 24, 31, 74, 114
Aron, Raymond, 7

Bacon, Francis, 11, 12, 53, 57, 73, 118, 156–158, 212, 215–217, 223–224, 236, 259–262 passim; Eden myth, 40–44, 52, 156, 224; forms, 14, 31–35, 45, 224; idolatry, 36, 38, see also Milton; idols of the mind, 16, 21, 36, 38–39, 41, 46, 47, 224; intuition, 18, 20–35, 40, 46, 217, see also Intuition; metaphor, 19–20; metaphysics, 44–45; poetry, 18–19, 36; Works: The Advancement of Learning, 17, 28, 36, 37, 45, 48; De augmentis scientiarum, 15, 16, 17, 37, 44, 45–46; De sapientia veterum, 14–16, 27; Description of the Intellectual Globe, 17; Essays, 51; The History of Henry VII, 51; Instauratio Magna, 15, 42, 50, 51; The Masculine Birth of Time, 20, 22, 28; The Natural and Experimental History for the Foundation of Philosophy, 37, 41, 43; The New Atlantis, 17, 48, 50; The New Organon, 17, 21, 22, 31, 32–35, 36, 38, 41, 46, 48; Principles and Origins According to the Fables of Cupid and Coelum, 15, 44, 45; The Refutation of Philosophies, 21, 37; Thoughts and Conclusions, 20–21, 36; Valerius Terminus, 17, 38, 40, 42 [Other references to these texts are cited in Essay I according to volume and page number in Spedding-Ellis ed.; see page 15, footnote 1.]
Barber, C. L., 186–187
Bateson, F. W., 2
Blake, William, 146
Boas, George, and A. L. Lovejoy: Primitivism and Related Ideas in Antiquity, 96–97
Bohr, N., 269
Bowers, Fredson, 77
Bradley, A. C., 206
Broad, C. D., 32
Brooks, Cleanth, 2, 4, 8
Browne, Sir Thomas: The Garden of Cyrus, 116
Bruno, G., 249
Burke, Kenneth: Attitudes Toward History, xvi; "Creation Myth," xv–xvi; The Philosophy of Literary Form, xvi; The Rhetoric of Religion, 120–121

Cambridge Platonists, 53
Campanella, Tommaso, 23
Campbell, L. B., 161
Cassirer, Ernst, 23; The Philosophy of Symbolic Forms, xvi, 244–245
Cicero, 16
Clevelandizing, 108
Coleridge, S. T., 206, 269
Colie, Rosalie L.: "My Ecchoing Song," 95, 101, 103, 106, 116; Paradoxia Epidemica, xvi
Collingwood, R. C., 6, 253; The Idea of History, xvi
Conrad, Joseph, 9
Croce, Benedetto, 6